The Last Year of the
Luftwaffe

Alfred Price

The Last Year of the Luftwaffe

May 1944 to May 1945

ARMS AND
ARMOUR

Arms and Armour Press
A Cassell Imprint
Villiers House, 41–47 Strand,
London WC2N 5JE.

First published 1991.
This paperback edition 1993.
Reprinted 1993.

Distributed in Australia by
Capricorn Link (Australia) Pty. Ltd,
P.O. Box 665, Lane Cove, New South Wales 2066.

British Library Cataloguing in Publication data
Alfred Price
The last year of the Luftwaffe:
May 1944 to May 1945
1. Germany. Air forces, history
I. Title
358.4

ISBN 1 85409 189 1

Edited and designed by Roger Chesneau.
Typeset by Typesetters (Birmingham) Ltd.,
Smethwick, West Midlands.
Camerawork by M&E Reproductions,
North Fambridge, Essex.
Printed and bound in Great Britain by
Mackays of Chatham PLC, Chatham, Kent

Cover Painting by Jim Mitchell,
supplied by Mirage Fine Art,
26 Megacre, Wood Lane, Stoke-on-Trent.

CONTENTS

MAPS

PREFACE

So much has been said and written about the *Luftwaffe*, but all previous accounts charting its path through the whole of the war seem to lose their thrust once they enter the final year. It is as if those writers, having delighted in describing the build-up of the force and its many triumphs, lost heart when the towering edifice began to come tumbling down. This book was written in an attempt to fill that gap, and it is directed particularly at those who already have a good general understanding of the history of the *Luftwaffe* but who wish to learn more about its demise.

A major problem facing anyone preparing an authoritative work on the *Luftwaffe* is the paucity of its official documents that survived the war. As the Soviet forces were tightening their grip on Berlin in April 1945, Hermann Göring ordered that all documents held in the archives of the *Luftwaffe*'s historical branch were to be destroyed. In general that order was rigorously carried out, and as a result very few unit war diaries have survived – and those that did are all incomplete. There is a similar shortage of official documents describing air operations. Of the documents that survived, many did so only because they were held by individuals in official positions at the end of the war, who simply kept hold of their unit's records afterwards. The tracking down of such documents has been a 'hit-and-miss' business, though deeply rewarding when successful.

In writing this book I was able to draw on material and photographs from several good friends and archives. I am particularly grateful for the use of documents from the Bundesarchiv in Freiburg; as mentioned above, the collection held there is far from complete but it contains several gems, notably the detailed orders of battle for the entire *Luftwaffe* assembled at ten-day intervals throughout the war. J. Richard Smith allowed me to use material he collected during his own researches, while Hanfried Schliephake and Tom Willis kindly let me use photographs from their collections. The following ex-members of the *Luftwaffe* kindly gave me their time and allowed me to tape-record interviews which are used in this account: Horst Bucholz, Roderich Cescotti, Adolf Dilg, Hans-Ulrich Flade, Werner Gail, Horst Goetz, Gordon Gollob, Walter Hagennah, Willi Herget, Hajo Herrmann, Bernhard Jope, Diether Lukesch, Horst von Riesen, Oskar-Walter Romm, Horst Rudat, Erich Sommer, Max Wachtel and Helmut Wenk. I am most grateful to all of them.

Alfred Price

AUTHORS' NOTE

Luftwaffe **ground fighting units** During the war the *Luftwaffe* raised three types of unit for ground fighting. Numerically the largest part of this force comprised the 22 *Luftwaffe* Field Divisions raised during the mid-war period from redundant ground personnel combed from flying units. In many cases hastily formed, these were low-grade infantry units intended for static roles. When *Luftwaffe* field divisions got caught up in the ground fighting they usually suffered heavy losses, and one by one they were disbanded and the survivors incorporated into the Army. By the autumn of 1944 only a couple of the field divisions remained in existence.

On a quite different level were the paratroop units, the *Fallschirmjäger*, high-grade units which throughout the war were part of the *Luftwaffe*. Even after large-scale airborne operations were no longer being contemplated these units continued to be formed. During the war ten divisions of paratroops were raised and these units served as shock troops in several critical areas.

Finally there was the *Hermann Göring Panzer Korps*, another high-grade unit, which comprised one *Panzer* and one *Panzer Grenadier* division, both of which were raised and equipped by the *Luftwaffe*.

When they went into action the *Luftwaffe* ground fighting units almost invariably operated under the control of the local Army commander and fought in the same way as normal German Army units. Where this is the case the *Luftwaffe* ground units will not be considered further in this book. The sole exception was the airborne assault operation mounted in support of the Ardennes Offensive in December 1944. This paratroop attack was mounted solely under *Luftwaffe* control and it is covered in this book.

CHAPTER 1

MAY 1944

IN MAY 1944 the Empire forged by Adolf Hitler extended from the French Atlantic coast in the west to the Ukraine in the east, from the North Cape at the tip of Norway to Rome in the south. Although Germany was beset by enemies on all sides and her forces had suffered severe reverses during the previous eighteen months, militarily she was still extremely strong. Her army could field 295 combat divisions and retained a reputation for awesome fighting power. Moreover Germany's European allies – Finland, Rumania, Hungary, Bulgaria and the Italian Socialist (Fascist) Republic – all contributed armies of varying size and effectiveness to support her war effort. At sea the German Navy's surface fleet had suffered heavy losses, and its operations were now confined to areas close to its ports. Its U-boat arm had suffered heavily also, but was husbanding its strength to meet the long-expected Allied invasion of western Europe.

THE *LUFTWAFFE*

Grounds for optimism At the end of May 1944 the *Luftwaffe* had a total strength of about 2,800,000 men and women. The force possessed about 4,500 combat aircraft, and although it had recently taken hard knocks there were grounds for optimism for the future. Great hopes were placed on the Messerschmitt Me 163 and Me 262 jet fighters and the Arado Ar 234 jet bomber/reconnaissance aircraft, which were on the point of entering service in large numbers. After many vicissitudes the Heinkel He 177 heavy bomber was at last in large-scale production, and several *Gruppen* were in the process of re-equipping with the type. Mass production of the Fi 103 (V-1) flying bomb and the A-4 (V-2) bombardment rocket had begun and both weapons were within a few weeks of making their operational débuts. These and other new German aircraft and weapons will be described in greater detail in the next chapter of this book.

The German aircraft industry had taken a terrible pounding from American heavy bombers during the early part of the year, but, thanks to the efforts of the *Jägerstab* (Fighter Committee) set up under Albert Speer's Ministry of War Production, the industry emerged from this pummelling with fighter production higher than ever before and still rising. Production had been rationalized by reducing the number of aircraft types and sub-types being built. At the same time airframe production was being dispersed out of the 27 main complexes, into more than ten

Acceptances of combat aircraft by the *Luftwaffe*, May 1944

The table shows the new combat aircraft accepted by the *Luftwaffe* from the manufacturers during May 1944, excluding repaired types returned to service. Examination of the figures reveals the parlous state of the *Luftwaffe*'s equipment programme at that time, however. Three types in large-scale production, the Junkers Ju 87, the Messerschmitt Bf 110 and the Heinkel He 111, were obsolescent as combat aircraft but had been kept in production because of the slow development of their intended replacements.

The Heinkel He 177 four-engined bomber had at last overcome its teething troubles and was in full production. Of the new jet-propelled aircraft, the Messerschmitt Me 163 and Me 262 fighters were being prepared for large-scale production: the first production aircraft were flying, and these types were about to enter service. The Arado factory at Brandenburg was tooling up for mass production of the Ar 234 jet bomber/reconnaissance aircraft, but production aircraft had not yet flown.

Factories were tooling up to mass-produce the Dornier Do 335 heavy fighter and the Junkers Ju 388 bomber.

Aircraft	No	Remarks
Fighters		
Messerschmitt Bf 109	1,065	Includes tactical reconnaissance version
Focke Wulf Fw 190	841	Includes tactical reconnaissance and ground-attack versions
Messerschmitt Bf 110	158	Night fighter version
Messerschmitt Me 410	89	Includes reconnaissance version
Messerschmitt Me 163	1	First production aircraft
Messerschmitt Me 262	7	Early production aircraft
Heinkel He 217	17	Night fighter
Bombers		
Heinkel He 177	71	
Junkers Ju 88	268	Includes night fighter version
Junkers Ju 188	47	Includes reconnaissance version
Dornier Do 217	2	End of production
Heinkel He 111	100	
Junkers Ju 87	129	
Transports		
Junkers Ju 52	57	
Junkers Ju 352	6	
Gotha Go 242	20	Transport glider
DFS 230	1	Transport glider; end of production
Miscellaneous types		
Fieseler Fi 156	49	Liaison aircraft
Junkers Ju 290	2	Maritime reconnaissance aircraft
Henschel He 129	35	Ground-attack aircraft
Dornier Do 24	14	Reconnaissance/rescue flying boat
Arado Ar 196	8	Reconnaissance floatplane
Total	2,987	

times that number of small factories distributed throughout the country. There was a similar dispersal of aero-engine production. Thus the industry was far less vulnerable to air attack than it had been earlier in the year.

Simultaneously, other important production facilities sought safety from the bombs by moving underground. The largest such underground factory was at Kohnstein near Nordhausen in the Harz Mountains. Originally constructed as a storage depot for oil and other strategic materials, its seven miles of tunnels gave a floor area of 1.27 million square feet. Protected from above by 140ft or more of solid rock, the complex was proof against the heaviest bombs. Speer's Ministry requisitioned the tunnels and allocated them to armament firms. The Mittelwerk GmbH was turning out V-1 flying bombs (less wings) and V-2 bombardment rockets (less warheads). The rest of the complex was given over to the Junkers aero-engine company, which was setting up production lines for Jumo 004 jet engines and Jumo 213 piston engines. Furthermore, to provide the workforce necessary to secure the increased levels of production, large numbers of foreign workers and slave labourers had been drafted into the aircraft industry.

As a result of these moves, during May 1944 deliveries of fighters of all types were 50 per cent greater than in the preceding January – 2,213 aircraft compared with 1,550. Göring was in a bullish mood when he discussed the new programme with senior officers and officials during a conference in Berlin on 23 May:

I must have two thousand fighters in the shortest possible time, even if the battle fronts get nothing at all . . . The schools will have to make do with repaired aircraft. And then I shall want the two thousand to be increased to two thousand five hundred. I must be in a position to meet any incursion into the Reich with two thousand fighters. Then heaven help you if you don't send the enemy to blazes! . . .

If we can stop these enemy incursions it will help the battle fronts. If the enemy is still contemplating invasion, we'll give him something to think about when he suddenly finds himself confronted with a thousand fighters within the next fortnight, just when he thinks he has settled accounts with our fighter force!

OTTO SAUR (in charge of the new fighter production programme): We shall be turning out a thousand aircraft during the next eight days alone.

GÖRING: Every one shall go to defend the Reich.

Hindsight has shrivelled the *Reichsmarschall*'s jaunty predictions, but it is important to note that at the time they appeared to point the way to the future.

The *Luftwaffe* had other grounds for satisfaction. The production of aviation fuel, which had imposed a brake on air operations from time to time, had reached an all-time high during March 1944 at just under 200,000 tons. Since then it had fallen back slightly but, coupled with the seasonal fall in air operations, this enabled stocks to rise to 580,000 tons – greater than at any time since the summer of 1941.

Elements of weakness Although there were some grounds for optimism for the future of the *Luftwaffe*, that service also suffered from several deep-seated weaknesses. Every German city or industrial complex wrecked by an Allied air attack gave further proof that the *Luftwaffe* was unable to fulfil its primary duty of protecting the Reich. One result was that the immense personal popularity and prestige enjoyed by *Reichsmarschall* Göring earlier in the war, both within the military and outside it, had dwindled almost to nothing. The rotund leader was now the butt of many jokes, and with increasing frequency the failures of the *Luftwaffe* placed him on the receiving end of outbursts from the *Führer*. The vast range and depth of the problems facing Göring defied solution, and his self-awarded periods of leave became increasingly frequent. Thus at the very time when the *Luftwaffe* most needed imaginative and energetic leadership from the top it received neither.

The Chief of Staff of the *Luftwaffe, General* Günter Korten, had assumed office the previous August after its earlier incumbent, *General* Hans Jeschonnek, had committed suicide. Like his predecessor, Korten was having a very bumpy ride as he found that the responsibilities that went with the post were not balanced by the powers to carry them out.

The most serious problem facing Korten was the declining fighting power of his force compared with that of its enemies. Each of the major enemy air forces facing the *Luftwaffe* in action – the Royal Air Force, the US Army Air Forces and the Soviet Air Force – was numerically much larger, and each enjoyed the support of a much larger industrial base than did the *Luftwaffe*. (To put this inferiority into perspective, even at its peak the monthly output of the entire German aircraft industry – measured in airframe pounds – was far exceeded by three American plants, those at Boeing-Seattle, Douglas-Long Beach and Consolidated-San Diego.) Moreover, at this stage of the war the best of the aircraft operated by the *Luftwaffe* had little qualitative edge over those operated by their opponents, and many of the types flown by front-line units were obsolescent or obsolete. In the case of the single-engined fighter units, for example, the majority operated the Messerschmitt Bf 109G which was outclassed by the latest enemy fighters; the remainder were equipped with the Focke Wulf Fw 190, which had lost the edge in performance it had once had over Allied fighters. Thirteen bomber *Gruppen* operated the Heinkel He 111 and fourteen operated the Ju 88, both of which were thoroughly outdated.

Within the German aircraft industry, the increasing numbers of impressed foreign workers and slave labourers imposed new problems on the production process. As anyone connected with the building of aircraft will testify, it is difficult enough to achieve quality even when everyone in the organization is trying to attain that end. In the German industry a small proportion of the workforce was willing to sabotage products if an opportunity presented itself, despite the summary execution meted out to offenders if they were caught. *Feldwebel* Adolf Dilg had been wounded in action earlier in the war and was no longer fit for combat flying. During the final year of the war he served as a Focke Wulf Fw 190 production test pilot at the Arado plant at Warnemünde, and described the sort of things that happened:

> Aircraft were sabotaged in all sorts of ways. Sometimes we would find metal swarf in electrical junction boxes, or sand in oil systems. On two or three occasions brand new Focke Wulfs took off for their maiden flights and as they lifted off the ground one of the wheels fell off; the pin holding the wheel retaining ring had 'accidentally' come adrift. Once, when I was delivering an aircraft, the engine suddenly burst into flames. I baled out and the aircraft crashed into a marshy area where the water rapidly extinguished the flames. When the wreckage was examined, it was found that somebody had jammed a couple of pyrotechnic flares between cylinders Nos 7 and 9, the two at the bottom of the rear row which became hottest when the engine was running. During the delivery flight the cylinders had duly heated up, 'cooked off' the flares, and up went the engine. Every time we had such an incident the *Gestapo* would make a lot of fuss, but although they would take the odd scapegoat the problem of sabotage was one we had to live with.

The *Luftwaffe* possessed a core of battle-hardened aircrews and experienced combat leaders, but these were wasting assets. There were no replacements for experienced pilots or crewmen as they were lost, and each time that happened the operational effectiveness of their unit declined by a corresponding amount. New pilots emerging from the training organization were being sent to front-line units with only 160 hours' total flying time – about half that given to their British or American counterparts.

Oberfähnrich Hans-Ulrich Flade went through the Bf 109G conversion course at Rechenbach in southern Germany in the spring of 1944, and described the conditions he found:

> I had almost completed my training as a reconnaissance pilot before I was posted to the fighter force, so my level of flying experience was well above the average for students. In general the standard of instruction at the school was low: the front-line units were desperately short of experienced and capable fighter pilots, so the training schools had to make do with what was left. Many of the instructors had been 'flown out' in action, and they were nervous, twitched and tired men who in many cases had spent up to three years in action and had crashed or bailed out many times.

In the hands of an inexperienced pilot the Bf 109G could be a vicious beast, especially at low speed. If the pilot opened the throttle too quickly during take-off, or if he attempted to lift the fighter off the ground before it had reached flying speed, the fighter was liable to roll on its back and smash into the ground. There was a high accident rate at the conversion schools, and of nearly a hundred students that started the course with Flade about a third had suffered death or serious injuries before the end. Another complicating factor was that each time an American attack force entered German airspace, the flying training programme had to be brought to a halt. Any student pilot who failed to hear or to heed the broadcasts ordering a return to base risked having to learn the finer points of air combat the hard way – from a flight of marauding Mustangs.

The Bf 109G conversion course provided only 30 flying hours on the type, barely sufficient to teach a pilot to take off and land the aircraft and carry out simple manoeuvres. In combat against a well-equipped foe, a pilot needed to operate his machine to the limits of its performance envelope. Putting pilots with such a sketchy training into action meant sending them to near-certain death – and that was the fate awaiting the majority of new pilots sent to German operational units during the final year of the war. **The flak arm** The greater part of this book is devoted to the *Luftwaffe*'s flying units and their operations. Yet mention must also be made of the flak arm, the *Flakwaffe*, which at this stage of the war employed about half of the personnel strength of the *Luftwaffe*. More than 1,125,000 men, women and boys served in that huge organization, which by May 1944 deployed 17,500 heavy anti-aircraft guns, 40,000 light flak weapons, 10,000 searchlights and 4,000 balloons in the defence of potential targets. The Army and the Navy operated their own flak batteries to defend their depots and port installations in Germany, but taken together they amounted to only a quarter of those operated by the *Luftwaffe*.

At the beginning of the war the *Flakwaffe* had been an élite arm of the *Luftwaffe*, but the demands of war had led to a steady drain of able-bodied men away from the static home defence units. At the same time the Allied bomber attacks on the German homeland had become progressively more powerful, leading to demands for a huge increase the number of batteries. The *Flakwaffe* tapped every possible source for personnel and by the spring of 1944 about a third of its strength was made up of auxiliaries, comprising Home Flak men (an organization rather like the British Home Guard, composed of factory workers who worked in shifts to man guns sited close to their places of work), the Reichs Labour Service (boys just too young for normal military service), *Luftwaffe* Assistants (15- and 16-year-old secondary school students who served as auxiliaries at gun and searchlight sites and who received their school lessons at the sites), female personnel engaged on staff duties, and foreigners (Croatian soldiers and volunteer Soviet prisoners).

THE *LUFTFLOTTEN*

Within the *Luftwaffe* the major air fighting formation was the *Luftflotte*, a combination of combat flying units of all types and their supporting services, based within a defined geographical area. At this stage of the war the combat units of the *Luftwaffe* were divided between seven *Luftflotten*, one *Luftwaffenkommando* and one independent *Fliegerkorps*. A detailed listing of the individual flying units in each major formation, and their equipment, is given at the end of this chapter.

For the moment things were relatively quiet on the battle fronts in the east, the west and the south, but when things hotted up the *Luftwaffe* was likely to find itself severely overstretched. In the absence of any reserve of combat units, one battle front could be reinforced only at the expense of one or more of the others.

Luftflotte Reich By far the strongest of the *Luftflotten*, *Luftflotte Reich* was based at airfields in the area known as 'Greater Germany', comprising Germany itself and the annexed territories of Austria and western Czechoslovakia. This formation was responsible for the day and night air defence of the homeland and it controlled the lion's share of the fighter units. The commander of *Luftflotte Reich*, *Generaloberst* Hans-Jurgen Stumpff, had commanded *Luftflotte 5* in Norway and Denmark during the Battle of Britain. Now the fates had placed him in the position of having to fight a 'Battle of Britain in reverse' against the huge formations of US heavy bombers, supported by swarms of escort fighters, that were systematically wrecking German industry.

With only 515 serviceable single-engined and twin-engined day fighters available at the end of May, the air defence forces of *Luftflotte Reich* were far too small to defend the German homeland against the increasingly heavy American daylight attacks. Moreover the fighters it had available, for the most part Bf 109Gs, Fw 190s and Me 410s, were outclassed by the latest versions of the P-47 Thunderbolt and the P-51 Mustang they met in combat. As a result, the defenders had suffered a fearful mauling.

The night fighter force controlled by *Luftflotte Reich* was smaller than its day fighter counterpart, with 421 serviceable aircraft. In addition it could call on three *Gruppen* of *Jagdgeschwader 300*, with 69 Bf 109s and Fw 190s; these aircraft, which have been included in the day fighter force listed above, were designated as day and night fighter *Gruppen* and went into action in either role.

On paper *Luftflotte Reich* also possessed 21 *Gruppen* of bombers, with 302 serviceable aircraft. But five of those *Gruppen* were converting to the Heinkel 177, and one more was re-forming with the type after suffering heavy losses in action. I./KG 66, a specialized pathfinder unit equipped with Junkers Ju 188s, had also suffered heavy losses during attacks on England and it too was in the process of re-forming. One *Gruppe*, III./KG 3, was converting to a version of the Heinkel He 111 modified to carry and launch a Fieseler Fi 103 flying bomb. A further thirteen *Gruppen*, the 'IV. Gruppe' in each bomber *Geschwader*, were in fact operational training units which providing replacement crews for the operational *Gruppen* of their *Geschwader*. At this time, therefore, *Luftflotte Reich* did not possess a single combat-ready bomber unit. The sole ground-attack unit, III./SG 3, had returned to Germany to re-equip with Fw 190s and was earmarked to return to the Eastern Front as soon as it was ready.

Included in *Luftflotte Reich* were two special units under the control of the *Oberkommando der Luftwaffe* (Ob.d.L. – the *Luftwaffe* High Command) which included captured aircraft on their strengths. One of these, *Versuchsverband Ob.d.L.*, conducted trials and demonstration flights with captured aircraft. The other special unit, *I./KG 200*, operated transport aircraft of various types to insert and supply agents in enemy territory. The unit operated several captured aircraft for this purpose, including a few B-17 Flying Fortresses, a Douglas DC-3 and some French-built Lioré et Olivier 246 flying boats; the captured

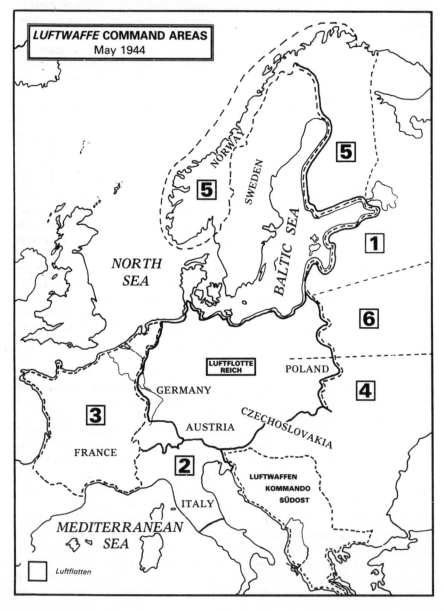

aircraft were used because they had superior range and/or load-carrying abilities to available German types, rather than to deceive the enemy. All captured aircraft flown by *Versuchsverband Ob.d.L.* and *I./KG 200* carried *Luftwaffe* markings and, contrary to what some accounts have suggested, none of them flew on operations wearing Allied markings.

Luftflotte 3 in the West *Luftlotte 3*, responsible for air operations on the Western Front, was braced to meet the long-awaited Allied invasion of northern France that would be backed by overwhelming numerical and technical superiority in the air. The commander of the formation, *Generalfeldmarschall* Hugo Sperrle, had headed it since 1940 when it supported the spectacular *Blitzkrieg* campaign in the west.

In contesting an Allied seaborne invasion, much would depend on the effectiveness of *Fliegerkorps X*, the specialized anti-shipping force. At the end of May this possessed 93 serviceable aircraft and was based in central and southern France. Two-thirds of the aircraft were Focke Wulf Fw 200s, Heinkel He 177s and Dornier Do 217s modified to carry Henschel 293 and Fritz X guided missiles. These radio-controlled weapons had proved their effectiveness in earlier operations over the Atlantic and the Mediterranean. The remainder of the aircraft were Junkers Ju 88 torpedo-bombers. In addition to the specialized anti-shipping units, *Luftflotte 3* included *Fliegerkorps IX* with 137 conventional bombers, Junkers 88s, Ju 188s and Dornier 217s. Based at airfields in eastern France, Belgium, Holland and western Germany, this force was within range of any likely invasion point.

Considering the magnitude of the task ahead, the anti-shipping and bomber units attached to *Luftflotte 3* were grossly inadequate. Yet these were the more effective components of Sperrle's force. His greatest weakness was in single-engined day fighters, with only six *Gruppen*, with 115 serviceable Messerschmitt Bf 109s and Fw 190s, in place. He also had two *Gruppen* of Junkers Ju 88 long-range fighters for the protection of U-boats passing through the Bay of Biscay, but these aircraft were too unwieldy to operate in areas where they might meet enemy single-seat fighters.

The *Luftwaffe* had laid elaborate plans for the transfer of fighter *Gruppen* from *Luftflotte Reich* to northern France as soon as the invasion began. Designated landing grounds had been stocked with fuel and munitions, so that the incoming units could go into action immediately on arrival. This shift of units would leave the homeland almost unprotected but it was expected, correctly, that during the initial phase of the landings the Allied heavy bombers would shift their attack to support the troops ashore. In the beach-head area *Luftflotte 3* would also have to provide close air support for a major land battle, and Sperrle's other great weakness was in specialized ground-attack units. Thanks to the insatiable demands of the Eastern Front, he possessed only two *Gruppen* of these aircraft, with 48 serviceable

Focke Wulf Fw 190F fighter-bombers. With reconnaissance aircraft, night fighters and other types, *Luftflotte 3* possessed just over 500 serviceable combat aircraft at the end of May 1944. Nearly every one of its units had taken a battering during the previous six months, and it showed. All were short of experienced crews, average serviceability was below 50 per cent.

That there would be an invasion was not in doubt; the only questions that remained were the precise time and place where the blow would fall. Nor could there be any doubt that once Allied forces had been committed to such a venture, the fight to establish a bridgehead would probably decide the outcome of the war. If the invasion succeeded, the Germans faced the chilling prospect of being squeezed between major battle fronts in both the east and the west. Yet *Luftflotte 3* was, in every respect, in poor shape to meet its great test.

Luftflotten 1, 4, 5 and 6 on the Eastern Front On the Eastern Front the spring thaw had reduced the ground to a muddy morass, rendering land operations virtually impossible over much of the area during May. There was, however, no shortage of pointers that the Soviet Army was gathering itself for a powerful offensive once the ground hardened.

Four *Luftflotten* in the east were deployed along a battle front of more than 1,500 miles, extending from the Arctic Ocean to the Black Sea. *Luftflotte 5*, based in Norway and Finland, operated over the northern part of the front; *Luftflotte 1* flew from bases along the southern shore of the Baltic and operated in the Leningrad area; *Luftflotte 6* operated over the central part of the front; and *Luftflotte 4* operated over the southern part of the front down to the Black Sea. Because of the steady withdrawal of fighter units during the previous nine months for the defence of the homeland, by the end of May the four *Luftflotten* had between them only thirteen *Gruppen* of single-engined fighters to cover the entire front.

Commanded by *General* Josef Kammhuber, *Luftflotte 5* possessed only 193 serviceable aircraft and was so weak that it did not really warrant the title of *Luftflotte*. Its day fighter force comprised just two *Gruppen* of Bf 109s and a *Staffel* of Bf 110s, and it possessed one *Gruppe* with Fw 190s and Ju 87s for ground-attack and a further *Gruppe* of Ju 87s for night harassment operations. There were three *Staffeln* of Ju 88s and Ju 188s operating in the long-range reconnaissance role, a *Staffel* of Fw 189s for short-range reconnaissance and a transport force comprising a *Gruppe* of Junkers 52s and a *Staffel* of Ju 52 floatplanes.

With 317 serviceable aircraft, *Luftflotte 1*, commanded by *General* Kurt Pflugbeil, was little better off. It possessed two *Gruppen* of single-seat day fighters, two *Staffeln* of night fighters, a *Staffel* of Heinkel He 111 bombers, two *Gruppen* of Junkers Ju 87s for ground-attack and three *Gruppen* for night harassment operations. In addition there were specialized units for long-range, short-range and night reconnaissance.

Commanded by *Generaloberst* von Greim, *Luftflotte 6* controlled operations over the central area, by far the largest part of the Eastern Front. Even so, that *Luftflotte* also possessed only two *Gruppen* of day fighters, plus two *Staffeln* of night fighters. In terms of offensive aircraft it was somewhat better off, with eleven *Gruppen* of Heinkel He 111 bombers, three *Gruppen* of Fw 190 and Ju 87 ground-attack aircraft, and a single *Gruppe* of Ju 87s operating in the night harassment role. Its remaining units comprised three long-range reconnaissance *Staffeln*, three *Gruppen* and two *Staffeln* of short-range reconnaissance aircraft and a *Gruppe* of Ju 52 transports.

Operating over the southern part of the Eastern Front, *Luftflotte 4* was commanded by *Generaloberst* Desloch. This area would be the first to dry out after the spring thaw and it was therefore likely to see the earliest resumption of fighting, so the *Luftflotte* was the strongest in terms of day fighter and ground-attack units. It possessed seven *Gruppen* of single-engined fighters, ten *Gruppen* of ground-attack aircraft and two of night harassment aircraft. For reconnaissance there were three *Staffeln* of long-range reconnaissance aircraft and one of night reconnaissance aircraft, and two and a half *Gruppen* of short-range reconnaissance aircraft. There were also two *Gruppen* of transport aircraft, one equipped with Junkers Ju 52s and one an Italian-manned unit operating Savoia Marchetti SM 82s.

Luftflotte 2 in the South *Luftflotte 2* (*Generalfeldmarschall* Wolfram von Richthofen), based in Italy, was responsible for air operations over the central and western Mediterranean. Starved of resources and operating in an area considered to be of secondary importance, this *Luftflotte* was, except in name, far removed from the force that had brought such devastation to Britain in 1940 and 1941. Now its combat strength comprised just four *Gruppen* of day fighters, three of bombers, two of ground-attack aircraft and one night harassment *Gruppe*. Backing these were two *Staffeln* of long-range and one of short-range reconnaissance aircraft, and a *Gruppe* of transport aircraft.

Luftwaffenkommando Südost was an *ad hoc* formation operating from bases in Jugoslavia, Albania and Greece. It possessed two *Gruppen* of day fighters and a *Gruppe* of night harassment aircraft, a *Staffel* of Junkers Ju 88 long-range fighters, a *Staffel* of Ju 88 night fighters, a *Staffel* of Ju 87 ground-attack aircraft and three *Staffeln* of short-range reconnaissance aircraft. The responsibilities of the *Luftwaffenkommando* included supplying the garrisons on the Greek islands, and for this purpose its transport element comprised a *Gruppe* of Messerschmitt Me 323s and two *Staffeln* of Junkers Ju 52 floatplane transports.

Fliegerkorps XIV (*General der Flieger* Cöler), a centralized pool of air transport units, completed the line-up of forces. It possessed nine operational *Gruppen* with 250 serviceable aircraft: four *Gruppen* of Junkers Ju 52s, one of He 111s, one of Me 323s, one of Savoia Marchetti SM 81s, one of SM 82s and one equipped with captured French Lioré et Olivier LeO 451 bombers converted into high-speed transports. *Fliegerkorps XIV* detached transport aircraft to operational theatres as and when required, and maintained courier services between them.

By the end of May 1944 the problems heaped on the *Luftwaffe* during the previous four years of war placed that service in a intractable position. For the future the only hope lay in the deployment against the enemy of the range of 'secret weapons' – a threat long heralded by Adolf Hitler's propaganda machine. The weapons will be discussed in the next chapter.

TOTALS OF SERVICEABLE AIRCRAFT, 31 MAY 1944

Luftflotte	Reich	1	2	3	4	5	6	LK SüdOst	FK XIV	Total
Fighters (single-engined)	444	90	81	115	138	63	66	54	–	1,051
Fighters (twin-engined)	71	–	–	37	–	16	–	16	–	140
Night fighters	421	21	–	56	9	–	19	13	–	539
Bombers	302	8	48	137	34	–	312	–	–	841
Anti-shipping	–	–	–	93	–	–	–	–	–	93
Ground attack	25	51	15	48	302	19	106	7	–	573
Night ground-attack	–	100	21	–	70	22	48	24	–	285
Strategic reconnaissance	–	17	7	29	31	28	26	–	–	138
Tactical reconnaissance	2	30	8	24	28	8	67	20	–	187
Transports	9	–	35	–	76	37	44	104	250	555
Special units	74	–	–	–	–	–	–	–	–	74
Totals	**1,348**	**317**	**215**	**539**	**688**	**193**	**688**	**238**	**250**	**4,475**

DEPLOYMENT OF COMBAT FLYING UNITS, 31 MAY 1944

LUFTFLOTTE REICH

Geschwader	Unit	Aircraft	Total	Serviceable
Day fighter units				
JG 1	Stab	Fw 190	2	2
	I. Gruppe	Fw 190	44	15
	II. Gruppe	Fw 190	42	20
	III. Gruppe	Bf 109	48	21
JG 3	Stab	Bf 109	4	2
	I. Gruppe	Bf 109	26	9
	II. Gruppe	Bf 109	29	23
	III. Gruppe	Bf 109	31	9
	IV.(Sturm) Gruppe[1]	Fw 190	54	1
JG 5	I. Gruppe	Bf 109	43	36
	II. Gruppe	Bf 109	44	36
JG 11	Stab	Bf 109	4	3
	I. Gruppe	Fw 190	28	20
	II. Gruppe	Bf 109	31	14
	III. Gruppe	Fw 190	28	11
	10. Staffel	Fw 190 Bf 109	10	7

JG 27	*Stab*	Bf 109	4	4
	I. Gruppe	Bf 109	41	31
	II. Gruppe[2]	Bf 109	24	12
	III. Gruppe	Bf 109	26	20
	IV. Gruppe	Bf 109	18	12
JG 53	*II. Gruppe*	Bf 109	31	14
JG 54	*III. Gruppe*	Fw 190	23	8
ZG 1	*II. Gruppe*	Bf 110	33	15
ZG 26	*I. Gruppe*	Me 410	20	6
	II. Gruppe	Me 410	52	24
	III. Gruppe[1]	Me 262	6	1
ZG 76	*I. Gruppe*	Me 410	47	25
	II. Gruppe[1]	Me 410	36	0
JG 104	*Einsatzstaffel*	Bf 109	4	4[3]
JG 106	*Einsatzstaffel*	Bf 109	5	3[3]
JG 108	*Einsatzstaffel*	Bf 109	12	6[3]
JG 301	*I. Gruppe*	Bf 109	25	21
JG 302	*I. Gruppe*	Bf 109	27	11
JG 400	*I. Gruppe*[1]	Me 163	10	0

Day/night fighter units

JG 300	*Stab*	Fw 190	2	1
	I. Gruppe	Bf 109	29	19
	II. Gruppe	Fw 190	32	24
	III. Gruppe	Bf 109	27	25

Night fighter units

NJG 1	*Stab*	He 219	2	1
		Bf 110		
	I. Gruppe	He 219	33	26
		Me 410		
	II. Gruppe	He 219	21	16
		Bf 110		
	III. Gruppe	Bf 110	17	17
	IV. Gruppe	Bf 110	23	14
NJG 2	*Stab*	Ju 88	4	4
	I. Gruppe	Ju 88	31	21
	II. Gruppe	Ju 88	33	16
	III. Gruppe	Ju 88	28	18
NJG 3	*Stab*	Ju 88	3	3
		Bf 110		
	I. Gruppe	Bf 110	26	23
	II. Gruppe	Ju 88	37	13
	III. Gruppe	Bf 110	29	20
	IV. Gruppe	Ju 88	32	21
		Bf 110		
NJG 5	*II. Gruppe*	Bf 110	19	13
	IV. Gruppe	Bf 110	18	12
NJG 6	*Stab*	Bf 110	2	1
	I. Gruppe	Bf 110	24	21
	II. Gruppe[4]	Bf 110	10	8
	III. Gruppe	Bf 110	18	13
	IV. Gruppe	Bf 110	23	18
NJG 7	*I. Gruppe*	Ju 88	21	9[5]
NJG 101	*I. Gruppe*	Bf 110	39	39
		Ju 88		
	II. Gruppe	Do 217	38	28
NJG 102	*I. Gruppe*	Bf 110	39	14
	II. Gruppe	Bf 110	39	16

–	*Nachtjagdgruppe 10*	Bf 109, Fw 190, He 219, Ta 154, Ju 88, Bf 110	25	16

Bomber units

LG 1	*IV. Gruppe*	Ju 88	30	18
KG 1	*Stab*	He 177	2	1
	I. Gruppe[1]	He 177	30	11
	II. Gruppe[1]	He 177	29	0
	III. Gruppe[1]	He 177	30	12
	IV. Gruppe[1]	He 177	34	12
		Ju 88	12	9
KG 3	*I. Gruppe*[1]	He 177	0	0
	II. Gruppe[1]	He 177	0	0
	III. Gruppe	He 111	35	21
	IV. Gruppe	Ju 88	23	14
KG 26	*IV. Gruppe*	Ju 88	34	15
KG 27	*II. Gruppe*[2]	He 111	15	12
	IV. Gruppe	He 111	39	33
KG 30	*IV. Gruppe*	Ju 88	22	12
KG 51	*I. Gruppe*[1]	Me 410	0	0
	IV. Gruppe	Me 410	12	5
KG 53	*IV. Gruppe*	He 111	39	21
KG 54	*IV. Gruppe*	Ju 88	13	9
KG 55	*IV. Gruppe*	He 111	34	17
KG 66	*I. Gruppe*	Ju 188	31	12
KG 76	*III. Gruppe*[1]	Ar 234	0	0
	IV. Gruppe	Ju 88	28	10
KG 77	*II. Gruppe*[2]	Ju 88	31	21
	IV. Gruppe	Ju 88	38	24
KG 100	*II. Gruppe*[1]	He 177	30	0
	IV. Gruppe	He 177	38	13
		Do 217		

Ground-attack unit

SG 3	*III. Gruppe*[1]	Fw 190	28	25

Strategic reconnaissance unit

–	*FAGr. 122*[2]	Ju 188	11	0

Tactical reconnaissance unit

–	*NAGr.8*	Bf 109	2	2
–	*NAGr.14*[2]	Bf 109	2	0

Transport unit

TG 2	*II. Gruppe*	Ju 52	12	9

Special units under control of *Oberkommando der Luftwaffe*

–	*Versuchsverband Ob.d.L.*	Ju 88	7	3
		Ar 240	1	1
		Ju 86	3	0
		Bf 109	3	1
		Fw 58	1	1
		Fh 104	1	0
		Mosquito	1	0
		P-38 Lightning	1	1
		P-47 Thunderbolt	1	1
		Spitfire	2	0
		P-51 Mustang	3	0
		Typhoon	1	1

KG 200	*I. Gruppe*	Ju 290	2	0
		Ju 252	2	1
		Ju 352	1	0
		Ar 232	1	1
		Bloch 160/162	2	0
		Ju 188	4	2
		He 111	15	10
		He 59	2	2
		He 115	2	2
		Fw 189	1	1
		Ar 96	2	2
		Si 204	1	1
		Fw 58	1	1
		Boeing B-17	6	0
		Douglas DC-3	1	0
		Amiot 143	3	1
		Loire 246	3	1
		Various glider types	20	15
KG 200	*II. Gruppe*	Ar 96	7	7
		Hs 126	1	1
		Fw 44	2	2
		Bü 181	4	4
		Bf 108	3	3
		Kl 35	2	2
		Ju W 34	1	1
		Si 204	2	2
		Bü 131	3	3

LUFTFLOTTE 3 IN THE WEST

Day fighter units

JG 2	*Stab*	Fw 190	3	0
	I. Gruppe	Fw 190	19	14
	II. Gruppe	Bf 109	13	11
	III. Gruppe	Fw 190	29	19
JG 26	*Stab*	Fw 190	2	2
	I. Gruppe	Fw 190	33	23
	II. Gruppe	Fw 190	32	25
	III. Gruppe	Bf 109	37	21
ZG 1	*I. Gruppe*	Ju 88	30	25
	III. Gruppe	Ju 88	22	12

Night fighter units

NJG 4	*Stab*	Bf 110	2	0
	I. Gruppe	Ju 88	16	7
	II. Gruppe	Bf 110	20	12
		Do 217		
	III. Gruppe	Bf 110	18	9
NJG 5	*Stab*	Bf 110	15	9
	III. Gruppe	Bf 110	18	8
NJG 6	*II. Gruppe*	Bf 110	13	11

Bomber units

KG 2	*I. Gruppe*	Ju 188	12	9
	II. Gruppe	Ju 188	5	0
	III. Gruppe	Do 217	7	1
	IV. Gruppe	Ju 188	31	15
		Do 217		

KG 6	*I. Gruppe*	Ju 188	22	15
	II. Gruppe	Ju 88	3	2
	III. Gruppe[1]	Ju 188	25	5
	IV. Gruppe	Ju 88	33	18
KG 26	*II. Gruppe*[6]	Ju 88	37	27
	III. Gruppe[6]	Ju 88	35	14
KG 30	*I. Gruppe*[2]	Ju 88	2	1
	II. Gruppe[2]	Ju 88	0	0
KG 51	*II. Gruppe*	Me 410	24	17
KG 54	*I. Gruppe*	Ju 88	11	5
	III. Gruppe	Ju 88	14	8

Anti-shipping units

KG 40	*I. Gruppe*	He 177	30	21
	II. Gruppe[7]	He 177	30	26
	III. Gruppe[7]	Fw 200	29	1
	IV. Gruppe	He 177	17	7
		Fw 200		
KG 77	*I. Gruppe*[6]	Ju 88	28	17
	II. Gruppe[6]	Ju 88	25	8
KG 100	*III. Gruppe*	Do 217	30	13

Ground-attack units

SG 4	*III. Gruppe*	Fw 190	34	29
SKG 10	*I. Gruppe*	Fw 190	33	19

Maritime reconnaissance unit

–	*FAGr.5*	Ju 290	11	4

Strategic reconnaissance units

–	*FAGr.33*	Ju 188	7	3
		Ju 88		
–	*FAGr.121*	Me 410	9	3
–	*FAGr.122*	Ju 188	8	2
		Ju 88		
–	*FAGr.123*	Ju 88, Bf 109,	36	17
		Fw 190, He 111,		
		Ju 188, Do 217		

Tactical reconnaissance unit

–	*NAGr.13*	Bf 109	42	24

LUFTFLOTTEN 1, 4, 5 AND 6 IN THE EAST

Luftflotte 1
Day fighter units

JG 54	*Stab*	Fw 190	4	4
	I. Gruppe	Fw 190	42	36
	II. Gruppe	Fw 190	54	50

Night fighter unit

NJG 100	*II. Gruppe*	Ju 88	29	21
		Do 217		

Bomber unit

KG 55	*14. Staffel*[1]	He 111	11	8

Ground attack units

SG 3	*Stab*	He 111	1	1
	I. Gruppe	Ju 87	27	24
	II. Gruppe	Ju 87	30	26

Night ground-attack units

–	*NSGr.1*	Go 145	32	25
		He 46		
–	*NSGr.3*	Go 145	36	34
		Ar 66		
–	*NSGr.11*	He 50	22	19
		Fokker CV		
–	*NSGr.12*	Ar 66	16	14
–	*1. Ostfliegerstaffel*	Go 145	9	8
		Ar 66		

Strategic reconnaissance units

–	*FAGr. 22*	Ju 188	6	2
–	*FAGr.122*	Ju 188	7	7
–	*4. Nachtauf. Staffel*	Do 217	12	8

Tactical reconnaissance units

–	*NAGr.5*	Bf 109	30	24
–	*NAGr.31*	Fw 189	12	6

Luftflotte 4

Day fighter units

JG 51	*IV. Gruppe*	Bf 109	35	22
JG 52	*Stab*	Bf 109	1	1
	I. Gruppe	Bf 109	31	10
	II. Gruppe	Bf 109	23	18
	III. Gruppe	Bf 109	26	23
JG 53	*I. Gruppe*	Bf 109	33	30
JG 77	*III. Gruppe*	Bf 109	31	24
JG 301	*II. Gruppe*[4]	Bf 109	11	10

Night fighter unit

NJG 100	[2]	**Bf 110**	15	9

Bomber units

KG 4	*I. Gruppe*	He 111	34	27
KG 27	*14. Staffel*	He 111	12	7

Ground-attack units

SG 2	*Stab*	Ju 87	1	1
	I. Gruppe	Ju 87	31	18
	II. Gruppe[1]	Fw 190	42	22
	III. Gruppe	Ju 87	39	27
	10. Staffel[8]	Ju 87	12	12
SG 3	*10. Staffel*[8]	Ju 87	12	12
SG 9	*IV. Gruppe*[8]	Hs 129	67	66
SG 10	*Stab*	Fw 190	5	2
	I. Gruppe	Fw 190	26	9
	II. Gruppe	Fw 190	25	15
	III. Gruppe	Fw 190	34	24
SG 77	*I. Gruppe*[1]	Fw 190	28	26
	II. Gruppe	Fw 190	27	15
	III. Gruppe	Ju 87	33	29
	10. Staffel	Ju 87	12	12

Night ground-attack units

–	*NSGr.4*	Go 145	30	28
–	*NSGr.5*	Go 145	58	42
		Ar 66		

Strategic reconnaissance units

–	*2. Staffel/FAGr.4*	Ju 88	10	7

–	2. Staffel/FAGr.22	Ju 88	10	8
–	2. Staffel/FAGr.100	Ju 188	11	8
–	1. Nachtauf. Staffel	Do 217	12	8
		He 111		

Tactical reconnaissance units

–	NAGr.1	Fw 189	12	7
–	NAGr.2	Bf 109	23	15
–	NAGr.32	Fw 189	11	6

Transport units

TG 2	III. Gruppe	Ju 52	45	43
TG 3	IV. Gruppe	SM 82	41	33

Luftflotte 5
Fighter units

JG 5	III. Gruppe	Bf 109	33	33
–	IV. Gruppe	Bf 109	33	30
–	13. Staffel	Bf 110	16	16

Ground-attack unit

SG 5	I. Gruppe[1]	Ju 87	22	19
		Fw 190		

Night ground-attack unit

–	NSGr.8	Ju 87	24	22

Strategic reconnaissance units

–	FAGr. 22[2]	Ju 88	12	12
–	FAGr.120[2]	Ju 188	6	5
–	FAGr.124[2]	Ju 88	12	11
		Ju 188		

Tactical reconnaissance unit

–	NAGr.32[2]	Fw 189	12	8

Transport units

–	Transportgruppe 20	Ju 52	32	28
–	Seetransportstaffel 2	Ju 52	10	9

Luftflotte 6
Day fighter units

JG 51	I. Gruppe	Bf 109	44	34
–	III. Gruppe	Bf 109	40	32

Night fighter units

NJG 100	I. Gruppe	Ju 88	30	19
		Do 217		

Bomber units

KG 4	II. Gruppe	He 111	35	28
–	III. Gruppe	He 111	37	26
–	IV. Gruppe	He 111	37	22
KG 3	14. Staffel[9]	Ju 88	12	8
KG 27	I. Gruppe	He 111	37	37
–	III. Gruppe	He 111	37	33
KG 53	I. Gruppe	He 111	37	27
	II. Gruppe	He 111	34	28
	III. Gruppe	He 111	37	24
KG 55	I. Gruppe	He 111	35	27
	II. Gruppe	He 111	32	23
	III. Gruppe	He 111	34	29

Ground-attack units

SG 1	I. Gruppe	Ju 87	39	35
	II. Gruppe[1]	Fw 190	42	26
		Ju 87		
	III. Gruppe	Fw 190	42	33
	10. Staffel[8]	Ju 87	12	12

Night ground-attack unit

–	NSGr.2	Ju 87	65	48
		Ar 66		

Strategic reconnaissance units

–	FAGr.11[2]	Ju 188	11	7
		Ju 88		
–	FAGr.14[2]	Ju 188	8	6
		Ju 88		
–	FAGr.100[2]	Ju 88	12	5
–	2. Nachtauf. Staffel	Do 217	12	8
		Ju 188		

Tactical reconnaissance units

–	NAGr.4	Bf 109	38	24
		Fw 189		
		Hs 126		
–	NAGr.10	Hs 126	27	20
		Bf 109		
		Fw 189		
–	NAGr.15	Fw 189	19	16
–	NAGr.31[2]	Hs 126	14	7
		Fw 189		

Transport unit

TG 3	I. Gruppe	Ju 52	48	44

LUFTFLOTTE 2 IN THE CENTRAL MEDITERRANEAN AREA

Day fighter units

JG 4	I. Gruppe	Bf 109	13	10
JG 53	III. Gruppe	Bf 109	13	17
JG 77	Stab	Bf 109	4	3
–	I. Gruppe	Bf 109	21	10
–	II. Gruppe	Bf 109	54	41

Bomber units

LG 1	I. Gruppe	Ju 88	19	16
–	II. Gruppe	Ju 88	20	16
KG 76	II. Gruppe	Ju 88	36	16

Ground-attack units

SG 4	Stab	Fw 190	3	2
–	I. Gruppe	Fw 190	14	4
–	II. Gruppe	Fw 190	27	9

Night ground-attack unit

–	NSGr.9	Ju 87	33	21
		Cr 42		

Strategic reconnaissance units

–	FAGr. 122	Me 410	8	4
		Ju 88		
–	FAGr. 123	Ju 88	5	3

Tactical reconnaissance unit

–	*NAGr.11*	Bf 109	15	8

Transport unit

TG 1	*II. Gruppe*	SM 82	46	35

LUFTWAFFEN KOMMANDO SÜDOST IN THE BALKANS

Day fighter units

JG 51	*II. Gruppe*	Bf 109	55	46
JG 301	*II. Gruppe*	Bf 109	9	8
ZG 26	*11. Staffel*	Ju 88	16	16

Night fighter unit

NJG 100	[2]	Ju 88	15	13

Ground-attack unit

SG 151	*13. Staffel*	Ju 87	7	7

Night ground-attack unit

–	*NSGr.7*	Cr 42	28	24
		Ca 314, Ju 87,		
		He 46		

Tactical reconnaissance units

–	*NAGr.12*	Bf 109	15	5
–	*NAGr.2*	Bf 110	12	10
–	*NA Staffel Kroatien*	Hs 126	8	5
		Do 17, Do 215		

Transport units

TG 1	*IV. Gruppe*	Ju 52	45	41
TG 4	*II. Gruppe*	Ju 52	39	36
TG 5	*II. Gruppe*	Me 323	21	9
–	*Seetransportstaffel 1*	Ju 52	12	11
–	*Seetransportstaffel 3*	Ju 52	8	7

FLIEGERKORPS XIV, POOL OF TRANSPORT UNITS

TG 1	*I. Gruppe*	Ju 52	45	39
–	*III. Gruppe*	SM 82	16	5
TG 3	*II. Gruppe*	Ju 52	43	38
TG 4	*I. Gruppe*	Ju 52	47	47
–	*III. Gruppe*	LeO 451	31	13
TG 5	*II. Gruppe*	Me 323	21	13
–	*Transport Gruppe 10*	SM 81	28	25
–	*Transport Gruppe 30*	He 111	33	32
–	*Transport Gruppe 110*	SM 82	35	0
–	*Tr. Gruppe Bronkow*	Ju 52	41	38

[1]Forming.
[2]Re-forming.
[3]Operational unit at training school, fighters flown by instructors.
[4]Part unit.
[5]'Illuminating' unit to drop flares in vicinity of night bomber stream to assist night fighters. Idea unsuccessful, unit disbanded soon afterwards.
[6]Torpedo unit.
[7]Unit re-forming, and training in use of anti-ship guided missiles.
[8]Anti-tank unit.
[9]Rail attack unit.

CHAPTER 2

THE WHITE HOPES (1)

IF THE *LUFTWAFFE* were to remain an effective fighting force it needed to bring into service as rapidly as possible its new aircraft, 'secret weapons' and improved sub-types of aircraft already in production. Nobody in the *Luftwaffe* High Command nursed any illusions that the German aircraft industry could match production in Great Britain, the USA and the USSR plane for plane. But if the new equipment gave the *Luftwaffe* a large qualitative edge, that might enable the force to overcome its numerical deficiencies.

In the spring of 1944 the German aircraft and armament industries were pushing ahead with the development of a huge number of new and improved weapons systems. A detailed description of every project would fill a book very much larger than this one, and in any case work on most of those projects would cease in the next few months as resources were concentrated on a few vital areas. The account that follows is confined to a brief outline of those aircraft, new versions of aircraft and new weapons that were in production or about to enter production in May 1944.

NEW DEFENSIVE SYSTEMS

The Messerschmitt Me 262 The most important of the aircraft entering production, and the one planned to be built in the largest numbers, was the Messerschmitt Me 262 jet fighter. There were high hopes that it would enable the *Luftwaffe* to re-impose air superiority over its numerically superior enemies. The technical and operational history of this aircraft is complex, however, and in several previously published accounts it has been oversimplified. For this reason we shall examine the story of the Me 262 in some detail.

The Me 262 had a maximum speed of 540mph and it could climb to 30,000ft in seven minutes, giving it a substantial performance margin over any Allied fighter type in service or in production. Moreover, the new fighter wielded a hefty punch, with a built-in armament of four 3cm cannon providing sufficient firepower to tear apart any heavy bomber then in existence. This combination of superior performance and heavy armament promised a solution to the problem of the American daylight bomber attacks and how to defeat them.

During this period the Me 262 was suffering severe problems with its engines however. The Jumo 004 was the key to the new fighter's sparkling performance, but it was also the first turbojet engine in the world to enter large-scale production. It ran at much higher temperatures and greater rotational speeds than any previous aircraft engine, and a host of fundamental problems had to be solved during its design. Moreover the usual ingredients of high-temperature-resistant alloys, nickel and chromium, were in critically short supply in Germany and could not be used. Various substitutes were employed. The engine's combustion chambers, for example, were manufactured from ordinary steel with a spray coating of aluminium baked on in an oven to increase their ability to withstand high temperatures. Such palliatives, though in many cases clever, were only partially successful and the average running life of early production engines was little more than about ten hours. There were frequent failures and engine fires, and in May 1944 the new turbojet engine was ready neither for mass production nor for service with front-line combat units.

Such was the pressure of events, however, that the Me 262 had been ordered into production even before its engine problems had been solved. Pre-production aircraft were delivered to test establishments, where pilots amassed flying experience with the new fighter and its temperamental new engines. This was the position when Adolf Hitler delivered his much-publicized edict, that when it first went into action the Me 262 was to be employed as a fighter-bomber rather than as a fighter. To understand the thinking behind this decision and assess its validity, it is important to look briefly into the reasons.

In the autumn of 1943, as he laid his plans for the following year, Hitler saw that the outcome of the war would hinge on the success or failure of the Allied invasion of north-west Europe. He had invested huge resources in fortifying the more likely landing areas and believed that during the hours following the initial landings there would be considerable confusion among Allied troops seeking to establish a beach-head before the *Panzer* divisions delivered their counter-attacks. How much more difficult would things be for the invaders if throughout that time they were under repeated bombing and strafing attack from enemy fighter-bombers. Even a few hours' delay in establishing the beach-head might be decisive to securing the defeat of the landings.

Given that the Allies were certain to maintain a strong fighter umbrella over the invasion area, only a jet aircraft like the Me 262 was fast enough to charge through the defences and deliver the required attacks. During discussions of the new aircraft in the autumn of 1943, Hitler asked Göring whether the Me 262 could carry bombs. The *Reichsmarshall* passed the question to Willi Messerschmitt, the chief designer, who replied that if required the aircraft could carry one 1,100lb or two 550lb bombs and that the necessary modifications would take no more than a couple of weeks. Messerschmitt went on to say that the new aircraft could even carry a 2,200-pounder or two 1,100-pounders.

The Messerschmitt Me 262A

Role: Single-seat jet fighter or fighter-bomber.
Powerplant: Two 1,980lb thrust Junkers Jumo 004 jet engines.
Armament: Four MK 108 3cm cannon. Maximum bomb load 1,100lb,
   carried externally under fuselage.
Performance (at 19,500ft): Maximum speed (fighter version) 540mph.
   Maximum range (no reserves) 526 miles.
Weights: Empty equipped 9,742lb. Normal operational take-off weight
   14,100lb.
Dimensions: Span 40ft 11½in. Length 34ft 9½in. Wing area 234 sq ft.

It should be pointed out that by this stage of the war it was normal to fit bomb racks to fighter-type aircraft, and enquiries along these lines would not have been considered unusual.

On 26 November Hitler inspected two prototype Me 262s during a display of new equipment at Insterburg, and this time he posed his question to Messerschmitt himself: Could the new aircraft carry bombs? The aircraft designer assured the *Führer* that the new plane could carry a 2,200-pounder or two 1,100-pounders without difficulty. That was all Hitler needed to know: here was the 'Blitzbomber' he sought to defeat the enemy invasion.

From then on the Me 262 featured prominently in Hitler's anti-invasion plans. At a conference on 20 December he delivered a confident speech to senior *Wehrmacht* officers in which he stated:

> Every month that passes makes it more and more probable that we will get at least one *Gruppe* of jet aircraft. The most important thing is that they [the enemy] get some bombs on top of them just as they try to invade. That will force them to take cover, and in this way they will waste hour after hour! But after half a day our reserves will already be on their way. So if we can pin them down on the beaches for just six or eight hours, you can see what that will mean to us . . .

The Me 262 could certainly have performed the task the *Führer* had in mind for it (always provided, of course, that the engines kept running long enough). This author has found no evidence of *Luftwaffe* officers attempting to sway Hitler from this view. Some felt that the *Führer*'s scheme was far-fetched, however, and that if they said nothing it might be forgotten. Possibly, given his well-known penchant for secrecy, Hitler omitted to stress in the right quarters the pivotal role of the Me 262 in his counter-invasion plan. *Generalfeldmarschall* Milch, responsible for aircraft production for the *Luftwaffe*, acknowledged the importance of the new aircraft as a fighter-bomber but devoted his efforts to getting it into service with the fighter force as quickly as possible.

At the end of April 1944 personnel from *III./ZG 26* had begun assembling at Lechfeld in Bavaria for what was to become *Erprobungskommando 262*, the proving unit that was to introduce the Me 262 into service and train a core of pilots to fly it. *Leutnant*

Günther Wegmann, an experienced Bf 110 pilot serving with the unit, told the author that he found the Me 262 relatively easy to fly but that the engines were temperamental. With the early Jumo 004 the throttle had to be moved slowly, or the engine was liable to flame-out or overheat and catch fire. Once a pilot was established on the landing approach and throttled back, he was committed to landing. If he tried to abort the approach and re-opened the throttles, the engines took so long to build up power that it was likely that the aircraft would hit the ground first. Clearly the Me 262 was far from ready to be flown by inexperienced pilots.

About half a dozen Me 262s had been delivered to *EKdo 262* when, on 23 May 1944, the slow-burning fuse ignited the time bomb beneath the programme. On that day Göring, Milch and other senior *Luftwaffe* officers were summoned to Hitler's headquarters at Berchtesgaden to discuss the latest aircraft production plans. The *Führer* listened impassively until the Me 262 was mentioned. Then he asked, 'I thought the 262 was coming as a high-speed bomber? How many of the 262s already manufactured can carry bombs?' Milch replied, 'None, my *Führer*. The Me 262 is being manufactured exclusively as a fighter aircraft.' There was an awkward silence, then Milch dug himself further into the pit by saying that the new aircraft could not carry bombs unless there were extensive design changes.

At that, Hitler lost his composure. Excitedly he interrupted the *Generalfeldmarschall*: 'Never mind! I wanted only one 250-kilo [550lb] bomb.' As the *Führer* realized the implications of what he had been told, he became increasingly angry. After all the assurances he had been given concerning the ease with which the Me 262 could be modified to carry bombs, no preparatory work had been done to enable it to do so. Within the next few weeks the Allied invasion of north-west Europe might begin, and it seemed that the weapon on which the *Führer* had pinned his hopes had been snatched from his hands. Hitler savagely denounced the *Luftwaffe* officers present, and made Göring personally responsible for seeing that every possible Messerschmitt 262 was prepared for service in the fighter-bomber role – and as rapidly as possible.

In later chapters we shall follow in detail the introduction of the Messerschmitt Me 262 into front-line service, but at this stage two salient points require to be made. First, when Hitler delivered his edict that the Me 262 was to be used initially as a fighter-bomber, less than fifty had been built and all were engaged in test programmes or in pilot training. Second, at this time the poor reliability of the aircraft's 004 engines precluded the operational use of the Me 262 *in any role*.

The Messerschmitt Me 163 The second German jet aircraft to enter production was the rocket-powered Messerschmitt Me 163 target-defence fighter. This revolutionary machine had a swept-back wing and no tail, it had a maximum speed of 558mph and it could climb to 30,000ft in about three minutes. Production

---

The Messerschmitt Me 163B

Role: Single-seat target-defence fighter.

Powerplant: One Walter HWK 509 bi-fuel rocket motor developing 3,750lb thrust.

Armament: (Initial aircraft) two MG 151 2cm cannon. (Later aircraft) two MK 108 3cm cannon.

Performance (at 30,000ft): Maximum speed 596mph. Maximum running time of rocket motor (full throttle) 4min, (with some time at reduced throttle) 7½min. When the fuel was exhausted the aircraft would glide back to its airfield.

Weights: Empty equipped 4,200lb. Normal operational take-off weight 9,500lb.

Dimensions: Span 30ft 7¼in. Length 19ft 2¼in. Wing area 199 sq ft.

---

aircraft would carry two 3cm cannon, sufficient to give the aircraft a potent capability as a bomber-destroyer. The fighter's impressive performance was, however, offset by the drawbacks imposed by its rocket propulsion system. The motor ran on two chemical fuels: *C-Stoff* (a chemical combination of methyl alcohol, hydrazine hydrate and water) and *T-Stoff* (highly concentrated hydrogen peroxide). When they came together the fuels were dangerously explosive, and they required the most careful handling. *T-Stoff* was highly corrosive, and not its least unendearing quality was a propensity to burn human flesh on contact.

The fighter's tanks held nearly two tons of the chemical fuels, but that was sufficient for only four minutes' running of the rocket motor at full throttle. The normal operational procedure was to climb at full power, level out and accelerate to fighting speed, then shut down the rocket. The Me 163 then flew as a high-speed glider, and when it began to slow down the pilot cut in the rocket in short bursts to restore his speed. In this way the fighter's endurance under power could be extended to 7½ minutes. When the fuel was exhausted, the Me 163 would glide back to its airfield. The fighter's radius of action was about twenty-five miles from base – the Me 163 had been built without compromise as a target-defence interceptor, and it was incapable of performing any other task.

By the end of May 1944 a *Staffel* of the newly formed *Jagdgeschwader 400* was training pilots to fly the rocket fighter at Bad Zwischenahn in north-west Germany. The unit possessed ten pre-production Me 163s, none of which was equipped for operations. The first production Me 163 had flown, however, and the type would soon become available in useful numbers.

The Focke Wulf Fw 190 '*Sturmbock*' Until the new jet fighters became available in sufficient numbers, the *Luftwaffe* had to make the best use it could of its existing aircraft types to ward off the increasingly devastating American daylight bombing attacks. One such development was the new *Sturmbock* (battering ram) Fw 190, a heavily armed and armoured bomber-destroyer version of the fighter.

The Focke Wulf Fw 190 '*Sturmbock*'

Nicknamed the '*Sturmbock*' (Battering Ram), this version of the Fw 190 was specially modified to attack American heavy bomber formations from short range and from behind. Because it needed to be able to fly through heavy return fire from enemy bombers, the *Sturmbock* was fitted with additional armour plating around the cockpit and the ammunition boxes, and with extra panels of laminated glass on the sides of the cockpit. In place of two 2cm cannon usually carried in the outer wing positions, the *Sturmbock* was fitted with two MK 108 3cm cannon – low-velocity weapons but with a high rate of fire. The 3cm high-explosive shells were extremely destructive against aircraft at short range, and on average three hits were sufficient to bring down a heavy bomber.

The *Sturmbock* modifications added some 400lb to the weight of the Fw 190 and brought about a corresponding reduction in performance. Because of this, each *Sturmgruppe* was to be accompanied into action by two *Gruppen* of standard fighters to fend off the American escorts.

The Fw 190 *Sturmbock* formed the equipment of the *Sturmgruppe* unit preparing to go into action, and made possible radically new fighting tactics. Flying in close *Staffel* formations each of about a dozen aircraft, the fighters were to deliver massed attacks on the American heavy bomber formations. The extra armour around the cockpit of the Fw 190 would enable its pilot to survive in the defensive crossfire from a score or more bombers, close within a hundred yards behind the bomber chosen as target and deliver a *coup de grâce* with heavy cannon.

As well as special aircraft and special tactics, the élite *Sturmgruppe* units were manned by volunteer pilots. Before he was accepted into a *Sturmgruppe*, each pilot had to sign an affidavit which stated:

I, ——, do solemnly undertake that on each occasion on which I make contact with an enemy four-engined bomber I shall press home my attack to the shortest range and will, if my firing pass is not successful, destroy the enemy aircraft by ramming.

Leutnant Walther Hagenah who flew with *IV.(Sturm) Gruppe* of *Jagdgeschwader 3*, explained the terms of the affidavit:

It was made clear to us that, having signed the affidavit, failure to carry out its conditions would render us liable to trial by court martial on a charge of cowardice in the face of the enemy. No man was forced to sign, however, and there were no recriminations against those who did not wish to do so; they simply did not join the ranks of the *Sturmgruppe*.

The additional armour and heavier armament added about 400lb to the weight of the Fw 190 and imposed a corresponding reduction in its performance and manoeuvrability. Because of this, each *Sturmgruppe* was to be escorted into position behind the American bombers by two *Gruppen* of Bf 109s.

In May 1944 *IV.(Sturm)/JG 3* was based at Saltzwedel and in the latter stages of its training.

Other Focke Wulf Fw 190 developments In the spring of 1944 two further developments of the basic Fw 190 design were entering large-scale production. The first of these, the D or *Dora* version of the Fw 190, was fitted with a Junkers Jumo 213 in-line engine in place of the BMW 801 radial used by earlier versions. With the extra power this version promised a fighting performance comparable with those of the Spitfire XIV and the P-51D Mustang, the latest fighters to enter service with, respectively, the Royal Air Force and the USAAF. Although it would enable German fighter units to engage the best Western fighters on equal terms, within the *Luftwaffe* the Fw 190D was considered an interim type pending production later in the year of the Focke Wulf Ta 152, the definitive fighter derivative of the Fw 190 design. The Ta (Tank) 152H, the initial production version of that new fighter, featured a lengthened wing for improved performance at high altitude and was credited with a maximum speed of 472mph at 41,000ft. Deliveries from the company's Cottbus factory were scheduled to begin at the end of 1944.

Messerschmitt Bf 109 developments Although it was still being built in very large numbers, the Bf 109 had reached the end of its development potential. The airframe could not accommodate an engine larger than the Daimler Benz DB 605 already fitted, so no major improvement in fighting capability was possible. To enable the fighter to remain effective in front-line service for as long as possible, however, new sub-types were optimized to carry out specific combat roles. For example, many of the G-10s coming off the production lines were optimized for high-altitude fighter-*versus*-fighter combat and assigned to units providing top cover for bomber-destroyer *Gruppen*. This version was fitted with a DB 605D engine with an enlarged supercharger and the GM-1 nitrous oxide injection system, to provide maximum performance at high altitude, and to reduce weight it carried an armament of only one 2cm cannon and two 13mm machine guns.

The Messerschmitt Me 410 A-2/U4 To improve the effectiveness of the twin-engined Messerschmitt Me 410 in the bomber-destroyer role, a few of these aircraft were fitted with the BK 5

The Messerschmitt Bf 109G-10

Role: Single-seat fighter. (The figures refer to the version of the aircraft optimized for the high-altitude fighter-*versus*-fighter combat role, one of the main production versions during the final year of the war.)

Powerplant: One Daimler Benz DB 605D engine with enlarged supercharger and nitrous oxide injection, developing 1,800hp at take-off.

Armament: One MG 151 2cm cannon and two MG 131 13mm machine guns.

Performance: Maximum speed (at sea level) 324mph, (at 24,250ft) 426mph. Climb rate 19,700ft in 5.8min.

Weights: Normal operational take-off weight 6,834lb.

Dimensions: Span 32ft 6½in. Length 29ft 0½in. Wing area 174 sq ft.

The Dornier Do 335A-1

Role: Single-seat fighter-bomber.

Powerplant: Two Daimler Benz 603E engines each rated at 1,800hp for take-off, in a novel 'push-pull' layout with one at the nose and one at the rear of the fuselage.

Armament: One MK 103 3cm cannon, two MG 151 1.5cm cannon and up to 1,100lb of bombs.

Performance: Maximum speed (at 21,325ft) 474mph. Climb to 26,250ft, 14.5min.

Weights: Empty 16,005lb. Normal operational take-off weight 21,160lb.

Dimensions: Span 45ft 3½in. Length 45ft 5¼in. Wing area 414 sq ft.

Other roles envisaged: Two-seat night-fighter (A-6), single-seat long-range and escort fighter (B).

high-velocity cannon in a fixed installation in the fuselage. A modification of the 5cm gun carried by armoured vehicles, the airborne version of the weapon was fitted with pneumatic automatic loading and a new recoil system. The BK 5 had a maximum effective firing range of about 1,000yd and was aimed by the pilot using a telescopic sight mounted on his windscreen. Although the maximum rate of fire of the weapon was only three rounds in four seconds, its 3.5lb shell was sufficiently powerful to bring down a heavy bomber if one hit almost any part of the aircraft's structure. During the spring of 1944 *II.Gruppe Zerstörergeschwader 26* re-equipped with the new version of the Me 410. The unit was to operate from Königsberg/Neumark on the Baltic coast, where it was hoped it would be far enough to the east to be beyond the range of American escort fighters operating from England.

The Dornier Do 335 The Do 335 was a twin-piston-engined fighter of novel configuration, with one engine in the nose driving a conventional tractor propeller and the other in the rear fuselage driving a pusher propeller. To prevent the rear propeller striking the ground during take-off or landing, the aircraft was fitted with a cruciform fin with a sprung bumper at the base of the lower fin.

The Do 335 had a maximum speed of 474mph and a range in excess of 800 miles, and was remarkably agile for a large aircraft. It was planned that this type would be built in large numbers as a fighter-bomber, an escort fighter, a bomber destroyer and as a night fighter. The Do 335 programme suffered a setback in March 1944, however, when much of the production tooling was destroyed in an attack on the Dornier plant at Manzel. Work was now in progress to set up a new production line at the company's works at Oberpfaffenhofen.

Anti-aircraft guided missiles To improve the lethality of the ground anti-aircraft defences against enemy bombers, two new types of surface-to-air guided missile were in an advanced state of development and had been ordered into production: the *Schmetterling*, for engaging bombers at medium altitudes, and the much more complex *Wasserfall*, for use against bombers at high altitude. A third type of guided weapon being prepared for service was the X-4, an air-to-air missile for carriage by fighter aircraft.

In the forms in which they were planned initially to go into service, all three were first-generation weapons and lacked the means to home on targets automatically. The missiles employed visual command guidance, and were steered to their targets by a human operator using a simple 'joystick' controller. As a result these weapons were ineffective at night, or if weather conditions denied the operator a clear view of the target.

The Henschel Hs 117 *Schmetterling* (Butterfly) The Hs 117 *Schmetterling* was a small (14ft long) winged missile launched from an inclined ramp. The rocket-powered missile had a maximum range of about 20 miles against medium-altitude targets and carried a 90lb warhead. In its initial form the weapon was fitted with the Kehl-Strassburg radio command guidance system, a modification of that fitted to the Henschel Hs 293 and Fritz X anti-ship weapons which had already been used in action. A pilot batch of *Schmetterling* missiles was being built for testing, and flight trials began in May 1944.

Despite the limitations mentioned above, the *Schmetterling* was the most practical and likely to be the most effective of the many German designs for surface-to-air missiles.

The EMW *Wasserfall* (Waterfall) *Wasserfall* was an approximately half-scale version of the A-4 (V-2) bombardment missile (described below). The surface-to-air version of the weapon had cruciform 'wings' mid-way along its body to improve its manoeuvrability, and it was fitted with a new and smaller rocket motor which ran on different fuels (one of the fuels used in the A-4 rocket motor was liquid oxygen, which evaporated if the missile was held in a fuelled state for any length of time; it was unsuitable for use in a defensive missile that might have to be at readiness for long periods).

Like *Schmetterling*, *Wasserfall* in its early form employed the

---

The Henschel Hs 117 *Schmetterling*

Role: Surface-to-air missile for use against aircraft flying within the band of altitudes between about 6,000 and 33,000ft.

Guidance system: Optical, radio-command-guided on to line-of-sight to the target.

Powerplant: One BMW 109-558 liquid fuel rocket motor, developing an initial thrust of 825lb for 33sec, falling to 132lb for the final 24sec running time. For additional thrust during take-off, two Schmidding 109-553 solid fuel booster rockets were fitted to the missile; these developed 3,850lb of thrust for 4sec and were then jettisoned.

Warhead: 50lb high-explosive. Detonated on impact or by radio command signal.

Performance: Maximum speed Mach 0.77. Maximum altitude 32,800ft. Maximum horizontal range 19 miles.

Weight at launch: 924lb.

Dimensions: Span 6ft 6½in. Length 14ft 1in.

The EMW *Wasserfall*

Role: Surface-to-air missile for use against aircraft flying at high altitude.

Guidance system: Optical, radio-command-guided on to line-of-sight to the target.

Powerplant: One Peenemünde XI bi-fuel rocket developing 17,640lb initial thrust.

Warhead: 518lb high-explosive. Detonated on impact or by radio command signal.

Performance: Maximum speed 1,700mph. Maximum range depended on altitude of target and amount of manoeuvring carried out but was typically 22 miles at over 40,000ft.

Weight at launch: 7,720lb.

Dimensions: Span (tail rudders) 8ft 2½in. Length 25ft 8½in.

Note: This was essentially a scaled-down version of the A-4 bombardment rocket, with a new type of engine running on different fuels so that it could be held at standby for long periods.

Kehl-Strassburg system of radio command guidance, and it began flight trials early in 1944. The weapon was considerably more complex and expensive than *Schmetterling*, and its development was hindered by the need for continual design changes to cure faults.

The Ruhrstahl X-4 The X-4 air-to-air missile was a cigar-shaped weapon with cruciform wings mid-way along the body and at the rear. At launch it weighed 132lb, of which 44lb was warhead. Its maximum range was about 3,100yd. As the X-4 sped away from the fighter, electrical contact between the two was maintained by thin wires unreeled from a pair of bobbins. Command guidance signals were transmitted along the wires to the missile, to hold it on a collision course until it impacted with the target. Production had begun on a pilot batch of X-4 missiles, but flight trials had not yet started.

NEW OFFENSIVE SYSTEMS

The Fieseler Fi 103 (V-1) flying bomb The most important *Luftwaffe* bombardment weapon under development at this time was the Fieseler Fi 103 flying bomb, more familiarly known as the V-1 (*Vergeltungswaffe 1* – Retaliation Weapon No 1). Fitted with a 1,870lb high-explosive warhead, the Fi 103 was powered by an Argus pulse-jet engine which developed about 740lb of thrust at launch and had a running life of about half an hour. The missile was catapulted to flying speed from an inclined ramp, and after launch it accelerated to its cruising speed of between 300 and 400mph at altitudes around 3,000ft. By this stage of the war there were shortages of aluminium alloys in Germany, and wherever possible parts of the weapon were manufactured from steel pressings.

The Fi 103 was first fired from a ground ramp in December 1942, and in July the following year a test round flew a distance

---

The Ruhrstahl X-4

Role: Air-to-air guided missile.

Guidance system: Optical, command-guided on to line-of-sight to the target by signals transmitted down a pair of wires unreeled by the missile as it sped towards the target.

Powerplant: One BMW 548 liquid fuel rocket developing an initial thrust of 300lb, reducing to 66lb at the end of the 17sec running time.

Warhead: 44lb high-explosive. Mounted in the nose; impact fused.

Performance: Maximum speed 640mph.

Weight at launch: 132lb.

Dimensions: Span 1ft 10½in. Length 6ft 7in.

---

of 152 miles and impacted within half a mile of the aiming point (that was a lucky shot, and would prove to be far more accurate than the average for this weapon). That successful firing gave a fillip to the programme, and the Fi 103 was ordered into mass production.

Plans were laid to build scores of launching sites in northern France, in preparation for the bombardment of London and other cities in England. Responsibility for the operational deployment of the new weapon was entrusted to the *Flak* arm of the *Luftwaffe*, and *Flakregiment 155(W)* under *Oberst* Max Wachtel had been formed specially to bring it into service. In the autumn of 1943, while the *Regiment's* personnel underwent training and fired unarmed missiles over the Baltic, some 40,000 workers of the Todt organization had been hard at work constructing the sixty-four main and thirty-two reserve firing sites in northern France. Originally it had been planned that the bombardment with Fi 103s would open in December 1943, but its production programme had slipped badly and more than six months would elapse before flying bombs were available in the required numbers.

The conspicuous launching sites for the flying bombs, elaborately built from concrete to a standard design and in most cases aligned on London, did not escape the notice of the British Intelligence Service. Although exact details of the new German weapon were not known, there could be no doubting its intended purpose. Allied medium bombers struck at the sites and in a series of intensive attacks the majority were either wrecked or severely damaged; attempts to carry out repair work drew further attacks.

Following this débâcle German engineers devised a new type of launching ramp for the Fi 103 – one that was simpler, easier to erect from a kit of steel parts and far less conspicuous from the air than the earlier type. *Flakregiment 155(W)* began surveying new sites, with the intention of assembling the ramps and moving in the firing equipment a few days before the bombardment was due to commence. The revised preparations took place under elaborate security and all work was carefully camouflaged.

The Fieseler Fi 103 (V-1) Flying Bomb

Role: Pilotless bombardment weapon.

Guidance: Compass, automatic pilot, air log to count off distance flown.

Powerplant: One Argus pulse-jet engine developing approximately 560lb thrust at 400mph.

Warhead: 1,870lb (extended-range version 1,000lb) high-explosive. Detonated on impact.

Performance: Maximum speed 420mph (extended-range version 480mph) at 4,000ft. Maximum range 130 miles (200 miles). These weapons were not manufactured to aircraft tolerances, and flying speeds varied quite greatly between missiles.

Weight at launch: 4,858lb.

Dimensions: Span 16ft (17ft 6in). Length 25ft 4½in (29ft 1½in). Wing area 55 sq ft.

This time there was little direct interference from Allied bombers, though the systematic air attacks on rail networks in France and Belgium, carried out as part of the pre-invasion 'softening up' operations, did impose further delays on the German schedule.

As mentioned in the previous chapter, during May a Heinkel He 111 unit, *III./KG 3*, had begun converting to a new sub-type of this aircraft modified to launch the Fi 103. The option of air-launching would greatly extend the area that could be brought under attack using the new weapon.

By the end of May 1944 the Fi 103 flying bomb was in full production, stocks of missiles were building up rapidly and the ground work was almost complete for the bombardment to begin. The sustained flying-bomb attacks on London and other cities in the south of England could start within a few weeks.

The A-4 (V-2) bombardment rocket In parallel with the Fi 103 flying bomb, the A-4 (*Aggregat 4*, more commonly known as the V-2) ballistic rocket was also in an advanced state of development

The A-4 (V-2) Bombardment Rocket

Role: Unmanned long-range bombardment rocket.

Guidance: Self-contained, preset. System employed integrating accelerometers to measure the velocity at which the motor was shut down.

Powerplant: Liquid-fuelled rocket motor, running on liquid oxygen and 3:1 alcohol-water mixture. Maximum thrust 25 tons. Maximum burning time 65sec.

Warhead: 2,010lb high-explosive. Mounted on nose and impact-fused.

Performance: Maximum velocity 3,600mph. Velocity at impact 2,200–2,500mph. Maximum altitude reached in ballistic trajectory (long distance shot) 60 miles. Maximum range 200 miles. Flight time (to cover 200 miles) 3min 40sec.

Weight at launch: 28,373lb.

Dimensions: Length 45ft 11½in. Fin span 11ft 9in.

and about to be deployed for the bombardment of the British capital. While the Fi 103 was a *Luftwaffe* programme, the competing A-4 was an Army weapon. As such the latter falls outside the strict remit of this book, but for completeness it will be covered briefly.

The A-4 had made its first successful firing in October 1942, two months before the Fi 103, but the ballistic missile was a much more complicated and expensive weapon and some development problems remained to be solved. Mass production of the weapon had already started, and during May 1944 the underground factory at Nordhausen produced 300 missiles. In contrast to the flying bomb, the A-4 was launched from a small square of flat concrete that was easy to conceal. All the other equipment necessary for firing the weapon was easily transportable. Thus little preparatory work would be necessary in the launching areas, once the decision to open the A-4 bombardment of London was taken.

The Arado Ar 234 The third and largest of the jet aircraft types about to enter production for the *Luftwaffe* was the Arado Ar 234 jet bomber and reconnaissance aircraft. This single-seater was powered by two Jumo 004 turbojets similar to those fitted to the Me 262, and initially it suffered similar problems with engine reliability.

The Ar 234 was designed and equipped to carry out three types of visual bombing attack: shallow-dive, low-altitude horizontal and high-altitude horizontal. During shallow-dive attacks, the pilot aimed his bombs through a periscopic sight mounted on top of the cabin. During the low-altitude horizontal attack the pilot released his bombs 'by eye' as he ran low over the target. Technically the most interesting mode of bomb delivery by the Ar 234 was the high-altitude horizontal attack. The pilot navigated the aircraft to a point about 20 miles from the target using normal map-reading or radio navigational methods. He then engaged the autopilot and swung the control column away to his right. That done he loosened his shoulder straps and leaned forward into the bomb-aiming position over the eyepiece of the Lotfe bombsight. The controls on the Lotfe were connected to the aircraft's automatic pilot via what would now be called an analogue computer. During the bombing run the pilot adjusted the bombsight to hold the sighting graticule over the target, and the act of doing so fed appropriate signals to the autopilot which 'flew' the aircraft along the required path. When the aircraft reached the release point, the mechanism released the bombs automatically. His task complete, the pilot straightened himself up in his seat, tightened his shoulder straps, switched out the autopilot and recovered manual control of the aircraft.

The Ar 234 was also equipped to carry out blind bombing attacks using '*Egon*', a system in which the aircraft was controlled to the bomb release point by a pair of '*Freya*' ground radars (the working principle of '*Egon*' was similar to that of the British '*Oboe*' system).

The Arado Ar 234B

Role: Single-seat jet bomber or reconnaissance aircraft.
Powerplant: Two 1,980lb thrust Junkers Jumo 004 jet engines.
Armament: Maximum bomb load 3,300lb. Usual loads carried on operations comprised one 1,100lb bomb or cluster-bomb container under the fuselage, or two 550lb bombs under the engine nacelles. Some late-production Ar 234s were fitted with a self-defence armament of two 2cm cannon in the fuselage, fixed to fire rearwards.
Performance (at 19,500ft): Maximum speed (clean) 461mph, (with 1,100lb bomb) 430mph. Maximum range (no reserves) 970 miles.
Weights: Empty equipped 11,460lb. Normal operational take-off weight (with full internal fuel, one 1,100lb bomb and two take-off booster rockets) 20,870lb.
Dimensions: Span 46ft 3½in. Length 41ft 5½in. Wing area 284 sq ft.

In the spring of 1944 pilots and ground crews of *III. Gruppe Kampfgeschwader 76* began training to operate the jet bombers when they started coming off the production lines.

The Heinkel He 177 Just as the Arado Ar 234 was the 'white hope' of the *Luftwaffe*'s medium bomber force, the long-delayed Heinkel He 177 four-engined bomber was expected to restore the fortunes of the heavy bomber force. The He 177 had several features that were technically advanced, including the arrangement of two engines side by side in single nacelle in each wing and driving a single large propeller through a clutch and gearbox mechanism. The bomber had an excellent performance when everything worked, but at first that was not a common occur-

---

The Heinkel He 177A-5

Role: Heavy bomber.
Crew: Six members, comprising pilot, co-pilot/nose-gunner/bomb-aimer, navigator/wireless-operator/ventral gunner, dorsal gunner for remotely controlled barbette, gunner for manual dorsal turret, rear gunner.
Powerplant: Two Daimler Benz DB 610 engines each rated at 2,950hp at take-off. The DB 610 comprised two DB 605s joined together, driving a single propeller via a common gearbox.
Armament: Six defensive gun positions, comprising one MG 151 2cm cannon and one MG 81 7.9mm machine gun firing forwards from nose, a pair of MG 81s firing rearwards from ventral position, two MG 131 13mm machine guns in dorsal barbette, one MG 131 in manned dorsal turret and one MG 151 in rear position.
Bomb load: Up to 13,200lb could be carried internally. One Fritz X guided bomb could be carried under the fuselage or two Henschel Hs 293 radio guided missiles under the wings.
Performance (fully loaded): Maximum speed 270mph at 20,000ft. Maximum economical cruising speed 210mph at 20,000ft. Maximum range (with two Hs 293) 3,240 miles.
Weights: Empty 37,038lb. Normal operational take-off weight 68,343lb.
Dimensions: Span 103ft 2in. Length 66ft 11in. Wing area 1,098 sq ft.

The *Mistel*

The *Mistel* (Mistletoe) comprised a Junkers 88 bomber with a Messerschmitt Bf 109 or Fw 190 mounted rigidly above it. The bomber's crew compartment was removed, and replaced with an 8,400lb shaped-charge warhead. Other modifications to the bomber included the removal of all unnecessary equipment and the installation of additional fuel tanks in the fuselage. The controls of the two aircraft were linked electrically, to give the pilot of the fighter control over the ailerons, elevators and rudders of both aircraft. He flew the combination to the target area, aligned it on the target in a 15-degree descent and engaged the autopilot. Then, at a distance of between 1,000 and 3,000yd from the target, he fired explosive bolts to separate the fighter from the bomber. The Ju 88 continued straight ahead and, it was hoped, impacted the target while the fighter withdrew from the area at high speed.

Performance of *Mistel* combination at 20,000ft: Maximum speed 300mph. Maximum cruising speed 270mph. Maximum radius of action 480 miles (fighter used fuel from bomber's tanks on the outward flight and returned on its internal fuel plus that in the 66-gallon drop tank).

Weights: Bf 109 modified as control aircraft, 6,200lb. Ju 88 with explosive warhead, 26,500lb. Total weight of combination 32,700lb.

---

rence. The prototype had first flown at the end of 1939 (shortly before the maiden flights of the British Handley Page Halifax and the American B-24 Liberator, both of which were now in large-scale service), but during the four years following its first flight the He 177 suffered one disaster after another.

The coupled engine arrangement gave continual trouble, and unless the throttles were handled carefully the engines were liable to overheat and catch fire. Several aircraft were lost to this cause. An extensive programme was instituted to modify the engines to overcome the problems, and in the spring of 1944 the He 177 was finally considered reliable enough to take up its intended place as the mainstay of the German long-range bomber force.

In May 1944 only two *Gruppen* (*I.* and *II. Kampfgeschwader 40*, both based in France) were fully operational with the heavy bomber. Production was running at about seventy aircraft per month, however, and plans were well advanced to increase the He 177 force to nine *Gruppen*. One *Gruppe* was re-forming after suffering heavy losses in action over England earlier in the year, and the remaining six *Gruppen* were in various stages of re-equipping with the type.

The *Mistel* Another of the new weapons for which there were high hopes was the *Mistel* (Mistletoe) system, an imaginative method for delivering a large warhead against high-value targets. The novel weapon comprised a Junkers Ju 88 bomber with the crew compartment removed and replaced with the warhead, and a Bf 109 fighter mounted on rigid struts above the bomber. The pilot sitting in the fighter had full control over the combination, and would take off and fly it to the target area. He then aligned *Mistel* on the target in a 15-degree descent and fired explosive bolts to separate the fighter from the bomber. The idea was that the Ju 88 would continue straight ahead until it impacted against the target and the warhead detonated, while the fighter and its pilot withdrew at high speed.

By the spring of 1944 the testing of *Mistel* was complete and work began on the first fifteen conversions for operational use.

NEW ANTI-TANK WEAPON

Henschel Hs 129 with 7.5cm cannon By the spring of 1944 the *Luftflotten* on the Eastern Front possessed four *Staffeln* of Junkers Ju 87 tank-busting aircraft, each aircraft fitted with two modified 3.7cm anti-aircraft guns under the wings. In addition, *Luftflotte 4* possessed an oversized *Gruppe* of Henschel Hs 129s (*IV./SG 9*) also specializing in this role, each aircraft fitted with a single MK 101 3cm high-velocity cannon. During 1943 these airborne tank-busters had proved their effectiveness, particularly against enemy tanks and armoured vehicles that had broken through the battle front and outrun the protection of their anti-aircraft guns. The 3cm and 3.7cm rounds would penetrate the Soviet T-34 tanks if fired into the less thickly armoured rear areas, but something heavier was needed to pierce the thicker armour fitted to the latest Joseph Stalin heavy tank.

In response to demands from the Eastern Front for a more powerful anti-tank weapon for aircraft, engineers at the Weapons Development Centre at Tarnewitz modified a 7.5cm anti-tank gun with semi-automatic loading and designed an installation to fit under the fuselage of the Hs 129. The weapon fired 26lb shells at a muzzle velocity of 2,300ft, giving a considerable increase in firepower over earlier tank-busting aircraft. The new weapon was designated BK 7.5 and prototype installations were fitted to three aircraft for test firings against captured Soviet heavy tanks. If the weapon proved effective, it was planned to install it in large numbers of Hs 129s on the production line.

These were the new and improved weapons on which the *Luftwaffe* leaders staked their hopes of success during the critical months of the summer and autumn of 1944. If all or most of these systems could be deployed against the enemy in large numbers, there could be no doubt that they would confer a mighty increase in fighting power. In the pages that follow we shall observe how these aircraft and weapons fared when they became operational. To start with, in the next chapter, we shall observe how the modified Me 410s and Fw 190s fared in air defence operations over Germany itself.

CHAPTER 3

IN DEFENCE OF THE REICH

1 May to 31 July 1944

DURING THE SPRING of 1944 the heaviest and most costly air battles fought by the *Luftwaffe* were those against the US Army Air Forces over Germany itself. Two or three times a week, weather permitting, the Eighth and Fifteenth Air Forces sent raiding forces of several hundred bombers escorted by similar numbers of fighters to strike at important targets in the Reich. Such incursions could not be allowed to go unchallenged, and *Luftflotte Reich* was forced to send up every available fighter.

As mentioned previously, by far the greatest part of the fighter force was committed to the air defence of German homeland. Yet there were serious and growing problems. The Bf 109Gs, Fw 190s and Me 410s were outclassed qualitatively and quantitatively by the American P-47 Thunderbolts and P-51 Mustangs. Previous incursions had cost *Luftflotte Reich* dear, and at the end of April *Generalmajor* Adolf Galland was moved to report to his superiors:

> Between January and April 1944 our day fighter arm lost more than 1,000 pilots. They included our best *Staffel*, *Gruppe* and *Geschwader* commanders . . . The time has come when our force is within sight of collapse.

These losses in pilots far outstripped the ability of the German training organization to provide replacements. To maintain a viable defence for the German industrial centres it had been necessary to withdraw several fighter units from the battle fronts, and those that remained were starved of replacement pilots.

During these large-scale air battles the numerical losses in aircraft were roughly equal on each side. On the American side, most of the aircraft lost were heavy bombers carrying ten-man crews, and since these usually went down over enemy territory most crewmen that survived were taken prisoner. On the German side, the planes lost were relatively cheap fighters – and pilots and crewmen who bailed out usually came down on friendly territory and could return to their units.

Yet, in spite of these discrepancies, the *Luftwaffe* was inexorably losing the battle. The huge US aircraft industry and aircrew training organization could make good the losses and still produce an excess to expand the force; the German aircraft industry could produce sufficient new fighters, but the *Luftwaffe* training organization could not turn out effective fighter pilots as fast as they were being lost.

The large numbers of escorts surrounding the bomber formations posed other fundamental problems for the defending fighter force. The specialized German bomber-destroyer planes, the twin-engined Messerschmitt 110s and Me 410s which carried the firepower necessary to knock down the bombers, suffered particularly heavy losses whenever they came into contact with the American escorts; in contrast, the single-engined Bf 109s and Fw 190s had the performance to dog-fight with the American escorts but lacked the firepower to engage the heavy bombers effectively. Of course, the Messerschmitt 262 had both the firepower to destroy the heavy bombers and the performance to avoid the escorts, and when it entered service in large numbers the problem would be rapidly solved. But the new fighter was not yet available and now the need was for stop-gap measures, to maintain an effective air defence of the German homeland until it was.

At this time the usual procedure for engaging American heavy bomber formations was to assemble large formations of up to a hundred fighters, which were positioned by ground control for a head-on attack. Such attacks, made at a combined closing speed of about 500mph, allowed German pilots time for only a single half-second burst before they had to pull up to avoid colliding with the bomber under attack. For their success these tactics required considerable skill, and only a few outstanding pilots were able to build up a sizeable victory score that way.

During May the new version of the Messerschmitt Me 410 fitted with the BK 5 high-velocity cannon began operations against the US bombers, serving with II./ZG 26. The automatic reloading system of the heavy cannon gave continual trouble, and rarely allowed more than a couple of rounds to be fired before it jammed. Nevertheless, when the Me 410s reached firing positions about 1,000yd behind the bombers – safely beyond the reach of the defensive fire – they picked off the bombers with individually aimed rounds.

By this stage of the war the Mustangs were accompanying the heavy bombers everywhere they went, and if they caught the lumbering bomber-destroyers they exacted savage retribution. That happened on 13 May when the bombers made one of their deepest penetrations so far to Posen (now Poznan in Poland), 1,470 miles from their bases in England. Thinking itself far enough east to be safe, II./ZG 26 rose to engage and was bounced by Mustangs which shot down twelve of the twin-engined fighters in quick succession. The Me 410 continued operating against the American heavy bombers for a few more weeks and then the unit was disbanded. The lesson was clear enough: no area of Germany was safe from the American escort fighters, and any weapon system or tactical method that could not survive in their presence was doomed to fail.

On 6 June Allied forces landed on the north coast of France, and for most of that month the Allied heavy bombers concentrated their attacks on tactical targets in support of the invasion.

The P-51B Mustang compared with its adversaries

The arrival of the American long-range escort fighters in force over Germany, during the spring of 1944, sealed the fate of the *Luftwaffe*. The USAAF quickly established air superiority over the enemy homeland and held it for the rest of the war. In a large measure this superiority was due to better pilot training and, later, superior numbers of fighters in operation. But it was also due to the superlative performance of one type of aircraft, the P-51C Mustang fighter. The Mustang escorted bombers to Berlin and beyond, proof of its remarkable range; but this would have counted for little had the fighter not been able to hold its own in combat.

How did the Mustang compare with the Messerschmitt Bf 109G and the Focke Wulf Fw 190A, the two types which bore the brunt of the battle to defend Germany during the spring and summer of 1944? Combat reports provide part of the picture, but unrelated factors such as pilot training, numbers involved and the tactical situation distort the assessment. Fortunately we know in great detail how they compared, for the Air Fighting Development Unit of the RAF flew trials between a P-51B, and captured examples of the Bf 109 and Fw 190; parts of the report on the trial are reproduced below:

Brief comparison with the Focke Wulf Fw 190 (BMW 801D motor)
Maximum speed
The Fw 190 is nearly 50 mph slower at all heights, increasing to 70 mph above 28,000 feet. It is anticipated that the new Fw 190D (DB 603 motor) might be slightly faster below 27,000 feet, but slower above that height.

Climb
There appears to be little to choose in the maximum rate of climb. It is anticipated that the Mustang will have a better climb than the new Fw 190D. The Mustang is considerably faster at all heights in a zoom climb.

Dive
The Mustang can always outdive the Fw 190.

Turning circle
Again, there is not much to choose. The Mustang is slightly better. When evading an enemy aircraft with a steep turn, a pilot will always outturn the attacking aircraft initially because of the difference in speeds. It is therefore still a worthwhile manoeuvre with the Mustang when attacked.

Rate of roll
Not even a Mustang approaches the Fw 190.

Conclusions
In the attack, a high speed should be maintained or regained in order to regain the height initiative. A Fw 190 could not evade by diving alone. In defence a steep turn followed by a full throttle dive should increase the range before regaining height and course.
Dogfighting is not altogether recommended. Do not attempt to climb away without at least 250 mph showing initially. Unfortunately there is not enough information on the new Fw 190D for any positive recommendations to be made.

Brief comparison with the Messerschmitt Bf 109G
Maximum speed
The Mustang is faster at all heights. Its best heights, by comparison,

are below 16,000 feet (30 mph faster, approximately) and above 25,000 feet (30 mph increasing to 50 mph at 30,000 feet).

Maximum climb
This is rather similar. The Mustang is very slightly better above 25,000 feet but inclined to be worse below 20,000 feet.

Zoom climb
Unfortunately the Me 109G appears to have a very good high-speed climb, making the two aircraft similar in a zoom climb.

Dive
On the other hand in defence the Mustang can still increase the range in a prolonged dive.

Turning circle
The Mustang is greatly superior.

Rate of roll
Not much to choose. In defence (in a tight spot) a rapid change of direction will throw the Me 109G's sight off. This is because the 109G's maximum rate of roll is embarrassing (the slots keep opening).

Conclusions
In attack, the Mustang can always catch the Me 109G, except in any sort of climb (unless there is a high overtaking speed). In defence, a steep turn should be the first manoeuvre, followed, if necessary, by a dive (below 20,000 feet). A high-speed climb will unfortunately not increase the range. If above 25,000 feet keep above by climbing or all-out level flight.

Combat performance with long-range tanks
Speed
There is a serious loss of speed of 40–50 mph at all engine settings and heights. It is, however, still faster than the Fw 190 (BMW 801D) above 25,000 feet, though slower than the Me 109G.

Climb
The rate of climb is greatly reduced. It is outclimbed by the Fw 190 and the Me 109G. The Mustang is still good in a zoom climb (attack), but is still outstripped (defence) if being followed all the way by the Fw 190 and definitely outstripped by the Me 109G.

Dive
So long as the tanks are fairly full, the Mustang still beats the Fw 190 (BMW 801D) and the Me 190G in a power dive.

Turning circle
The tanks do not make quite so much difference as one might expect. The Mustang can at least turn as tightly as the Fw 190 (BMW 801D) without stalling out, and therefore definitely more tightly than the Me 109G.

Rate of roll
General handling and rate of roll are very little affected.

Conclusions
The performance of the Mustang is greatly reduced when carrying drop-tanks. Half-hearted attacks could still be evaded by a steep turn, but determined attacks would be difficult to avoid without losing height. It is still a good attacking aircraft, especially if it has the advantage of height.

The majority of single-engined fighter *Gruppen* belonging to *Luftflotte Reich* were immediately transferred to forward bases in France to provide air cover for German ground forces. (The move and subsequent events will be described in the next chapter.)

On 8 June, two days after the invasion, General Carl Spaatz commanding the US Strategic Air Forces in Europe issued orders that henceforth the primary aim of his forces would be the denial of oil supplies to the enemy. The Eighth Air Force in England was to attack refineries in central and eastern Germany, while the Fifteenth Air Force in Italy was to attack those in Austria, Hungary, Rumania and southern Germany. Simultaneously, Royal Air Force Bomber Command was to attack oil plants in the Ruhr area.

Also at this time, the *Luftwaffe* prepared to employ its new *Sturmgruppe* tactics against the American formations when they resumed attacks on Germany itself. Each *Gruppe* of *Sturmbock* Fw 190s was to be escorted into action by two *Gruppen* of Messerschmitt Bf 109s fitted with uprated engines and reduced armament, to hold off the American escort. The American bombers flew in columns up to a hundred miles long, and the escorts could not be present everywhere in strength. The German plan was to assemble a *Gefechtsverband* (battle formation) comprising the *Sturmgruppe* and its two escorting *Gruppen* and direct it against the bomber stream midway along its length.

The first successful use of the new tactics occurred on 7 July. That day a force of 1,129 Fortresses and Liberators of the US Eighth Air Force set out from England to bomb aircraft factories in the Leipzig area and the synthetic oil plants at Böhlen, Leuna-Merseburg and Lützgendorf. As the bombers droned into Germany the fighter controller passed a stream of intercept vectors to *Major* Walther Dahl at the head of a *Gefechtsverband* comprising *IV.(Sturm) Gruppe JG 3* escorted by two *Gruppen* of Bf 109s from *JG 300* – a total of about ninety aircraft.

Just west of the target Dahl caught sight of his quarry: box after box of bombers heading east. Dahl swung his force in behind the Liberators of the 492nd Bomb Group which, as luck would have it, were temporarily without fighter cover. The *Sturmgruppe* closed on the American Group's Low Squadron, as *Hauptmann* Wilhelm Moritz split his force into its three component *Sturmstaffeln* and directed them against different parts of the enemy formation. *Leutnant* Walther Hagenah, one of the German pilots who took part in the attack, described the tactics employed:

> Once a *Sturmstaffel* was in position about 1,000yd behind 'its' squadron of bombers, the *Staffel* leader would order his aircraft into line abreast and, still in close formation, they would advance on the bombers. At this stage our tactics were governed by the performance of our wingmounted 3cm cannon. Although the hexogen high-explosive ammunition fired by this weapon was devastatingly effective, the gun's relatively low muzzle velocity meant that its accuracy fell off rapidly

with range – and since we carried only 55 rounds per gun, sufficient for about five seconds' firing, we could not afford to waste ammunition in wild shooting from long range. It was essential that we held our fire until we were right up close against the bombers. We were to advance like Frederick the Great's infantrymen, holding our fire until we could see 'the whites of the enemy's eyes'.

During the advance each man picked a bomber and closed in on it. As our formation moved forwards the American bombers would, of course, let fly at us with everything they had. I remember the sky being almost alive with tracer. With strict orders to withhold our fire until the leader gave the order, we could only grit our teeth and press on ahead. In fact, with the extra armour, surprisingly few of our aircraft were knocked down by the return fire; like the armoured knights in the Middle Ages, we were well protected. A *Staffel* might lose one or two aircraft during the advance, but the rest continued relentlessly on. We positioned ourselves about 100yd behind the bombers before opening fire. From such a range we could hardly miss, and as the 3cm explosive rounds struck home we could see the enemy bombers literally falling apart in front of us. On average, three hits with 3cm ammunition would be sufficient to knock down a four-engined bomber, and the shortest burst was usually sufficient to achieve that.

The German pilots made the most of their opportunity, and within about a minute the entire squadron of eleven B-24s had been wiped out. The US 2nd Air Division lost 28 Liberators that day, the majority to the *Sturmgruppe* attack. Walther Hagenah was credited with the destruction of one of them. *IV./JG 3* lost nine fighters shot down, and three more suffered damage and made crash landings; five of the unit's pilots were killed. By the standards of the time it had been a highly successful operation for the *Luftwaffe*, and following this success a further two *Jagdgeschwader*, *JG 4* and *JG 300*, each converted one *Gruppe* to the Fw 190 *Sturmbock* aircraft and began training in the new tactics.

Walther Hagenah was in action with *Sturmgruppe JG 3* on 18 and 20 July, and was credited with the destruction of a B-17 on each occasion. Despite the fact that each of them had signed the affidavit indicating their readiness to ram the enemy bombers if all else failed, it was rare for *Sturmgruppe* pilots to take this course. Hagenah never rammed a bomber, nor did he ever see anyone else do so:

If we held our formation, ran the gauntlet of the bombers' defensive fire and reached a firing position 100yd behind a bomber, with our powerful cannon it was a relatively simple matter to get a kill. There were a few occasions when people reached a firing position and found, for example, that their weapons had jammed. They then opened their throttle, pulled up a little, dived down and rammed. By and large, however, our weapons were very reliable and that was rarely neces-sary. We received no detailed instructions from our High Command on how best to ram the enemy bombers though the matter was, of course, the subject of several discussions in our crewroom. Of the pilots who made ramming attacks, about half escaped without serious injury.

For the Americans, the answer to the new German tactics was to send large numbers of fighters to sweep the areas ahead and to

---

A *Sturmgruppe* pilot looks back

Walther Hagenah flew Focke Wulf Fw 190 Sturmbock *fighters with IV. Gruppe of* Jagdgeschwader 3. *Speaking in 1975, he summed up his time with the élite* Sturmgruppe *in these words:*

Thinking about it now, sitting in the comfort of an armchair after more than thirty years of peace, it is easy to overemphasize the personal danger of being a *Sturmgruppe* pilot. But it should be remembered that we were in the front line in wartime, where conditions of absolute safety did not exist. Certainly the risks to us were no greater than, say, those accepted by an infantryman charging an enemy position.

As members of a *Sturmgruppe* we knew that we were a tough unit, something special, and morale was high. There were no shirkers; people like that did not accept the harsh conditions of membership. The enemy was systematically destroying our homeland and we were determined to hit back hard. I am proud to have been numbered amongst the *Sturmgruppe* pilots. If the conditions were ever repeated, I would do the same thing again.

---

the flanks of the bombers, to catch the unwieldy German formations and break them up before they reached the bombers. Once a *Gefechtsverband* had been broken up, it was almost impossible to re-form it in the presence of the enemy and the operation had to be abandoned.

In general, the American countermeasures were successful, as is borne out by the disconcertingly gloomy figures that appeared in a *Luftwaffe* staff paper written on the daylight air defence operations by *Luftflotte Reich* during August 1944. In the course of 22 major attacks on targets in Germany, the defenders claimed to have shot down 307 US bombers – an average of fourteen bombers during each incursion. But to achieve that mediocre result the *Luftwaffe* lost 301 fighters destroyed and 270 pilots killed. Day after day defending fighter units were being hurled against the enemy formations. They suffered terrible losses but were doing nothing to reduce the strength, the frequency or the destructiveness of the enemy attacks. Clearly the German fighter force was failing in its intended purpose.

Meanwhile, what of the new jet fighter units? During July the first unit equipped with Messerschmitt Me 163 rocket-propelled fighters, *I./JG 400*, moved from its training base at Bad Zwischenahn to its operational base, Brandis, near Leipzig. On 28 July, as a force of 652 heavy bombers ran in to attack the oil refinery complex at Leuna-Merseberg, six Me 163s took off to engage. Colonel Alvin Tacon leading a flight of Mustangs of the 359th Fighter Group had a brush with two of the rocket fighters and afterwards reported:

The two I had spotted made a diving turn to the left in close formation and feinted towards the bombers at six o'clock, cutting off their jets as they turned. Our flight turned for a head-on pass to get between them and the rear of the bomber formation. While still 3,000yd from the bombers, they turned into us and left the bombers alone. In this turn they banked about 80 degrees but their course changed only about 20 degrees. Their turn radius was very large but their rate of roll appeared excellent. Their speed I estimated was 500 to 600mph. Both planes passed under us, 1,000ft below, while still in a close-formation glide. In an attempt to follow them, I 'splitS'd'. One continued down in a 45-degree dive; the other climbed up into the sun very steeply and I lost him. Then I looked back at the one in a dive and saw he was five miles away at 10,000ft. Other members of my flight reported that the one which went up into the sun used his jet in short bursts as though it was blowing smoke rings. These pilots appeared very experienced but not aggressive.

Tacon's final comments were perceptive. In fact some of the German pilots had their rocket motors cut out when they nosed over too rapidly at the top of the climb – it was difficult to be aggressive when that happened. Those Me 163 pilots able to get near the bombers were harried by the escorts to such an extent that none was able to press home an attack. The action ended in a draw, with no loss to either side.

After the rocket fighters had exhausted their fuel they came gliding back to Brandis singly, and that gave rise to a new problem. The Me 163s arrived at the airfield nearly simultaneously, all committed to landing. There were several tense moments, and some near misses, before all were back on the ground. It was a clear pointer to the sort of problem that would arise if, as planned, larger operations were attempted with the Me 163.

After reading Tacon's report, Major General Kepner, commanding the VIIIth Fighter Command, instructed his operational units thus:

It is believed we can expect to see more of these aircraft immediately and we can expect attacks on the bombers from the rear in formations or waves. To be able to counter and have time to turn into them, our units are going to have to be in positions relatively close to the bombers to be between them and our heavies. It is believed these tactics will keep them from making effective, repeat effective, attacks on the bombers.

Tactically the American plan was sound: by forcing the jets to maintain high speed, it ensured that any which got through to the bombers would make only very brief firing passes. And if a German pilot slowed down to engage more effectively, the Mustangs would have a good chance of catching him.

In parallel with the American daylight attacks, the Royal Air Force was sending in similarly large raiding forces to attack Germany at night. The night fighter force controlled by *Luftflotte Reich* was numerically smaller than its day fighter counterpart, and in the spring of 1944 it was at the peak of its effectiveness. During the previous summer, by the use of 'Window' aluminium foil and other countermeasures, the Royal Air Force bombers had come close to bringing the German night air defence system to its knees. Since then, following an expansion of the night fighter force and the installation of the new detection systems in their night fighters, the defenders restored and then surpassed their previous effectiveness.

The technical improvement of the night fighter force hinged on the development and introduction of three new electronic devices into its aircraft, and in keeping the RAF ignorant of their existence. The most important of these was the SN-2 airborne interception radar, which operated in the 85–90MHz band and was invulnerable to the types of 'Window' that had been so effective previously. SN-2 worked in the same part of the frequency spectrum as the *Freya* early-warning radar and its signal characteristics were similar, making the equipment difficult to identify. RAF intelligence officers thought the *Luftwaffe* had probably introduced a new type of airborne radar, but until the set's parameters were known nothing could be done to counter it. Electronic reconnaissance aircraft scoured the frequency spectrum for its signals, but when they searched in the right place they picked up numerous pulse trains seeming to come from the old and familiar *Freya* radars.

The other two new German electronic systems, code-named *Naxos* and *Flensburg*, were passive devices which enabled night fighters to home, respectively, on emissions from the bombers' H2S ground-mapping radar and on the 'Monica' tail warning radar. The night-fighter force abandoned the earlier tactic of using close ground control and fighting over limited geographical areas, which was vulnerable to jamming. Instead, night fighters ranged far and wide after the bombers, using the new homing devices to find their prey.

During the spring of 1944 the German defences had inflicted heavy losses on the night raiders, culminating on 30–31 March when 94 bombers were shot down during an attack on Nuremburg. Soon afterwards the RAF bombers switched their main attack to targets in occupied Europe to support the forthcoming invasion. To reach their targets the bombers made only shallow penetrations of the defences, and this reduced the time available for the night fighters to engage. Yet so long as the three new German systems remained secret, there was every likelihood that the *Luftwaffe* would inflict further heavy losses on the night bombers when they resumed their attacks on Germany.

Two of the new German electronic systems were soon to be revealed, however. During the early morning darkness on 13 July a fully equipped Junkers Ju 88G night fighter landed at the RAF airfield at Woodbridge in Suffolk. Its inexperienced pilot had been ordered to fly the night fighter from its base in Holland to Germany for engineering work but had inadvertently steered a reciprocal compass course and arrived in England by mistake. Examining the windfall the next day, Royal Air Force intelligence officers found that the Ju 88G carried two ominously unfamiliar systems: the SN-2 radar and the *Flensburg* homer. So that was why the German night fighter force had been so successful during the previous months!

The Ju 88 was flown in a series of tests to determine the

strengths and weaknesses of the two new German electronic devices. SN-2 was found to be vulnerable to 'Window' of a longer length than that previously used, and the new type of metal foil was ordered in large quantities. Tests with *'Flensburg'* against a stream of seventy Lancaster bombers running 'Monica' revealed that the German receiver's tuning was so fine that its operator could single out individual aircraft and guide his pilot to within visual range (at night) from distances of up to 45 miles. For the RAF that was a horrifying discovery, and following the test the tail warning radar was removed from all aircraft in Bomber Command.

Soon afterwards the RAF got an inkling of the existence of *'Naxos'* as well, and the use of the H2S bombing radar was restricted. In rapid succession SN-2, *'Flensburg'* and *'Naxos'* were either negated entirely or else rendered far less effective. The German night fighter force would never recover from this triple blow.

Having looked at the problems of defending the German homeland, we shall now direct our attention to events taking place in France. Following the Allied landings in Normandy the *Luftwaffe* was engaged in a life-and-death struggle, as will be described in the next chapter.

CHAPTER 4

THE SECOND BATTLE OF FRANCE

6 June to 31 August 1944

WHEN ALLIED SEABORNE TROOPS began landing on the coast of Normandy, shortly after dawn on 6 June, the *Luftwaffe* was taken completely by surprise. No reconnaissance aircraft had been in position to observe the approach of the huge invasion armada, and initially there was no reaction from the defences. Throughout the day the troops coming ashore enjoyed the protection of more than three thousand fighters and fighter-bombers patrolling the beach-head, flying in relays from airfields in southern England.

In the face of this powerful aerial umbrella *Luftflotte 3* was unable to mount any effective attacks during the critical period immediately following the initial landings. The total *Luftwaffe* effort during the daylight hours amounted to about a hundred sorties, mostly by fighters and fighter-reconnaissance aircraft. No Me 262 operated over the beaches in the fighter or any other role, for its jet engine was still not ready for mass production.

The influx of combat units to airfields in the area of the invasion, planned so assiduously beforehand, had little effect during the critical initial phase of the landings. *III. Gruppe Schlachtgeschwader 4*, a ground-attack unit with some fifty Focke Wulf Fw 190Fs at Clastres near St-Quentin, and at Le Luc and Frières in the south of France, was one of the units now pitch-forked into the battle and its experiences were more or less typical of those enjoyed by units moving forwards. (Part of the War Diary of this *Gruppe* during the period immediately following the invasion is included at the end of this chapter.)

Although the first reports on the invasion reached the *Gruppe* at 3 a.m. on the morning of 6 June, not until 9.35 a.m. did it receive the executive order to begin the move to its designated forward operating bases at Laval and Tours. The *Gruppe Stab, 7.* and *9. Staffeln* left for Laval and *8. Staffel* left for Tours. In accordance with the standard procedure during rapid operational deployments of this type, each Focke Wulf carried its mechanic in the rear fuselage. To reduce the likelihood of encountering enemy fighters, the *Gruppe Stab* and *9. Staffel* flying in from St-Quentin to the west of Paris were ordered to take a wide detour round the south of the capital and remain at low altitude. In spite of these precautions the Focke Wulfs were intercepted by American Mustangs and Thunderbolts which shot down five, killing eight out of the ten men on board. The mechanics had no way of abandoning the aircraft in flight, and when aircraft were hit their pilots refused to bail out and leave their mechanics to certain death.

During the late afternoon *9. Staffel* mounted three attacks against the landing area near the mouth of the Orne, with a total of thirteen aircraft. Allied fighters prevented one raiding force from reaching its target, and the other two were restricted to fleeting attacks and pilots were unable to assess the damage caused.

With the onset of darkness, *Fliegerkorps X* launched about 40 aircraft to attack the concentrations of Allied shipping off the beach-head. Certainly there were targets aplenty: off the coast that night were seven battleships, 23 cruisers, 105 destroyers, more than a thousand smaller vessels and more than four thousand landing craft. Göring had termed the units equipped with guided missiles 'the spearhead of the anti-invasion force', but in the event the cutting edge proved dull and the aircraft accomplished little. *Fliegerkorps IX* flew about 130 sorties with conventional bombers, but it too failed to achieve any tangible results. During their approach flights the attackers suffered casualties not only from the Allied night fighters but also from German flak units long accustomed to regarding any aircraft that came within range as hostile. Those bombers that reached the beach-head area encountered such a violent reception from guns ashore and afloat that in many cases attacks had to be broken off prematurely. Whenever Hs 293 glider bombs were launched against the ships, escort vessels in the area radiated a cacophony of jamming to blot out their radio guidance system. All the missiles splashed into the sea safely clear of their intended victims, and on that first night not a single ship was lost to air attack.

On the following day, 7 June, the fighter-bomber unit *III./SG 4* was again in trouble. Early that morning it sent twenty-four Focke Wulfs to attack British troops coming ashore near the mouth of the River Orne. Strong patrols of defensive fighters forced most of the German aircraft to jettison their bombs before they could reach their target. Also that morning, Mustangs strafed the airfield at Laval, shooting down one Focke Wulf and destroying four more on the ground. That evening, Mustangs shot down another Focke Wulf near the airfield.

Meanwhile fighter units were being transferred from *Luftflotte Reich* to France, for the express purpose of providing top-cover for the fighter-bombers and bombers attacking the beach-head. In his book *The First and the Last*, Adolf Galland described some of the problems they encountered:

> When the invasion finally came, the carefully made preparations immediately went awry. The transfer of the fighters into France was delayed for 24 hours because *Oberkommando West* would not give the order, expecting heavier landings to be attempted in the Pas-de-Calais area. The *Luftwaffe* finally issued the order on its own authority and the transfer began.
>
> Most of the carefully prepared and provisioned airfields assigned to

the fighter units had been bombed and the units had to land at other hastily chosen landing grounds. The poor signals network broke down, causing further confusion. Each unit's advance parties came by Junkers 52, but the main body of the ground staff came by rail and most arrived days or even weeks later.

The fighter units transferred from Germany suddenly found themselves in a situation quite unlike anything they had previously encountered. For all the problems of battling against the American heavy bombers and their escorts, there was at least the advantage of operating from well-stocked permanent airfields with established radar and fighter control systems to direct their activities. In France the fighter units flew from field landing grounds with minimal facilities. The system for ground control interceptions rarely worked, and on several occasions fighter pilots failed to find their assigned airfields because they had been carefully camouflaged to conceal them from the enemy.

Representative of the home defence units transferred to France, and initially luckier than most, was *II. Gruppe Jagdgeschwader 1*. On the afternoon of 6 June the unit moved with its twenty-five Fw 190s from western Germany to Le Mans. On the following day the *Gruppe* put up its full strength in a fighter sweep to cover the roads to the south-east of the beach-head, along which German reinforcements were passing. The *Gruppe* flew three such patrols that day, fortuitously without encountering a single enemy aircraft.

On the next day, the 8th, almost all serviceable aircraft were loaded with 550lb bombs for an attack on shipping off the coast. None of the pilots had previous experience of fighter-bomber operations, and now they received only a sketchy briefing on how to perform the specialized task. Over the invasion area the pilots ran into flak they described as 'terrific', released their bombs and sped out of the area at low altitude. All the Focke Wulfs got back to base, though some had minor damage. No results were observed, and from Allied records it appears that no ship was hit. A repeat operation on the following day was similarly unsuccessful, but the luck of the *Gruppe* held and again there were no losses.

On the next day, 10 June, Le Mans airfield was attacked by more than a hundred Lancasters and Halifaxes of the Royal Air Force. Several hundred bomb craters pock-marked the landing ground, and the operations room, three hangars and several buildings were demolished. The unit's Focke Wulfs had been dispersed and camouflaged in the surrounding fields at least 500yd from the airfield, however, and none was damaged. But owing to the absence of proper earth moving equipment, and the ever-present risk of attack from Allied fighter-bombers, it was six days before sufficient of the bomb craters had been filled in to allow the unit to resume flying.

On 16 June the unit moved to Essay, from which it flew fighting patrols over the battle area for the next four days. Then it transferred to the field landing ground at Semalle, south-east of Alençon. As the unit was establishing itself at the new base, the charmed existence it had enjoyed since its arrival in the battle area came to an abrupt end. A force of Mustangs swept over the airfield and, in a series of co-ordinated strafing runs, shot up everything in sight. Within the space of a few minutes fifteen Fw 190s had been destroyed, and *II./JG 1* was out of the battle.

As a result of this continual harassment of the *Luftwaffe* by the enemy air forces, German troops received minimal air support during the hard-fought actions to contain the Allied bridgeheads.

During the nights following the invasion, the *Luftwaffe* anti-shipping units smashed themselves vainly against the powerful defences that protected the Allied landing areas. In the ten days following the invasion, *III. Gruppe Kampfgeschwader 100*, which had started June with thirteen missile-carrying Dornier Do 217s serviceable, had lost ten aircraft and eight crews. In return for such heavy losses the anti-shipping units had few successes: during that period only two destroyers and three smaller vessels were lost to direct air attack.

For its part, *Fliegerkorps IX* soon gave up trying to bomb the ships and instead resorted to sowing many hundreds of the newly developed pressure mines in the shallow waters off the coast. The mines, detonated by the wake of a passing ship, caused considerable inconvenience to Allied shipping: they were difficult to sweep, and could be countered only by reducing speed to a minimum while in shallow water. The mines caused difficulties and delays, but these were not and could not be decisive.

Among the units that moved into France to engage the invasion force was a *Staffel* of *Kampfgeschwader 101* equipped with the highly secret *Mistel* weapon. From its base at St-Dizier, the unit launched its first attack with four *Mistel* combinations on the evening of 24 June. *Hauptmann* Horst Rudat, the unit commander, led the ungainly aircraft off the ground at dusk and, with their escort of Messerschmitts, they set course for the invasion area.

Flak units along the route should have received warning of the operation and been given instructions to hold fire. But one unit received no such instruction and it opened a vigorous fire on the *Misteln* as they climbed away from their base. One of its rounds knocked out the port engine of Rudat's Ju 88. Rudat told the author:

> I was able to maintain control of my combination, but my speed was reduced so I ordered the other three aircraft to continue without me. By then darkness had fallen, and as I moved west of Le Havre I saw a British night fighter approaching me. As I had nothing with which to fight back (the armament had been removed from the Messerschmitt to save weight), I aimed the combination in the direction of a collection of landing craft and ships near the shore and released the Ju 88. The automatic pilot did not hold the aircraft on one engine, however, and it dived into the sea.

Rudat's story is confirmed in the combat report of an RAF Mosquito on patrol near the beach-head that evening. The latter's crew noted:

> The Mosquito was on patrol 25 miles west of Le Havre at an altitude of 5,000 to 6,000 feet. Visibility was excellent and a large convoy was observed about four miles to the west. Both occupants of the Mosquito had a good view, lasting 15 to 20 seconds, of an unusual biplane about a mile away. This had the appearance of a small aircraft attached to the top of a larger twin-engined type. It was possible to see between the two aircraft and they appeared to be connected at the trailing edges of the mainplane.
>
> Although the Mosquito was flown on a parallel course and must have been seen, no avoiding action was taken by the composite which proceeded on a dead straight course in the direction of the convoy. Its speed was estimated to be between 200 and 250mph.

As those in the Mosquito tried to identify the unusual machine, the smaller aircraft suddenly lifted off the larger one and disappeared from view. The larger aircraft (the Ju 88) was seen to roll on its back and dive into the sea, exploding with a bright orange flash that lit up the sky for miles around. One of the explosive Ju 88s launched that night blew up near the head-quarters ship HMS *Nith*, causing extensive splinter damage. The ship had to be withdrawn for repairs.

During its operations against shipping off the coast of Normandy, *Kampfgeschwader 101* launched about ten *Mistel* combinations. At least one hit was claimed on 'a battleship', but apart from *Nith* there is no record of any Allied ship being damaged by the novel weapon. A possible explanation that would fit the known facts is that the Ju 88 had been launched against one of the old ships abandoned and sunk in shallow water as part of the breakwater for the 'Mulberry' artificial harbour. There is evidence that the old French battleship *Courbet*, which served in this role, might have been hit by one of the explosive Ju 88s.

A further revolutionary new weapon to see action during the Battle of Normandy was the Messerschmitt Me 262 jet aircraft; it will be remembered that at Hitler's insistence this aircraft had been modified to carry bombs, to provide a weapon to disrupt the invasion in its early stages. The first fighter-bomber unit to receive the Me 262, *3. Staffel Kampfgeschwader 51*, had begun training with the new aircraft on 20 June (exactly two weeks after the initial Allied landings). A month after its formation the unit was declared operational – far too short a time for pilots to become familiar with the foibles of the completely new machine – and, under the command of *Major* Wolfgang Schenk, it moved with nine Me 262s to Chateaudun to the south-west of Paris.

Operating in the fighter-bomber role, the Me 262 carried two 550lb bombs. In order to minimize the risk of one of these advanced aircraft being shot down and falling into enemy hands, their pilots had strict orders not to descend below 4,000m (13,000ft) while over enemy territory. Because the converted fighter had no downwards-looking bombsight, the bombs had to be released using the normal gunsight and accurate aiming was almost impossible from such an altitude against small battlefield targets such as bridges or vehicles moving along roads. In spite of a careful search of Allied records, this author has found no mention of German jet fighter-bombers operating over France during the summer of 1944. It seems that the speed and altitude performance of the Me 262 concealed its presence over the battle area even more effectively than the German High Command can have hoped, and the lack of any tangible result from these first jet fighter-bomber operations undoubtedly assisted in preserving the secret.

Throughout the Battle of Normandy Allied army commanders received frequent and comprehensive photographic coverage of the enemy positions in front of them. In stark contrast, German field commanders often received no warning of a build-up of Allied forces until the leading units came within view of their forward positions. During the battle *Luftwaffe* reconnaissance units endeavoured to fly two types of operation: high-speed low-altitude visual and photographic reconnaissance sorties by day, flown by Messerschmitt 109s of the tactical reconnaissance units; and high-altitude night photographic missions by Me 410s and Ju 188s of strategic reconnaissance units.

The tactics employed by the Bf 109 reconnaissance units were straightforward enough, though often hazardous in view of the magnitude of the opposition. Usually the aircraft operated in pairs, one of each pair conducting the reconnaissance while the other kept watch for enemy fighters. On rare occasions a fighter escort would be provided if a reconnaissance of a particularly heavily defended area were required, but usually the reconnaissance pilots had to penetrate the defences on their own.

In the nature of things, photographs taken at night gave considerably less information than those taken by day. However, the all-pervading Allied fighter patrols rendered high-altitude daylight photography too dangerous to be contemplated. During a night mission the aircraft would run through the target area at high speed, at altitudes of around 20,000ft, and release a photo-flash bomb fused to ignite at about 4,000ft above the surface. On ignition the bomb gave a flash of 6,000,000 candlepower lasting for a third of a second, and this automatically closed the shutter of the camera and wound on the film for the next photograph. Then the shutter opened again for the next shot. Usually four or five pictures were taken in this way, at ten-second intervals. By the end of that time the night fighter and gun defences in the area were thoroughly alerted and the German crew had to dive to low altitude and beat a hasty retreat.

As was to be expected, such reconnaissance methods produced only a fragmentary picture of the Allied dispositions. The powerful defences took a mounting toll of both aircraft and crews, and, if they were to survive, the latter had often to break off their missions at the first sign of trouble.

The lack of aerial reconnaissance had serious consequences.

At the end of July American troops broke out of the western side of the lodgement area and, unknown to the German High Command, advanced rapidly down the western side of the Cherbourg peninsula. On the last day of the month they seized intact the bridges over the Rivers See and Sélune at the southern end of the peninsula. News of the advance reached the German headquarters, but too late. General Patton, commander of the US Third Army, realized his heaven-sent opportunity and poured troops across the bridges and into the open countryside beyond to outflank the enemy defences. Of the incident, the famous historian Chester Wilmot later wrote:

> Patton did not wait to draw up movement plans or march tables. The bottleneck of the single road from Avranches to Pontaubault became a sheep race. At the mouth senior officers herded units through in any order. At the exit each division was allocated one of the roads radiating from Pontaubault and, as its units came through the race, they were drafted down the appropriate route . . . Defying field regulations and textbook rules, Patton moved seven divisions down this one road in 72 hours.

Once they were through the bottleneck the American armoured units fanned out, the majority swinging to the east in a right hook that aimed at the rear of the German troops containing the beach-head.

Here was a fighter-bombers' paradise – mile upon mile of vehicles moving slowly and jammed nose-to-tail along the narrow road between the two bridges, and a marvellous opportunity for the *Luftwaffe* to disrupt the operation. But the German fighter-bombers were quite unable to penetrate the web of defensive air patrols protecting Patton's troops. In a desperate attempt to stop the advance, Dornier Do 217s of *III./KG 100* attacked the bridges with Henschel Hs 293 glider bombs on the nights of 2, 4, 5 and 6 August. One hit was claimed on the bridge at Pontaubault, for the loss of six aircraft and crews, but the damage was not serious and the bridge continued in use.

In a bid to resolve the problems caused by the lack of effective aerial reconnaissance, near the end of July the *Luftwaffe* dispatched to France two Arado Ar 234 jet aircraft, the fifth and seventh prototypes, fitted for the high-altitude reconnaissance role. On the 25th the two aircraft had taken off from Oranienburg for their new operating base at Juvincourt near Reims, but almost from the start there were difficulties. That flown by *Oberleutnant* Horst Götz, the unit commander, suffered an engine failure during transit and had to return to Oranienburg for an engine change. The other pilot, *Oberleutnant* Erich Sommer, landed at Juvincourt without incident. To keep the arrival of the aircraft secret, it was immediately hoisted on to a low-loader and towed into a hangar. Then, despite the desperate need for its services, the world's most advanced reconnaissance aircraft had now to remain ineffective on the ground for more than a week. To save weight, the early production Ar 234s were not fitted with conventional undercarriages; instead, they took off from a special trolley that was released as they left the ground (only one trolley had been built for each aircraft and, because of minor differences between each of the Arados in the prototype series, the trolleys were not interchangeable among the aircraft). The new aircraft also required a pair of liquid fuel rocket booster pods if it were to get airborne with a full fuel load.

More than a week elapsed before the all-important trolley, rocket pods, ground equipment and spare parts reached Juvincourt from Oranienburg by rail – and not until the morning of 2 August was everything ready for Erich Sommer to take off on the world's first jet reconnaissance mission. After getting airborne Sommer headed west for Normandy and climbed rapidly to 34,000ft. High over the Cherbourg peninsula the German pilot turned on to an easterly heading, levelled off and let his speed build up to 460mph, then began his photo runs. As the invasion beaches passed beneath the Arado the two cameras in the rear fuselage, each fitted with a 50cm telephoto lens, took in a swathe of ground just over 6 miles wide. At 11-second intervals the cameras' shutters flicked open and closed.

It was a beautiful summer's day, with scarcely a wisp of cloud to hinder the operation. From the German pilot's lofty vantage point scarcely anything could be seen of the life-and-death struggle taking place on the ground. If any Allied fighter attempted to intercept the high-flying Arado, Sommer never noticed it. He was too busy concentrating on holding his wings level and flying a dead straight track. The first photographic run, taking in the coastal strip, lasted about ten minutes. Then Sommer turned to port through a semi-circle and flew a second run six miles inland and parallel to the first. Ten minutes later he began his third run, heading east, six miles further inland and parallel to the other two. Near the end of the third run the film ran out.

Sommer continued on his easterly heading and took the Arado back to Juvincourt in a high-speed descent, keeping a wary eye open for Allied fighters. Even before the new plane had slid to a halt on the grass, men were converging on it from all directions. The camera hatch above the rear fuselage was opened and the magazines bearing the precious film were lifted out and whisked away for developing. Again the Arado was hoisted on to the low-loader and driven back to its hangar.

In a single flight lasting less than 90 minutes Erich Sommer, alone, had achieved what had been beyond the entire *Luftwaffe* reconnaissance force in the west for the previous eight weeks: he had photographed almost the entire Allied lodgement area in Normandy. The 380 photographs he brought back caused an enormous stir: by then the Allies had landed more than 1½ million men and 300,000 vehicles in France. Working flat-out, it took a twelve-man team of photo interpreters more than two days to produce an initial assessment of what the photographs revealed. Detailed examination of the prints took some weeks.

Also on 2 August, Horst Götz finally reached Juvincourt in the other Arado. During the three weeks that followed the two aircraft flew thirteen further missions. At last the German army commanders received regular reconnaissance of the enemy rear areas, the vital information that had been denied to them for so long.

Like the Me 262 fighter-bombers, the Ar 234s appear to have escaped Allied notice and this author has found no report mentioning their operations over France at this time. For Sommer and Götz it was the highest possible compliment that could be paid: their task had been take the photographs and bring back the precious film, avoiding contact with the enemy. However, even as Sommer's initial batch of photographs was being analyzed, the time when such information might play a decisive part in the land battle was long past. By then the American troops had broken out of the beach-head area and were advancing southwards rapidly. The thousands of photographs brought back by the Arados did no more than provide a detailed picture of a battle already lost.

August saw the rout of the German armies in France. After their break-out from the beach-head, the American spearheads swung south and then east, aiming to encircle the German troops attempting to contain the eastern end of the Allied lodgement area. Unable to sustain their stubborn defence of Normandy any longer, the German forces began a headlong retreat to the east.

While all this was happening, events taking place outside France began to catch up with *Luftflotte 3*. The fuel crisis was starting to bite and in the first week in July it had been necessary to withdraw the Heinkel He 177 and Focke Wulf Fw 200 anti-shipping units to Germany. They were soon followed by the remnants of the twin-engined bomber force. Once back in Germany, many of the bomber units were disbanded.

On 11 August all units received orders to restrict flying in order to conserve stocks of fuel. Fighters were permitted to undertake unrestricted operations only against enemy heavy bombers. By the middle of August there were, in any case, only about 75 single-engined fighters available for operations in the whole of *Luftflotte 3*. As the German retreat turned into a rout, four more fighter *Gruppen* were rushed to France from *Luftflotte Reich* – at the expense of the strategic defence of the homeland – in an attempt to provide air cover for the badly mauled German ground forces. The new units made little difference. As one German soldier who took part in that retreat bitterly commented: 'If the aircraft above us were camouflaged, we knew that they were British. If they were silver, we knew that they were American. And if they weren't there at all, we knew that they were German!'

From time to time home defence fighter *Gruppen* were sent to France to replace units that had taken a beating and had to be withdrawn. One such newcomer was *II./JG 6*, an Fw 190 *Gruppe* formed recently with pilots from Messerschmitt Me 410 bomber-destroyer units that had been disbanded. When the *Gruppe* arrived at the field landing ground at Herpy near Reims on 23 August, *Feldwebel* Fritz Bucholz had less than eleven hours' flying time on single-engined fighters and no dog-fighting experience. Bucholz told the author:

> Our airstrip at Herpy was nothing more than a piece of flat cow pasture surrounded by trees in which our aircraft could be hidden; nearby was our tented accommodation. The Allied fighter-bombers seemed to be everywhere and our survival depended on the strictest attention to camouflage. As part of this we even had a herd of cows which we moved on to the airfield when no flying was in progress; as well as giving the place a rustic look, these performed the valuable task of obliterating the tracks made on the grass by the aircraft. Such attention to detail paid off and there were no attacks on Herpy while I was there.

II./JG 6 fought its first major action on 25 August, when *Hauptmann* Elstermann led the entire *Gruppe* with some forty fighters on an offensive patrol towards the battle area. Near St-Quentin the German force surprised a dozen P38 Lightnings of the 394th Fighter Squadron in the act of strafing the airfield at Clastres. Six American fighters were shot down in quick succession, but their distress calls summoned the P-38s of the other two squadrons of the 367th Fighter Group and when these joined the fight they quickly turned the tables. In the mêlée that followed, *II./JG 6* lost sixteen aircraft destroyed and several more damaged, and accounted for only one more Lightning. Numerically, the two forces had been almost equal and the Fw 190 should have been more than a match for the P-38. But, like Bucholz, the German pilots had little dog-fighting experience. One of those killed in the engagement was *Leutnant* Rudi Dassow, one of the most successful German bomber-destroyer pilots with 22 victories to his credit.

Although it had lost nearly half of its strength during its first disastrous action, *II./JG 6* was allowed no time to recover. On the following day its surviving aircraft and pilots were ordered to mount a fighting patrol to provide cover for German forces pulling back over the River Seine. Bucholz recalled:

> Again I led my *Schwarm* and we made for our briefed patrol area near Rouen. Soon after our arrival in the battle area, however, we were 'bounced' out of the sun by Mustangs. I never even saw the aircraft that hit me. All I heard was a loud bang and the next thing I knew my aircraft was tumbling out of the sky with part of the tail shot away. I blew off the canopy and struggled to get clear of the spinning aircraft, but my right foot became wedged under the instrument panel. After what seemed an age, I managed to wrench it away though I left my flying boot behind and my foot struck the tailplane as I was falling clear. My parachute opened normally and I landed on the west bank of the Seine near Duclair.

Bucholz was picked up by men from an SS rearguard unit and that night he crossed the Seine by ferry. His wounds would keep him out of action for six weeks. When he finally rejoined *II./JG 6* its complement of personnel had changed completely: of the forty or so pilots that had set out for France, only about four remained.

The losses suffered by *II./JG 6* were repeated in many of the German fighter units plunged into the maelstrom over France during the summer of 1944. Other units, perhaps with more experience in dog-fighting, remained intact for longer, but sooner or later the fates caught up with almost every one of them. Such was the general dislocation of forces, there were few serious attempts to conduct co-ordinated operations. Thanks to Albert Speer's energetic measures, the *Luftwaffe*'s fighter force had plenty of aircraft and ammunition. But it was desperately short of combat proficient pilots, and it had neither the time nor the fuel to train new ones.

By the beginning of September 1944 *Luftflotte 3* was a spent force. *Generalfeldmarschall* Sperrle was held responsible for the poor showing of his units and transferred to the reserve. Given the limited forces available, it is doubtful whether anyone else could have secured better results. *Generaloberst* Otto Desloch replaced Sperrle, but soon afterwards *Luftflotte 3* was downgraded to *Luftwaffenkommando West* and subordinated to *Luftflotte Reich*.

Now the depleted units that had fought in France prepared to hold the new line along the western frontier of Germany. But before we observe their performance, chronology demands that we shift our attention to events on the Eastern Front. These will be described in the next chapter.

WAR DIARY, *III. GRUPPE SCHLACHTGESCHWADER 4*

At the time of the invasion this ground-attack unit was equipped with some fifty Focke Wulf Fw 190Fs and its constituent Staffeln were based at Clastres near St-Quentin, and at Le Luc and Frières in the south of France. This excerpt from its war diary gives an insight into the confusion that reigned following the Allied landings.

6.6.44
At 03.00hrs the commander was informed by Derfflinger Ia [operations officer at headquarters] *Major* Fahrenburg that there had been landings by enemy airborne forces to the north of Caen and landings of seaborne forces near the mouth of the Seine. At 06.45hrs, on his own discretion, the commander ordered the *Gruppe* to come to Readiness State 1. At 07.45hrs Derfflinger Ia gave orders for the *Gruppe* to prepare to move to [forward airfields in] the Le Mans area. On the question of whether to begin moving immediately, the reply came that teleprinter confirmation should be awaited. One of the previously stated codewords for use in the event of an enemy landing had not been given. The order to prepare for the move was given to unit commanders by the [*Gruppe*] commander.

All airworthy combat aircraft were to prepare to leave, with their pilots and 1st mechanics. [It was standard procedure to carry mechanics in the rear fuselage of single-seat fighters during rapid operational deployments of this type.] Key personnel and the doctor will follow in two Ju 52s.

After the teleprinter order to move to Laval was received at 09.35hrs, the individual *Staffeln* took off as follows:
12.00hrs, *7. Staffel* from Le Luc to land at Laval at 19.00hrs.

12.15hrs, *Stab* and *9. Staffel* from Clastres, to land at Laval at 13.35hrs.
13.45hrs, *8. Staffel* from Frières, to land at Tours at 14.45hrs.

For security reasons [to reduce the risk of encountering enemy fighters] the machines which took off from St-Quentin were ordered to fly round the south of Paris at low level. In spite of this, all units were intercepted by the enemy and there were dog-fights with American Mustangs and Thunderbolts.

The losses of the *Gruppe* on 6.6.44 were:

Pilots:

Oblt. Pühringer	killed	*Uffz.* Speer	killed
Obfw. Kollburg	killed	*Lt.* Limberg	wounded
Fw. Brauneis	killed		

Mechanics:

Fw. Eidam	killed	*Obgef.* Ohlwein	killed
Uffz. Krüsmann	killed	*Obgef.* Kleinker	wounded
Uffz. Ebert	killed		

From 17.00hrs *9. Staffel* mounted *Schwarm*-strength [four to five aircraft] attacks against enemy landings and vehicle concentrations near the mouth of the Orne, with a total of three operations with thirteen aircraft. In one case it was not possible to reach the target area owing to the presence of strong enemy defences. Lessons learned from the move:

1. The *Gruppe* could have deployed earlier, if the order to begin the move had been issued earlier by *Korps*.
2. In view of the superiority of the RAF and the USAAF over France, it is unwise to carry mechanics in combat aircraft.
3. The airfield at Laval was quite unprepared for the arrival of the ground-attack unit. There were no refuelling vehicles, no bomb loading trolleys, no personnel to assist and, above all, no airfield defence at all. The airfield commander had been told not to expect the unit to arrive until evening, and that missions would be flown only from the following morning. There was little room to disperse [the aircraft] and accommodation had been prepared too close to the airfield.

7.6.44

At 04.30hrs the two Ju 52s took off from Clastres carrying key personnel for Tours; they should have taken off at 13.00hrs the previous day but then they arrived eight hours late. When they arrived it was impossible to go further by road, in spite of strenuous efforts: further flights by Ju 52 [to take the personnel nearer to the combat area] were out of the question. Not until two days later, on 9 June, did the servicing team arrive at Laval.

From 06.00hrs four operations were mounted, in which 24 aircraft were sent against landings and tank concentrations in the area of the mouth of the River Orne [where British troops were coming ashore]. Because of the strong fighter defences, three of the operations had to be broken off before reaching the target and the bombs jettisoned.

At about 10.00hrs ten Mustangs carried out a strafing attack on the airfield. *Lt.* Essau was shot down and severely wounded, and four Fw 190s were destroyed on the ground.

At about 21.00hrs there was an attack on aircraft of *8. Staffel* as they were coming in from Tours, by three Mustangs. *Oblt.* Dahle was shot down and wounded.

In spite of favourable weather our operations achieved little, because successful operations were impossible without effective fighter protection. The losses in pilots and aircraft on this day can all be blamed on the absence of any flak defence at the airfield.

8.6.44

At 12.40hrs three operations with seventeen aircraft were flown against the enemy troops landing near Riva Bella and the Orne Bridge near Benouville. Owing to the strength of the fighter defences one of these operations had to be broken off prematurely. *Fw.* George is missing. For the first time there was a fighter escort, provided by *I./JG 11* [with Bf 109s]. On the whole these operations achieved little, because it was impossible to keep to the planned rendezvous points and routes ordered by *Fliegerführer West.* Because of continuous enemy air activity over the airfields, individual units could not meet their assigned take-off times; and because of dog-fights on the approach routes it was not possible to keep rendezvous times. At 22.00hrs the vehicle column arrived from Clastres. Losses due to air attack: one car, one lorry, one mobile workshop with trailer.

During the evening the *Kommandeur* attended a conference to discuss operational policy, held at [headquarters] *Fliegerführer West.* The operations planned by *II. Fliegerkorps* the previous day could not be carried out at the times given. Operational matters such as the strength of attacks, timing, routing, defensive tactics in the light of the prevailing weather situation, should be left to *Fliegerführer West* [commander of the fighter and fighter-bomber units] or, better still, to the *Gruppe* commanders. The last order, for the attack on Arromanches approaching from Trouville along the whole length of the invasion coast, was nonsensical and disregarded the fact that the flight distance [to the target] was more than 200km [125 miles]. It could have been ordered only by people who had no idea of the situation or the strength of the enemy defences. *II Fliegerkorps* will not be argued out of its previous inflexible way of giving orders. [For a unit war diary, this is a remarkably forthright criticism of the conduct of a higher formation.]

9.6.44

06.10hrs. Early operation in poor weather at the lowest possible altitude. The target was not reached. A late attack, at 20.10hrs, was made against the landings at Riva Bella. The *Gruppe* commander made an emergency landing at Falaise. Altogether fourteen aircraft operated. During the night there was a heavy attack by four-engined bombers [on the airfield]. The runway was cut in several places by bomb craters.

10.6.44

Released from operations, airfield still cannot be used. *Hptm.* Wedekind and *Lt.* Limberg visit *Fliegerführer West.*

11.6.44

Released from operations, work on runway.

12.6.44

06.35hrs. Operation by four aircraft against the landing area at Riva Bella. The target could not be reached and bombs were jettisoned. *Ofw.* Schopper made an emergency landing. Operations should have started to fly supplies to *Luftwaffe* personnel at the strong point at Douvres [a radar station near the coast, which was still holding out after being encircled by British troops]. But at the take-off point all four Fw 190s were destroyed in a strafing attack by eight Spitfires. Two fighters (Bf 109s) were shot down. After that the unit was stood down.

Ten pilots were sent to Le Bourget to pick up new aircraft.

CHAPTER 5

DISASTER IN THE EAST

1 June to mid-October 1944

AT THE BEGINNING of June 1944, as their counterparts in the west battled to prevent British and American troops securing a foothold in Normandy, *Luftwaffe* units on the Eastern Front braced themselves to meet the expected summer offensive by the Red Army.

A last-minute though very welcome addition to the *Luftwaffe*'s strength was *Kampfgeschwader 1*, now declared operational with three *Gruppen* of Heinkel He 177 heavy bombers and based at airfields around Königsberg. With a strength of about a hundred four-engined bombers, the *Geschwader* was the most powerful strategic striking force possessed by either side on the Front. The heavy bombers went into action almost immediately but, although several strategic targets lay within range, *KG 1* made no attempt to hit them. Even in normal times the limited supply of fuel imposed a major constraint on heavy bomber operations. No reserves of fuel were held at the bomber airfields, and the exact amount needed for specific operations and training flights was delivered by rail the day before it was required.

Nevertheless, when fuel was available, *KG 1* operated as effectively as it could. With the Soviets making obvious final preparations for their summer offensive, the German Army needed all possible help to soften the blow when it came. The Heinkels delivered formation attacks by day on supply centres and troop assembly areas, flying at altitudes of around 20,000ft. The Soviet Air Force, equipped primarily for the low-level interception and ground-attack roles, could do little to hinder the activities of the high-flying bombers. Those fighters which did claw themselves up to the He 177's attack altitude showed the greatest respect for the defensive cross-fire put up by the bombers, and rarely would they press home their attacks.

In the course of these operations *KG 1* carried out several pattern-bombing attacks. During the most powerful of these the *Geschwader* commander, *Oberstleutnant* Horst von Riesen, led a formation of eighty-seven Heinkel 177s against the important rail centre at Velikye Luki, 300 miles west of Moscow. The force made an impressive sight as it attacked in a formation of three closely spaced vee-shaped waves, each wave comprising a *Gruppe* of about thirty heavy bombers.

On 10 June, four days after the initial landings in Normandy, Soviet ground forces opened their summer offensive. Contrary to German expectations, the blow fell not on the Central Front

THE
EASTERN
FRONT
May 1944

Leningrad

BALTIC SEA

ESTONIA

Riga

LATVIA

LITHUANIA

East
Prussia

Moscow

Dnieper

Smolensk

Minsk

Warsaw

SOVIET UNION

POLAND

Pinsk

Pinsk
Marshes

Kursk

Kiev

Kremenchug

Theiss

Ukraine

HUNGARY

Dniester

Bug

Pruth

Iasi

Dnieper

Odessa

RUMANIA

Ploesti

Bucharest

Sevastopol

BLACK   SEA

Front line,
1 May 1944

or in the south, but on the Finnish frontier at Karelia on the Gulf
of Finland. Initially the weak *Luftflotte 5* forces in this area had
to bear the brunt of the fighting, reinforced only with a couple
of *Gruppen* of Junkers Ju 87s from *Luftflotte 1*. The German High
Command had suspected, rightly, that the attack in the north was
merely a diversion and the main reserves were held in place
further south.

On 21 June the He 111 medium bomber units of *Luftflotte 6*
enjoyed a rare success. On that day a force of 163 Flying
Fortresses of the Eighth Air Force took part in Operation

'Frantic': after attacking the oil refinery at Schwarzheide, the formations continued eastwards over Poland with their escorting Mustangs. The bombers landed at Poltava and Mirgorod, and the fighters at Pirjatin, in the Soviet Union. It was intended to carry out a similar shuttle mission in the opposite direction a couple of days later and land in Italy. The *Luftwaffe* had other plans, however.

A Junkers Ju 88 reconnaissance aircraft of *Fernaufklärungs-gruppe 100* followed the American bombers to the Soviet airfields and photographed them on the ground. At their bases in Poland, He 111s of seven *Gruppen* of *General* Rudolf Meister's *Flieger-korps IV*, drawn from *KG 4, KG 53* and *KG 55*, were ordered to prepare an immediate riposte. That night about 200 Heinkels took off to attack Poltava and Mirgorod, the machines of *KG 4* being loaded with flares to serve as pathfinders for the rest of the force. Poor weather in the target area led to the attack on Mirgorod being abandoned, and all units attacked Poltava. After releasing their high-explosive and incendiary bombs, several of the Heinkels descended to low altitude to carry out strafing runs on the parked aircraft lit up by the flares.

Daylight revealed the success of the German attack. Of the 72 Flying Fortresses dispersed around the airfield, 44 were wrecked and 26 damaged – only two heavy bombers had survived un-scathed. Of the other US and Soviet aircraft on the airfield, five were destroyed and 28 damaged. The airfield's fuel dump had been set ablaze and some 400,000 gallons of aviation fuel destroyed.

Ignorant of the raiders' intention to attack Mirgorod, but fearful of this possibility, the US commander ordered his surviving B-17s to move to Zaporozhe 150 miles to the south to put them beyond the reach of the German bombers. It was a wise move. The following evening *Fliegerkorps IV* delivered a heavy attack on Mirgorod which caused considerable damage to ground installations. When the US heavy bomber force left the Soviet Union on 26 June, to attack Drohobyz in Hungary before flying on to airfields in Italy, it was without more than half of the 162 Flying Fortresses that had flown in. Never again would the Americans attempt a shuttle operation of this type.

Luftflotte 6 was allowed little time to savour its victory at Poltava for, two days later on 23 June, the main Soviet offensive opened with a series of powerful attacks on the Central Front. The Soviet planners had realized that the key to the land battle lay in the defeat of the German artillery; because of the weakened state of German infantry and armoured units, on the Eastern Front there was great reliance on artillery concentra-tions to provide the necessary firepower to stiffen the defences. If attacks by the Soviet Air Force could prevent the German gunners from engaging the armoured thrusts effectively, the Front might collapse. During the previous six months several fighter *Gruppen* had been withdrawn from the *Luftflotten* in the east for the defence of the German homeland; now there were insufficient fighters left on the Eastern Front even to provide local air superiority in times of crisis. When the offensive began, the German fighter force was quite unable to stem the heavy attacks on artillery and other forward positions by Soviet bombers and ground-attack aircraft, nor could it provide cover for German aircraft attempting similar attacks on enemy forces moving forward. In his book *Hitler's War on Russia*, Paul Carell wrote:

> By means of well-prepared air strikes, the Russians succeeded in eliminating the previously reconnoitred or rapidly pinpointed gun positions of the German artillery. The backbone of the German defence was broken. The German infantry was helpless against any motorised or mechanised enemy. The same dilemma arose as in the West. Soviet ground-support aircraft bombed the retreating columns of the German rearward services and reserve units at bridges and road bottlenecks. The effect was devastating. There was chaos on the roads. No switching of units was possible, no movement was feasible. Faced with this sudden enemy superiority in the air, the German divisions were desperate and, in view of their defencelessness, frequently panicked. There was nothing the German command could do.

The powerful onslaught smashed through the German lines in several places, turning defeat to rout. Like an avalanche pounding down a mountain and sweeping all before it, the Soviet Army stormed forward.

Too little and too late, the *Luftwaffe* dispatched forces from the Western Front, Germany and the Mediterranean in an attempt to shore up the breach. The reinforcements amounted to four *Gruppen* of fighters and three of fighter-bombers, while *Luftflotte 4* transferred in several of its 'tank-busting' units.

As well as being heavily outnumbered by their Soviet opponents, the German fighter units had to switch their airfields frequently, both to keep ahead of the enemy advance and to meet the successive crises at different parts of the Front. For example, during an eight-day period following the opening of the Soviet offensive, the Bf 109s of *I./JG 51* made no fewer than seven changes of base:

23 June: At the start of the offensive the *Gruppe* was based at Orsha, and had a strength of 28 aircraft.

25 June: As Orsha was threatened by the Soviet advance, the *Gruppe* left for Dokudovo at 21.00hrs.

26 June: *Gruppe* ordered to move from Dokodovo to Bojary at 04.30, to be ready for operations at 10.00hrs. Made a further move at 17.30hrs to Skobrovka, but owing to a lack of fuel stocks at the airfield it was unable to conduct operations from there and the *Gruppe* returned to Bojary. Later that evening the unit, by now down to twenty aircraft, flew to Baranovicki to support an attack by bombers of *KG 1*.

27 June: Transfer at 12.00hrs to Minsk. At 18.00 a further transfer from Minsk to Pukhovichi. Now down to eighteen aircraft.

1 July: Withdrawal from Pukhovichi to Pinsk.

During each change of base, the *Gruppe* was effectively out of action. Moreover, during the moves to keep ahead of the Soviet advance, several aircraft with minor unserviceablities that prevented them getting airborne had to be blown up to prevent their falling intact into enemy hands.

When the Soviet offensive began, *Leutnant* Werner Gail of *III./Schlachtgeschwader 3* was in Germany where his unit was re-equipping with Fw 190Fs. The ground-attack unit was immediately recalled to the east and was soon in the thick of the fighting, operating from Idriza in western Russia. Gail recalled:

Our task was to do all we could to delay the thrusts, to give the German ground forces time to improvise defensive positions to stop the rush. Wherever there was a hole in the Front, it was our job to try to plug it.

During this period the ground situation was so fluid that we had to start each day with an armed reconnaissance: two or three *Schwarme* were sent to patrol different parts of the area assigned to our *Gruppe*, to see if the enemy had moved and if so where. Since we soon came to know our area well and we knew where the enemy had been the night before, we had a good idea where to start looking for him the following morning. Also, whenever enemy armoured units had broken through, they would advance through open country, which made the task of finding them much easier.

Once the reconnaissance *Schwarme* had returned and its pilots had reported on the latest enemy positions, the *Gruppe* was allocated its targets for the day in order of importance.

Our Focke Wulfs were armed with two 13mm machine guns and two 2cm cannon, which we used for strafing attacks. The bombs we used during these operations were mainly 550 and 1,100lb and also SD-2, SD-4 and SD-10 bomblets carried in large numbers in containers.

When we found enemy units moving forwards unopposed, as a matter of policy we concentrated our attacks on the soft-skinned supply vehicles; these were relatively easy to knock out with machine-gun and cannon fire and we knew that without frequent replenishments of fuel the tanks spearheading the advance would not get far. If the enemy armoured units were actually in contact with our ground forces, however, then the tanks themselves were our main target.

The normal unit during these attacks was the four-aircraft *Schwarm*, though against the larger enemy troop concentrations sometimes as many as twelve aircraft would be used. Usually we would approach our target at altitudes around 6,000ft, above the effective reach of the enemy light flak, though if there were much cloud about we would keep underneath it so as to maintain contact with the ground. Against the enemy tanks and armoured vehicles we usually made skip-bombing attacks, running in at speeds of around 300mph at between 15 and 30ft above the ground and releasing the bomb as the tank disappeared beneath our engine cowling. The 550lb bombs used during these attacks would either skip off the ground and into the tank, or else smash straight into the tank; the bombs were fused with a one-second delay, to give us time to get clear before they went off. It was a very accurate form of attack and we used it often against the tanks we caught in open country. Once we had released our bombs, we would use up our cannon and machine-gun ammunition against suitable targets round about.

During the first part of the Russian offensive the pace of operations of our *Gruppe* was very high, sometimes with as many as seven or eight sorties per day. On average the sorties lasted only about half an hour;

the enemy was never very far away. Sometimes we caught Russian units that had outrun their flak cover and then we could do a lot of damage and suffer hardly any losses ourselves. But if the enemy units did have proper flak cover our losses were sometimes heavy. Only rarely did we come into contact with Russian fighters. I personally saw them on only two occasions and on neither did we lose an aircraft. Even so, the general view of the more experienced people on the Eastern Front was that in the summer of 1944 the Russian fighters were much more active than they had been during previous years.

The reinforcement of fighter-bombers to the Central Front was insufficient to stem the tide, and the Soviet troops began to advance on a wide front. Among the combat units heavily committed were the specialized tank-busting units equipped with Henschel Hs 129s and Junkers Ju 87Gs fitted with 3cm and 3.7cm cannon. *Major* Hans Rudel, commander of *Schlachtgeschwader 2*, described this type of attack with the Ju 87G:

> Sometimes we dive on to the steel monsters from behind, sometimes from the side. The angle of attack is not too steep to prevent us flying in quite close to the ground, and so also when pulling out from getting into any trouble in case the aircraft overshoots. If it overshoots too far it is hardly possible to avoid contact with the ground with all its dangerous consequences.
>
> We always to try to hit the tank in one of its most vulnerable places. The front is always the strongest part of every tank; therefore every tank invariably tries as far as possible to offer its front to the enemy. Its sides are less strongly protected. But the best target for us is the stern. It is there that the engine is housed, and the necessity for cooling this power centre permits only a thin armour plating. In order to assist the cooling, this plating is perforated with large holes. This is a good spot to aim at because where the engine is there is always petrol. When its engine is running a tank is easily recognizable from the air by the blue fumes of the exhaust . . .
>
> I go out with aircraft of my anti-tank *Staffel* carrying the 37mm cannon on tank hunts at the lowest possible level . . . Generally there are none of our fighters there; the Russians realize their enormous numerical superiority over us alone.

Rudel was the leading exponent of tank-busting operation with the cannon-armed Ju 87G, and would end the war credited with the destruction of 519 Soviet tanks.

Also heavily committed to contain the Soviet summer offensive were the three *Nachtschlachtgruppen* (night harassment *Gruppen*) assigned to *Luftflotten 4* and 6. Apart from a few Ju 87s, the force was equipped with Arado Ar 66 and Gotha Go 145 two-seat biplane trainers modified to carry machine guns and racks for small bombs. Each night these slow-flying aircraft flew nuisance raids over the enemy rear areas, where they bombed and strafed any enemy movement they detected on the ground. These operations used relatively little fuel, incurred few casualties and exerted a continual pressure on the enemy, but they were unable to put down the concentrated firepower necessary to inflict a major blow.

As the situation on the ground became progressively more

desperate, it became necessary to employ almost every available aircraft in the close-support role to arrest the Soviet rush westwards. Horst von Riesen even received orders from Göring in person to send his big He 177 bombers into action against the advancing enemy tanks. It was a reckless way to employ such large aircraft, for to stand much chance of hitting small moving targets the bombers had to attack from low altitude. But Göring ignored von Riesen's protests to this effect and insisted that the operation be mounted.

Von Riesen sent his He 177s out in pairs to engage the enemy tanks, in the hope that the combined firepower from a couple of aircraft would be sufficient to provide adequate protection from the fighter attack. It was not, and the use of the four-engined heavy bomber in this role was a fiasco. *KG 1* lost nearly a quarter of the forty or so He 177s it committed in this way, most of them to Soviet fighters, before it was released from the commitment. It is doubtful whether a single Soviet tank was destroyed during the unit's low-altitude attacks.

Kampfgeschwader 1 resumed attacks from high altitude, whenever the fuel supply allowed. On 20 July the unit put up almost every serviceable bomber it had, the three *Gruppen* attacking separate targets. During their assembly into formation, the He 177s circled over one of the distinctive lakes in the area. Near to Königsberg was Rastenburg, Adolf Hitler's war headquarters, a heavily wooded area which *Luftwaffe* aircraft were not to overfly without special permission. Von Riesen told the author of the events of that day as he saw them:

> At mid-day we assembled over one corner of the lake to the east of the Rastenburg prohibited area. To assemble 80 aircraft into three formations takes a lot of time, and as luck would have it a couple of the aircraft developed engine fires. My crews had been previously briefed that in this event they were to release their bombs 'safe' [i.e. set so that they did not go off on impact] and aimed into the lake. This the crews did, and I set off with one of my *Gruppen* to make the attack.
>
> It was about five o'clock in the afternoon when I landed at Prowehren, and I did not get to my headquarters until six o'clock. There I was met by my adjutant who looked very serious. He ushered me into an empty office and said, 'A terrible thing has happened. One of our machines obviously did not drop its bombs "safe"; moreover they landed on the *Führer*'s headquarters and caused an explosion there'.

Von Riesen telephoned his Corps headquarters, and was told that an officer from the legal branch was on his way to collect evidence for a possible court martial – Von Riesen's. Then came a news-flash on the radio, announcing the explosion at Hitler's headquarters but giving no details. The anxious commander tried to get in touch with the two crews who had dropped the bombs into the lake. One of the aircraft had made a forced landing many miles from base but the crew could not be contacted; the other crew had baled out of their bomber and nobody knew where they were.

There followed a very worrying couple of hours before von Riesen's Corps commander telephoned and told him that he was 'off the hook'. The explosion had been a deliberate attempt on Hitler's life – the famous 20 July assassination attempt – and von Riesen was cleared of any complicity in it. Hitler survived the assassination attempt but one of those in the room with him, *Generaloberst* Günter Korten, the Chief of Staff of the *Luftwaffe*, was seriously injured and died a few days later. *General der Flieger* Werner Kreipe replaced Korten as Chief of Staff.

The operation on 20 July was one of the final large-scale attacks mounted by *Kampfgeschwader 1*, or by any other *Luftwaffe* heavy bomber unit for that matter. With the fuel shortage biting progressively more deeply, even the previous hand-to-mouth supply of fuel could no longer be maintained. *KG 1* received orders to cease operations and fly its four-engined bombers to airfields in central Germany, and the *Geschwader* was disbanded.

Rapidly the fuel famine impinged on every type of air operation in the east, and units were ordered to take the most stringent steps to conserve stocks. Horses or oxen were used to tow aircraft from their dispersals to the take-off point, and after landing pilots had to shut down their engines immediately and await the arrival of the animals to tow them back to their dispersals.

By the end of July the losses suffered by the *Luftflotten* on the Eastern Front had more than offset the reinforcements they had received since the Soviet offensives began. With the situation turning from bad to worse on the Central Front, on 20 August Soviet forces opened their long expected offensive in the south. In Rumania this was the signal for a well-planned *coup d'état* which immediately deposed the President, Ion Antonescu, who had been friendly to Germany. The new government immediately made peace with the Soviet Union, and declared war on its erstwhile ally. The most serious consequence of the Rumanian defection was the loss of that nation's oilfields, the last major source of natural oil available to the German war economy. This change in the strategic position was to bring about another, secondary effect that would be almost as important. Relieved of the need to continue its sustained attack on the Rumanian oil industry, the US Fifteenth Air Force based in Italy could now devote the whole of its energies to the bombardment of synthetic oil refineries in other areas of southern Europe.

Luftflotte 4, now too weakened to hold up the Soviet advance in the south, was forced to pull back to airfields in Bulgaria. Its stay there was to be brief, however, for on 6 September that nation followed Rumania's example and declared war on Germany. Yet another strip of territory had suddenly become untenable, and yet again the *Luftflotte* had to make a precipitate withdrawal.

Meanwhile, in the northern and central sectors of the Front, the collapse of German resistance continued. During the final week in August, in an act of political rather than military importance, Red Army units crossed the frontier of Germany itself and secured a narrow toehold in East Prussia. A week later, Finland joined those nations that changed sides and was now at war with Germany.

By mid-October the Soviet offensive had largely spent itself, having in some places secured gains of up to 300 miles. The huge tracts of territory won so easily from the Soviets in 1941 had been wrested back, and Germany's military position on the Eastern Front was vastly weaker than it had been at the beginning of June 1944. Three erstwhile allies, Finland, Rumania and Bulgaria, had been forced to change sides, tearing a large hole in the German defensive line in each case. *Luftflotte 5* withdrew to Norway and *Luftflotte 1* was cut off with German forces isolated in the Courland peninsula in Latvia. Henceforth neither *Luftflotte* would play much part in the fighting.

Now operating from bases in East Prussia and eastern Poland, *Luftflotte 6* was down to about 1,000 combat aircraft of all types. *Luftflotte 4*, based in Hungary and Yugoslavia, was down to about 200 planes. Outnumbered by the Red Air Force by more than five to one and lacking reserves, the *Luftwaffe* on the Eastern Front was in a poor position to meet the next Soviet offensive when it came.

For the time being we must leave the Eastern Front, and in the next chapter we shall examine the bombardment of Britain using the most important of Hitler's 'secret weapons' – the Fi 103 flying bomb and the A-4 bombardment rocket.

CHAPTER 6

THE ROBOT BOMBARDMENT

13 June 1944 to 19 March 1945

SHORTLY BEFORE 3.50 a.m. on the morning of 13 June 1944, on a camouflaged launching ramp near Hesdin in the Pas-de-Calais, a Fieseler Fi 103 (V-1) flying bomb sat on its wheeled cradle ready for firing. (German records of the launching of this particular flying bomb have not survived, but from the laid-down firing procedure and British records of the night's events, it is possible to reconstruct an accurate picture of what took place.)

Working flat out during the previous six days, the firing crew, part of *II. Abteilung Flakregiment 155(W)*, had brought their launcher to operational status. Now the missile selected for the initial firing sat silently on its cradle at the base of the launching ramp, fully fuelled and with its electrical circuits checked. The benign scene gave no indication of the dramatic succession of events that had gone before, nor of those that would follow during the next 25 minutes.

The *Oberleutnant* commanding the firing troop ordered his men to take cover, then joined his firing NCO and radio operator in the concrete *Kommandostand* near the base of the launching ramp. When he was satisfied that everyone was clear of the launcher or under cover, the commander told his NCO to commence the launching sequence. At the flick of a switch, a hiss of compressed air forced 75-octane petrol up to the burners of the Argus pulse-jet mounted above the fuselage. A spark plug crackled, the fuel ignited and flames belched from the rear of the engine as it roared to life.

Simultaneously, below the base of the launching ramp, a separate supply of compressed air forced *T-Stoff* (hydrogen peroxide) and *Z-Stoff* (calcium permanganate) from their tanks into the combustion chamber built into the base of the ramp. As the two liquids came into contact there was a violent chemical reaction producing super-heated steam and oxygen at rapidly increasing pressure.

During the seven seconds after the pulse-jet engine came to life, it reached maximum thrust. In the meantime the pressure of steam and oxygen built up rapidly. At the forward end of the combustion chamber was a firing piston, held in place by a ¼in (6mm) diameter steel pin. When the combination of engine thrust and chemical reaction produced sufficient force, the retaining pin sheared.

With nothing to restrain it, the firing piston shot forwards up the launching ramp, taking the flying bomb with it. The missile accelerated rapidly and when it left the end of the 156ft ramp it was moving at about 250mph, comfortably above minimum flying speed. Once the missile was airborne, the firing piston and launching cradle fell away and thudded into the ground in front of the ramp. Trailing flame, the missile rumbled away from the launching site and was soon out of sight and sound of those who had worked so hard to send it on its way. Now the firing crew returned to the ramp and began preparing it for the next launch.

The Fi 103 flew straight ahead, climbing at a shallow angle and building up speed. Three minutes after launch the compass took control of the missile and, with a small correction to allow for the forecast wind along the route, the nose swung on to the pre-set course for its designated target – Tower Bridge in London.

Six minutes after launch the missile reached its pre-set cruising altitude of about 3,000ft and levelled off. Shortly after that, at 3.57 a.m., it crossed the French coast near Etaples and rumbled out to sea. (Whether the Hesdin missile was the first one fired that night is not known – four of the initial salvo of flying bombs crashed immediately or shortly after leaving their launchers. But there is no doubt that the Hesdin weapon was the first to come within view of Britain's defences.)

At 4.01 a.m., four minutes after the flying bomb had left the French coast, operators at the radar station at Swingate near Dover had their first unknowing glimpse of the new form of attack. For a few sweeps of their scanner they tracked an approaching 'aircraft', then lost it. The first visual sighting came four minutes later: the crew of a Royal Navy motor torpedo boat on patrol in mid-channel reported seeing a 'bright horizontal flame' moving north-westwards from the French coast near Boulogne.

At 4.07 p.m. an Observer Corps post near Dymchurch reported the incoming object heading north-west towards the coast. That sighting was immediately linked to intelligence warnings circulated previously on the expected attack by 'pilotless aircraft', and the code-word 'Diver' was issued. After the 'Diver' crossed the coast it was tracked by other observer posts as it continued its unswerving journey across Kent at a speed of between 250 and 270mph. The noise made by the pulse-jet was quite different from that of an aircraft, but it was sufficiently like other sounds for the watchers to describe it vividly: the clatter was likened to 'a motor boat', 'a two-stroke motorcycle without a silencer' or 'a Model T Ford going up a hill'.

The flying bomb continued relentlessly towards London, the small wind-driven propeller on its nose driving a counter that logged the distance flown. At 4.20 a.m. the counter reached the previously set figure at which the flight was to be terminated. A pair of electrical contacts closed and fired a couple of detonators in the tail of the missile, to lock the elevator and rudder in the neutral position. Simultaneously, spoilers under the tailplane sprang out, thrusting upwards the tail of the missile and forcing it into a steep dive. The harsh negative-G forces resulting from this bunting manoeuvre hurled the remaining petrol to the front of the almost-empty tank, uncovering the feed pipe and causing the pulse jet to flame out. The engine roar ceased and, whistling quietly, the weapon crashed into open land at Stone near Dartford. On impact the 1,870lb high-explosive warhead detonated, excavating a shallow crater and causing blast damage over a large area. There were no casualties. The weapon had fallen about fifteen miles to the east of Tower Bridge, its intended target.

During the next hour three more flying bombs came over the coast of England. Two crashed on open land and caused no casualties, but the third fell on a built-up area of Bethnal Green – within two miles of the aiming point – killing six people and injuring nine. Of the ten flying bombs launched against London early on the morning of 13 July, six suffered failures of one sort or another that caused them to crash short of the English coast.

So began the robot bombardment of London that had been predicted by the British Intelligence services for more than a year. The War Cabinet had been led to expect a much heavier initial onslaught, and such was the anti-climax that Lord Cherwell, Mr Churchill's scientific adviser, was moved to comment: 'The mountain hath groaned, and given forth a mouse!'

On the afternoon of 6 June, immediately following the Allied landings in Normandy, the German High Command's assessment had been that these were probably part of a diversionary operation intended to draw away German forces from the Pas-de-Calais area where the main invasion was expected. If there were landings in the Pas-de-Calais area, the Fi 103 launching sites situated there might be lost even before they began firing. Preparations for the bombardment of London with flying bombs were well advanced, but they were still several days from completion. Nevertheless that afternoon *Oberst* Max Wachtel, commander of *Flakregiment 155(W)* and in charge of the ground launching operation, received orders to commence firings against London late on the afternoon of the 12th.

It was an almost impossibly tight schedule, but Wachtel and his men did their best. Working round the clock, they moved into position and installed the necessary equipment at 55 of the *Regiment*'s 64 firing sites. At that time the Allied air forces were concentrating their attacks on the French rail network, however, and the disruption was such that when Wachtel's deadline was reached many sites lacked essential supplies. Of the *Regiment*'s four firing *Abteilungen*, each responsible for sixteen missile launchers, one had no diesel fuel for its generators and another lacked *Z-Stoff* for the launching ramps; neither *Abteilung* took part in the initial firings. The other two *Abteilungen* did little better and, as we have seen, only four missiles reached England.

Following the initial débâcle, Wachtel was allowed a three-day respite in which to bring all the firing units to full readiness. When the bombardment reopened on the evening of 15 June, the results were more gratifying from the German point of view. Up to midnight on the 16th, the *Regiment* had fired 244 flying bombs. Of that total, 45 (18 per cent) failed to launch properly and came down in the vicinity of their ramps, in ten cases causing severe damage to them. It would appear that a further 40 missiles came down in the sea, for only 153 (62 per cent of those fired) crossed the coast of England or were otherwise seen by British observers.

During the lull following the initial attack, fighters and anti-aircraft guns had been deployed to the south of England to counter the new threat. The fighters and guns shot down 22 bombs, and about 50 more fell on open ground clear of the capital. But 73 of the bombs (30 per cent of those fired) fell on the Greater London built-up area, where they caused widespread damage and casualties.

During the sixteen-day period, between the resumption of firings and the end of June, *Flakregiment 155(W)* launched 2,442 flying bombs. Roughly one-third of these crashed or were shot down before they reached the English coast, one-third crashed or were shot down over southern England before reaching the target area, while the remaining one-third, about 800 missiles, crashed on Greater London. In total, the flying bombs caused 2,441 deaths and 7,107 cases of serious injury. On average 153 missiles were launched each day and each one launched caused, on average, one death and three cases of serious injury in England. Considering the indiscriminate nature of the Fi 103 bombardment, it is remarkable that the most serious single incident in June occurred at a military target. On the 18th, a flying bomb crashed into the Guards' Chapel at Wellington Barracks while a service was in progress. Of the 121 people killed, 63 were soldiers.

Whenever Allied reconnaissance aircraft located the Fi 103 launching sites, the latter came under repeated air attack. But the elaborate camouflage discipline practised by Wachtel's men stood them in good stead. Few sites suffered serious damage, and following repairs most of these were able to resume firing. From German records, we know that during the period 12 June to 1 July only two out of the 64 launching sites were completely destroyed; a further 22 suffered heavy damage, 8 had moderate damage and 10 sites suffered slight damage. Casualties among firing crews totalled 28 killed and 80 wounded.

The most serious effect of the Allied air attacks against the Fi 103 bombardment was the hindrance to the rail and road transport systems used to move weapons to the launching sites. Sites fired off their stock of missiles, then sometimes had to wait days for the next batch to arrive. Throughout this bombardment, the ability of the supply organization to deliver missiles fell far short of the *Regiment*'s capacity to fire them. One result of this failure was that the average time interval between shots was 1 to 1½hrs, compared with a minimum firing interval of 26min demonstrated by sites with a full complement of missiles.

The flying-bomb attack on England continued unabated

throughout the whole of July. On 2 August *Flakregiment 155(W)* launched what was to be its heaviest attack of all during a 24hr period, when 316 bombs were fired at London from its 38 serviceable launchers. About 107 of the missiles impacted in the Greater London area. As in the case of previous weapons, the aiming point was Tower Bridge and on that day, for the first time, one of the weapons scored a direct hit on the famous landmark, causing damage to the roadway.

By now the German Army's days in western France were numbered. On 7 August the War Diary of *Flakregiment 155(W)* recorded the first reference to this fact, when orders were received that construction was to cease on all sites situated to the south of the River Somme, and only minimum repair work was to be done on damaged sites. At the same time, new sites were to be surveyed and constructed as far east as the range of the flying bomb permitted. In the third week in August the Front collapsed, and German forces began a headlong retreat to the east. On the 25th, troops of the British 21st Army Group crossed the River Seine and moved rapidly towards the Pas-de-Calais. One by one the flying bomb launching sites were abandoned and Wachtel's men joined the withdrawal east.

At 4 a.m. on the morning of 1 September, the last of 8,617 flying bombs was dispatched from a launching site in northern France. That marked the end of the initial, and what was to be by far the most destructive, phase of the Fi 103 bombardment.

The ground launching sites in the Pas-de-Calais area had dispatched the majority of the flying bombs launched against England, but there was another source. Since 9 July the specially modified Heinkel He 111s of *III. Gruppe Kampfgeschwader 3*, commanded by bomber ace *Major* Martin Vetter, had joined in the bombardment operating at night or in bad weather from Gilze Rijen and Venlo in Holland and Beauvais in France.

As modified for the new role, the Heinkels carried special equipment to carry and launch the flying bomb as well as a FuG 101 radio altimeter and a '*Lichtenstein*' tail-warning radar. The 2½-ton weight and the drag of the externally carried flying bomb imposed a severe penalty in performance. On their approach flights the bombers would cruise over the sea at 170mph, keeping to altitudes below 300ft where they were out of sight of the British coastal radars.

As it neared the launching point, the bomber turned on to its attack heading and begin a slow climb to the minimum safe launching altitude of 1,700ft. Once there, the aircraft levelled out and accelerated to 200mph, the minimum flying speed for the Fi 103. Ten seconds before release the flying bomb's pulse-jet was started, the flame lighting up the sky for miles around and making the bomber crew feel very vulnerable indeed. After final checks were completed, the missile was released. It fell about 300ft before the autopilot took control and established the weapon in the climb for its pre-set cruising altitude. While that was happening the Heinkel was in a high-speed descending turn, as its crew endeavoured to put as much distance as possible between themselves and the highly visible missile they had unleashed.

During July, August and the first week of September, *III./KG 3* launched about 300 bombs at London, 90 at Southampton and a score at Gloucester. The final attack during this phase of the action was during the early morning darkness on 5 September, with a nine-bomb salvo aimed at London. Air-launched flying bombs proved considerably less accurate than those fired from ground launchers. The attacks on the two smaller cities were complete failures: not a single flying bomb hit Gloucester, while the craters south of Southampton covered so large an area that British Intelligence took it to be an unsuccessful attempt to strike at Portsmouth!

The citizens of London enjoyed only a week's respite following the end of the Fi 103 bombardment from ground launchers in France, then the second of the German retaliatory weapons went into action. Late on the afternoon of 8 September, giving no warning of its approach, the first A-4 (V-2) bombardment rocket crashed on Chiswick to the west of London and exploded, killing three people and injuring seventeen. The weapon had been fired from a launching site near The Hague in Holland, some 200 miles from the target.

The complex and entirely novel technology required to make the bombardment rocket work was close to the limits of what was possible at this time, and the A-4 programme had been beset with technical difficulties. Moreover, once firings had begun, the launching sites in Holland came under almost continual threat – actual or perceived – from Allied ground forces. In its intensity, its concentration and its effects, the A-4 bombardment of London fell far short of what the weapon's enthusiastic proponents had led the *Führer* to expect. Between 8 September 1944 and 27 March 1945, a total of 1,054 rockets fell on England (an average of about five a day); of that total, 517 rockets (an average of less than three a day) hit London. Just over 2,700 Londoners were killed in the attacks. As an act of petty terrorism the A-4 bombardment was successful, but its consequences fell far short of what was necessary to achieve decisive results.

Meanwhile the bombardment of Britain with flying bombs launched from modified He 111s continued through the autumn and winter of 1944. Following the loss of ground launching sites in France, the relative importance of air launching for this weapon increased greatly. The unit that had pioneered this form of attack, *III./KG 3*, was forced by the Allied advance to pull back to northern Germany, but operations continued from the airfields at Aalhorn, Varelbusch, Zwischenahn and Handorf-bei-Münster.

As in the case of that with A-4s, however, the attack by air-launched Fi 103s failed to achieve any degree of intensity. Following release, between a third and a half of the flying bombs failed to function correctly and crashed soon afterwards; many of the remainder were shot down by fighters or guns; and, as mentioned earlier, the accuracy of air-launched missiles was far worse than that achieved from ground launchers.

As an example of this type of operation, let us take a look at that on 16 September 1944. Weather conditions over the North Sea were perfect for the operation: there was a thick overcast, with the cloud base between 700 to 1,200ft and light drizzle. Shortly after dark that evening fifteen Heinkels took off at five-minute intervals from their bases in northern Germany and headed for the missile launching area in the Thames Estuary. Nine Fi 103s got under way satisfactorily, of which three were destroyed by British ships and aircraft before they reached the coast of England. Over land, two more of the flying bombs were shot down by fighters. Two of the remaining four missiles came down in open countryside in Essex. Only two Fi 103s reached the Greater London area, of which one fell on Woolwich and the other on Barking. No launching aircraft was lost.

As might be expected, the Royal Air Force spared no effort to engage the missile launchers. Each night when operations were considered likely, Mosquito intruders patrolled over the bases used by the German bombers. At the same time, Mosquito night fighters mounted standing patrols in the areas from which the Heinkels launched their missiles.

In the autumn of 1944 the Fi 103 launching force was expanded from a *Gruppe* to a full *Geschwader, KG 53. III./KG 3* was re-designated as *I./KG 53*, and *II.* and *III. Gruppen KG 53* converted to the role and became operational in November. By the time the extra *Gruppen* were ready for operations, however, the fuel famine imposed restrictions on the activities of the *Geschwader*.

Remarkably, after the beginning of September there was little attempt to exploit the flexibility conferred by air launching, by attacking targets other than London. Had it been necessary for the defenders to protect a greater area, the fighter and gun defences would have had to be spread correspondingly more thinly. Yet after August there was only one attack on a target in England other than London – Operation '*Martha*', a large-scale venture against Manchester during the early morning darkness on 24 December. From launching points over the North Sea some fifty Heinkels fired their missiles, thirty flying bombs crossing the coast between Skegness and Bridlington and rumbling westwards. Eleven bombs came down within fifteen miles of the centre of Manchester, but only one impacted within the city limits. As a result of the attack 37 people were killed and 67 seriously injured. One Heinkel was shot down by a night fighter. The only significant effect of the German attack was that it forced the redeployment of anti-aircraft guns from the south of England, to provide continuous cover of the east coast as far north as Yorkshire.

On 10 January 1945 *KG 53* reported that it had 79 serviceable He 111s on strength. Four days later the unit ceased operations on account of the fuel shortage. From first to last the stand-off bombing force had lost 77 Heinkels. Of these, sixteen were shot down by night fighters, most of the others succumbing to accidents resulting from the hazards of flying at low altitude at night and in bad weather.

In the final stages of the war, the bombardment of London was resumed using a new, extended-range version of the Fi 103 with a larger fuel tank and a smaller warhead. With a maximum range of 200 miles the missile could reach the capital from ground launching sites in Holland. The new phase of the attack opened on 3 March and closed at the end of the month with the firing of 275th and final bomb. The longer flight time meant that more bombs crashed into the sea or were shot down by fighters, and by this time the British fighter and gun defences had reached such a peak of efficiency that only thirteen bombs – less than one in five of those launched from Holland – reached the London area.

Altogether, just over ten thousand Fieseler Fi 103 flying bombs were launched against England. The great majority of these, about 85 per cent, came from ground launchers. Of that total, 7,488 crossed the British coast or were otherwise observed by the defences and 3,957 were shot down short of their targets. Of the 3,531 which eluded the defences, 2,419 reached London, about thirty reached Southampton and Portsmouth, and one hit Manchester. Thus only about a quarter of the ground-launched bombs reached their intended target areas; of the air-launched bombs, the figure was about one-tenth. In England the flying bombs caused 6,184 deaths – an average of three deaths for every five bombs fired. A further 17,981 people were injured.

So ended the flying-bomb and rocket bombardment of England. Had it been possible to co-ordinate these attacks with large-scale raids by manned bombers, and had *Flakregiment 155(W)* been able to deliver the planned daily attack rate of several salvo firings each of fifty or more missiles, the defences might have been seriously over-extended: many more flying bombs would have got through and much more damage caused. As it was, the defenders were able to deal with the threats individually and they achieved considerable success in bringing down flying bombs before they reached their targets.

And at the same time, people living in the target areas quickly got used to the distinctive rumble of the Fi 103's pulse jet. They learned that they were safe so long as the engine kept going. If it stopped, they had about ten seconds to get to cover; the author well remembers those exciting times, as a nine-year-old living in Ewell. Apart from staying under cover the whole time there was no way of avoiding the A-4 missiles, but the rockets arrived so infrequently that they came to be accepted as just another hazard of wartime living.

On 21 October 1944 a further phase in the Fi 103 bombardment began, with attacks on targets in Belgium. The first of these weapons fell on and around the city of Brussels, then the port of Antwerp came under attack followed shortly afterwards by the cities of Charleroi and Liège.

In the late autumn of 1944 Antwerp was the main supply port for Allied forces moving towards the German frontier, and in support of the German offensive in the Ardennes (see Chapter 9) the port came under intensive bombardment with missiles from mid-December. Between then and the end of the year more than 740 flying bombs and 924 rockets were launched at the port from sites in Holland. The hail of missiles caused considerable damage and greatly hindered the operation of the port, and the bombardment continued until the middle of March 1945.

In covering the whole range of attacks by the German retaliatory missiles, we have overrun the chronology of this account. In the next chapter we must return to the autumn of 1944, to examine the position in which the rest of the *Luftwaffe* found itself at that time.

CHAPTER 7

ATTACK ON THE OIL INDUSTRY

1 August to 30 September 1944

THE SHIFT OF THE FOCUS of the Allied bombing offensive against the German oil industry had immediate and far-reaching effects: compared with the 175,000 tons of aviation fuel it produced in April, in June the German oil industry turned out only 55,000 tons – less than a third of the previous figure. Unless something were done, and done soon, the *Luftwaffe* could find itself with insufficient fuel to continue sustained air operations.

As an initial move, large numbers of anti-aircraft guns were transferred from other areas to protect the oil refineries. *14. Flakdivision* was responsible for the defence of the industrial district round Leipzig, which included the important oil plants at Leuna-Merseburg, Böhlen, Tröglitz, Espenhain, Rositz and Mücheln. The moves to strengthen the *Division* typify those made at this time to render these targets harder to attack. At the beginning of May the *Division* possessed 374 heavy guns, 342 of 8.8cm calibre, 24 of 10.5cm and 8 of 12.8cm calibre. Immediately after the Allied offensive against oil industry began, the energetic *Generalmajor* Adolf Gerlach was appointed to the command of the *Division*. He received a visit from *Reichsminister* Albert Speer, who made it clear that unless the refineries were kept working the war was as good as lost. When Gerlach assumed command of the *Division* there had been 104 heavy guns protecting the large Leuna-Merseburg production complex; he demanded, and received, sufficient weapons to bring about a six-fold strengthening of the flak defences ringing that target.

Having secured the large numbers of guns he needed, Gerlach set about increasing their tactical effectiveness. During the attacks the US heavy bombers dropped huge quantities of 'chaff' and radiated a cacophony of noise jamming that effectively neutralized the German '*Würzburg*' flak-control radars. As a result, during daylight attacks, the gunners were forced to abandon the use of radar-laid fire and resort to optically predicted fire.

If cloud and enemy countermeasures prevented accurate predicted fire, the gunners would put up a box barrage. All guns would fire at the point in the sky just short of where it was calculated that the aircraft would release their bombs; by disrupting the bombing run in this way, the accuracy of the attack could be greatly reduced. The method was highly extravagant in the use of ammunition, however, and was permitted to be used only in the defence of high-priority targets such as the oil refineries. US bomber crews rated the oil refineries and chemical plants round Leipzig as the most heavily defended area they had to attack.

In addition to these active defence measures, passive measures were introduced to lessen the effects of the bombing. Concrete blast walls were built around items of vulnerable machinery, and a warren of deep shelters under the plants enabled workers to remain near at hand during the attacks and emerge afterwards to extinguish fires before they took hold. Although itself short of skilled manpower, the German Army transferred seven thousand engineers for employment in repair gangs at the refineries and a large slave labour force was drafted in to assist with this work. Finally, to ensure that morale at the refineries did not flag under the Allied bombardment, their work forces came under 'special supervision' from Heinrich Himmler's feared Security Service.

As a further measure to safeguard German oil production, Edmund Geilenberg was appointed head of a far-reaching programme to build a network of new refineries that would be far less vulnerable to air attack. For the production of aviation fuel, he and his staff laid plans for the construction of seven underground hydrogeneration plants. Lower grade motor fuel was to be produced in 41 much smaller plants situated above ground but widely dispersed in woods and quarries, each carefully camouflaged and individually too small to make an attractive target for bombers. Geilenberg made full use of his authority to take labour and materials from other industries, and his labour force was built up rapidly to more than a third of a million workers. It was planned to have several of the motor fuel plants operational by the autumn of 1944, but in spite of prodigious efforts by Geilenberg and his staff the first of the underground plants was not due to begin producing aviation fuel until well into 1945 (in fact no aviation fuel would come from this source).

During this period, German rocket fighters went into action several times in defence of refineries in the Leipzig area. On 16 August the US Eighth Air Force put up about a thousand bombers to attack a spread of targets in central Germany, including the oil refinery at Böhlen. Five Me 163s were scrambled, and two were promptly shot down without inflicting any damage on the raiding force.

The Messerschmitt 163 achieved its first aerial victories just over a week after that, on 24 August. Eight of the small fighters took off from Brandis to engage a force of 185 B-17s running in to attack the refinery at Merseburg. *Feldwebel* Siegfried Schubert carried out a successful interception and shot down two Flying Fortresses, other pilots from his unit bringing down two more. That day two Me 163s were damaged, one by return fire from the bombers and the other on landing. It had been a most successful day for the new rocket fighter and seemed to be a portent for its future as a bomber-destroyer. In the event, however, the Me 163's score of four bombers destroyed that day would mark the high point of its operational career.

On 24 September *JG 400* reported that it had nineteen Messerschmitt Me 163s on strength, of which eleven were serviceable. By then more than a hundred rocket fighters had been delivered to the *Luftwaffe*, and it is clear that the factor limiting operational employment was not aircraft but trained pilots. Clearly the hoped-for salvation for the German fighter force was not going to come from this quarter. During September *I./JG 400* operated on five occasions – on the 10th, 11th, 12th, 13th and 28th. The largest of these operations was the last one, when nine of the diminutive fighters were committed.

The short range of the Me 163 meant that accurate ground control was essential if the aircraft were to be used effectively. Such control was not always forthcoming, however, and only a small proportion of the fighters reached firing positions. During the operation on the 28th, for example, *Feldwebel* Rudolf Zimmermann was sent to intercept a bomber formation flying past Brandis. Afterwards he wrote:

> Four minutes after take-off I sighted the B-17s, about 45 aircraft at about 10 o'clock at 7,700m [25,000ft]. I myself was flying level at 9,200m [30,000ft] at about 800kph [500mph], in an excellent position. But about 1.5km [a mile] behind the formation my rocket motor shut down – my fuel was exhausted. In a flat dive I curved round to the left on the last B-17 in the box, and at 500m I fired one burst without visible result.

Zimmermann pushed down the nose of his fighter to build up speed, then pulled up for a final snap attack on the same bomber – only to have his guns jam at the critical moment. Seething with frustration, the German pilot broke away and headed back to Brandis.

During September the Me 163 programme suffered a disaster from which it would never recover. In bombing attacks on the towns of Leverkusen and Ludwigshaven that month, two of the main sources of hydrazine hydrate (*C-Stoff*) suffered serious damage and production was greatly reduced. For the remainder of the war shortages of this chemical fuel would dog the Me 163. (A major competitor for the limited supplies was the Fi 103 flying bomb programme, which used it to power the launching catapult. The Fi 103 enjoyed a higher priority for supplies than the Me 163.)

Meanwhile, the piston-engined fighter units continued to mount *Gefechtsverband* attacks, and from time to time they were able to pick their way past the American fighter screens and deliver their special brand of saturation attack on bomber formations. On 27 September, for example, *Jagdgeschwader 4* delivered a sharp attack on the 445th Bomb Group and in three minutes shot down 28 Liberators out of 37 dispatched; it would be the heaviest loss ever suffered by a US Bomb Group on a single mission. On the following day the *Gefechtsverband* from *JG 3* assailed the 41st Combat Wing and shot down eighteen Flying Fortresses before the arrival of strong forces of escorts prevented further slaughter. Just over a week later, on 6 October, a *Gefechtsverband* drawn from *JG 4* and *JG 300* fought a similarly brisk battle with the 4th Combat Bomb Wing and shot down fourteen B-17s.

Yet although such actions brought disaster upon the individual bomber units involved, their effect on the US bomber offensive as a whole was derisory. During the three days mentioned above heavy bombers of the US Eighth Air Force flew a total of 3,275 successful sorties for a loss of 81 of their number – less than 2.5 per cent of the total. And that, it must be stressed, was on three days when the defenders were relatively successful. Each day when the weather permitted, the US Eighth and Fifteenth Air Forces would send more than a thousand heavy bombers to attack targets in Germany and the occupied territories, and on most days losses were less than 1 per cent of the force involved.

The German night fighter force had not recovered from the neutralization of its airborne detection systems when it suffered a further calamity. The loss of French territory had torn a gaping hole in the German early warning radar chain, which the RAF now exploited by routing bombers from that direction during attacks on western and southern Germany. Even as signals personnel toiled to reposition radars to plug this breach there came a further blow: the fuel famine started to take effect and forced a curtailment of night fighter operations.

Then, to add to the misery, No 100 Group of the Royal Air Force began to make its presence felt during the night air battles. The Group operated five squadrons of heavy bombers modified into specialized jamming aircraft – B-17 Fortresses, B-24 Liberators, Halifaxes and Stirlings. These aircraft were able to carry large quantities of 'Window' of all types, as well as noise-jamming equipment to counter '*Würzburg*' fire control radar, the SN-2 night fighter radar, and the '*Freya*', '*Mammut*', '*Wassermann*' and '*Jagdschloss*' radars that made up the German early-warning chains. In addition, some of the aircraft carried 'Jostle' a high powered jammer to blot out the night fighters' radio communications channels.

No 100 Group's other element comprised six squadrons of Mosquito night fighters carrying special equipment to enable them to operate against their *Luftwaffe* counterparts deep inside Germany. Homing on radar emissions was a game that two could play, and in addition to AI radar some of the Mosquitos carried 'Serrate', which enabled them to home on emissions from the German night fighters' SN-2 radars. Other Mosquitos carried 'Perfectos', which transmitted interrogating pulses to trigger the identification friend or foe (IFF) sets of German aircraft in the area. When the German IFF sets replied, their signals betrayed the range and bearing of the aircraft and identified it to the Mosquito crews as hostile. Several German planes were shot down following 'Perfectos' contacts – and many others were lost when German crews, having heard of the device, flew with IFF switched off and were shot down by their own flak!

Despite the presence of the Mosquitos, the German night fighter force suffered a far lower rate of attrition than its day fighter counterpart. But No 100 Group's operations imposed considerable pressure on the defences, which combined with the other factors to allow RAF night bombers to operate at will over Germany with minimal losses.

Throughout this period the German oil industry was hit hard and it was hit repeatedly. The reader may get an idea of its sufferings from the fate of one of its largest units, the Ammoniakwerk Merseburg plant at Leuna. In the spring of 1944 it was the second largest producer of synthetic fuel, accounting for about one-sixth of the total German production. The huge plant sprawled over an area of 757 acres, and in addition to liquid fuels it produced ammonia, methanol and various types of industrial alcohol from coke and brown coal.

The first large-scale attack, by 224 Flying Fortresses of the Eighth Air Force, had taken place on 12 May even before the main offensive against German oil industry had begun. That initial attack brought a halt to fuel production. As can be seen from the accompanying table, during the next six months the plant came under attack twelve more times. The bout between the Leuna refinery and the US bombers can be likened to a prize fight. Time after time the plant was hit hard and production halted, as if one of the prize-fighters had been knocked to the ground. But each time it picked itself up and production resumed. At first the recovery was relatively rapid and almost complete, but as the accumulation of punishment began to tell the recovery became progressively slower and less complete.

Compared with the 175,000 tons of aviation fuel produced in

Attacks on the Leuna synthetic oil plant, 12 May–28 September 1944

Date	Force	Effect
12 May	224 × B-17	Production halted, repairs started.
28 May	63 × B-24	Repairs disrupted, resumption of production delayed.
3 June		Production resumed, rose rapidly until by the end of June it reached 75 per cent.
7 July	51 × B-17	Production again halted, but within eleven days it had returned to 51 per cent.
20 July	155 × B-17	No production for three days, then it resumed and rose to 35 per cent within five days.
28 July	652 × B-17	Heavy damage, production halted.
29 July	569 × B-17	Further heavy damage.
24 August	185 × B-17	Repair work disrupted before production resumed.
11 Sept.	111 × B-17	As above.
13 Sept.	141 × B-24	As above.
28 Sept.	301 × B-17	As above.

Note: Percentage production figures are relative to the level before the first attack on 12 May.

April, in August there was only 16,000 tons and in September a mere 7,000 tons. Throughout the summer the *Luftwaffe* kept going on its fat – the reserve of over half a million tons of aviation fuel it had accumulated previously. But with consumption running far in excess of production, by the beginning of September more than half this reserve had been consumed: from a high point of about 580,000 tons at the beginning of May, stocks were only about 180,000 tons at the end of September.

Now the harsh realities of the shortfall in fuel production could be avoided no longer. Operations by medium and heavy bombers were sharply curtailed; the use of aerial reconnaissance was limited; air operations in support of the Army were permitted only in 'decisive situations'; and the number of night fighter sorties was cut back. Only day fighter operations in defence of the Reich were allowed to continue at their previous level.

Meanwhile, as we shall observe in the next chapter, in Germany the production of combat aircraft, and in particular fighter types, had risen to unprecedented levels. The *Luftwaffe* was about to stage a remarkable recovery in fighting strength.

Above Adolf Hitler awarding the *Ritterkreuz* with Oakleaves to *Major* Anton Hackl, one of the leading fighter pilots in the *Luftwaffe*. Hackl survived the war and was credited with 192 victories; he was operational on all the main battle fronts and was shot down eight times and wounded in action several times. (Hackl)

LUFTWAFFE LEADERS

Left *Reichsmarschall* Hermann Göring being greeted by *General* Adolf Galland at the latter's headquarters. By the spring of 1944 Göring's status within the Third Reich had been eroded to the point where he had little further influence on events.

Right *Generalfeldmarschall* Hugo Sperrle commanded *Luftflotte 3* in the west and was charged with defeating the Allied invasion of Normandy.

Far right In May 1944 *Generaloberst* Hans-Jürgen Stumpff commanded *Luftflotte Reich* (at that time the largest *Luftwaffe* formation) and remained in that post until the end of the war.

Below left In May 1944 *Generaloberst* Günther Korten was Chief of Staff of the *Luftwaffe.* On 20 July he was a few feet from Hitler when a bomb exploded in the latter's headquarters, and a few days later he died from the injuries received.

Right *Generaloberst* Robert von Greim commanded *Luftflotte 6* on the Eastern Front in May 1944. In April 1945 he was promoted to *Generalfeldmarschall* and appointed Commander-in-Chief of the *Luftwaffe*, in succession to the deposed Hermann Göring. (IWM)

Far right After a distinguished career as a fighter pilot, Adolf Galland was appointed Inspector General of Fighters and in May 1944 held the rank of *Generalmajor.* His outspoken criticisms of the *Luftwaffe* High Command and the handling of the fighter force brought him into conflict with Göring. In January 1945 he was relieved of his staff duties and appointed commander of the élite Me 262 unit *Jagdverband 44.*

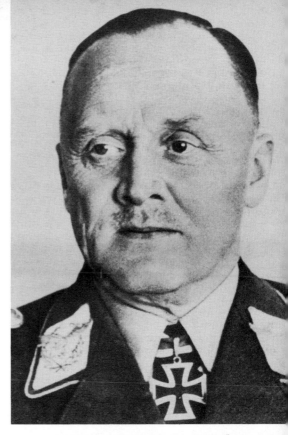

FIGHTER TYPES

Left and centre left
Messerschmitt 262 twin-jet
fighters of the operational
trials unit *Erprobungs-
kommando 262*, photo-
graphed at Lechfeld in
Bavaria in the summer of
1944.

Top right The Focke
Wulf Fw 190D entered
service in the summer of
1944. This sub-type of the
famous fighter was fitted
with the Jumo 213 in-line
engine, resulting in
lengthened nose contours.
The performance of the Fw
190D was similar to that of
the best Allied fighters of
the late-war period.

Above right Although the
Messerschmitt Bf 109 was
obsolescent by the summer
of 1944, it continued in
mass production. This
example, a G-14, served
with *III./JG 3*, providing top
cover for *Sturmgruppe*
attacks. (Romm)

Right The Dornier Do 335
heavy fighter, with its
unique push-pull engine
arrangement, was to have
been the most important
long-range fighter type in
the *Luftwaffe* but it suffered
delays in production and
never entered service.

Below left The rocket-
propelled Me 163 was the
first jet fighter to enter
service with any nation.
Although the type had a
sparkling turn of speed and
excellent climbing
performance, it had a
pitifully short radius of
action. This example
belonged to *Jagd-
geschwader 400*, the
only combat unit to receive
the type. (Via Ethell)

Right A Messerschmitt Me
410 heavy fighter fitted with
a BK 5 high-velocity 5cm
cannon for use against the
US heavy bombers. Note
the telescopic gunsight
fitted into the windscreen.
(Bucholz)

STURMGRUPPE UNITS

Above A heavily armoured Focke Wulf Fw 190A-8 *'Sturmbock'* of *IV./(Sturm) Gruppe* of *JG 3*, modified for close-range fire-fights with US heavy bombers. (Romm)

Below A close-up photograph of a *Sturmbock* Fw 190, showing the muzzle of the 3cm cannon in the outer wing position.

Above right Another close-up view of a *Sturmbock* Fw 190, showing the laminated glass mounted on the sides of the canopies of some aircraft. Part of the externally mounted armour providing the pilot with side protection can be seen in the bottom left of the photograph.

Above far right *Feldwebel* Hans Schäfer of *IV./JG 3* with the 'whites of the eyes' insignia worn by *Sturmgruppe* pilots on their flying jackets.

Centre right The *Sturmgruppe* Fw 190s carried out destructive attacks on the US bombers from close astern. This B-24 is on the receiving end of such an attack.

Below right Three leading exponents of the *Sturmgruppe* tactics against American heavy bombers: (from right to left) *Oberst* Walter Dahl, *Hauptmann* Wilhelm Möritz and *Leutnant* Oskar Romm. All three took part in the devastating attack by *IV./Sturm JG 3* on 7 July 1944.

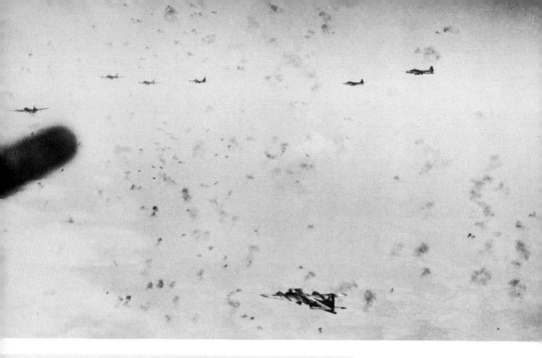

AIR DEFENCE MEASURES

Above Although German anti-aircraft guns shot down relatively few aircraft they damaged many, and by forcing the raiders to release bombs from high altitude they prevented accurate attacks. These B-17s under heavy fire belonged to the 457th Bomb Group of the Eighth Air Force.

Left With the gradual demise of the *Luftwaffe* day fighter force, the *Flak* arm underwent a steady expansion to provide target defence. The most powerful weapon employed by the *Flakwaffe* was the twin-barrelled version of the 12.8cm anti-aircraft gun.

Above Its nose blown away moments earlier by an anti-aircraft shell, a B-17 teeters before entering its final dive over Budapest, 14 July 1944.

Right A battery of 10.5cm guns mounted on railway flats, pictured engaging night bombers. (Lux)

Below right A quadruple-barrelled 2cm gun. These weapons were used in large numbers to protect airfields and other targets against attack from low-flying fighter-bombers.

DEFENSIVE GUIDED MISSILES

Left The Henschel Hs 117 *Schmetterling* surface-to-air weapon was intended for service deployment in the late spring of 1945.

Above right and right The Ruhrstahl X-4 air-to-air missile was wire-guided. The weapon was fitted with a 44lb warhead and had an effective maximum range of about 3,000yd. This example was fitted to an Fw 190 trials aircraft.

Left The EMW *Wasserfall* surface-to-air missile was a scaled-down version of the A-4 (V-2) bombardment rocket and was to have gone into service late in 1945.

NEW BOMBERS

Above A Heinkel He 177 of *KG 1*. Despite its appearance as a twin-engined aircraft, the aircraft was in fact a four-engined type with two coupled engines in each wing nacelle. The arrangement gave considerable trouble, however, and it was the spring of 1944 before the first full *Geschwader* went into action with the type.

Left Horst von Riesen, commander of *KG 1*, which operated with He 177s for a brief period on the Eastern Front.

Top right and centre right Arado Ar 234 bombers of *III. Gruppe Kampfgeschwader 76*, photographed at Burg-bei-Magdeburg in the autumn of 1944 when the unit was working up for operations.

Right *Major* Hans-George Bätcher (second from right) commanded *III./KG 76* when the unit re-formed with Ar 234s. On the far right is *Hauptmann* Diether Lukesch, the commander of *9. Staffel* which first flew the new bomber in action.

THE FIESELER Fi 103

Above An Fi 103 (V-1) flying bomb being man-handled on to the launching ramp.

Below An Fi 103 launching site at Vignacourt near Abbeville in France, photographed in June 1944. The only 'give-away' amongst the innocuous-looking cluster of apparent farm buildings is the launching ramp in the top right-hand corner, aligned on London.

Above and below left From July 1944 the *Luftwaffe* conducted desultory attacks on targets in England with V-1 flying bombs launched from He 111s. (Via Selinger)

Below right *Oberst* Max Wachtel commanded *Flakregiment 155(W)*, the unit which manned the ground launchers for flying bombs during the bombardment of targets in Great Britain in 1944 and 1945. (Wachtel)

THE *MISTEL*

Left The *Mistel* comprised an unmanned Junkers 88 fitted with a 7,800lb warhead in place of the crew compartment. The combination was flown by a pilot sitting in a Bf 109 (later an Fw 190) mounted rigidly on top of the bomber. The pilot aligned the combination on the target, switched on the bomber's automatic pilot and then fired explosive bolts to release the lower component which continued straight ahead until it impacted on, it was hoped, the target.

Centre left and below left A remarkable photograph taken through trees surrounding the airfield at St-Dizier by a member of the French resistance, showing a *Mistel* at one of the dispersal points.

Above right A close-up view of a *Mistel* earmarked for Operation 'Iron Hammer', the attack on the power stations around Moscow, pictured at Oranienburg early in 1945. Note the large jettisonable fuel tanks fitted to both the Fw 190 control aircraft and the Ju 88 explosive aircraft. (Schliephake)

Right *Hauptmann* Horst Rudat led the first *Mistel* attack, against shipping off the Normandy coast on 24 June 1944. (Rudat)

Far right Seven *Mistel* combinations photographed by an Allied reconnaissance aircraft at Prague/Ruzyne, during the preparations for 'Iron Hammer' in February 1945. The Fw 190 fighters on top of the Ju 88s are hardly visible, but the shadows betray their presence.

THE BATTLE FOR FRANCE

Above An Fw 190 of an unidentified ground-attack unit pictured in France in 1944. For their survival, these units were forced to operate from widely dispersed landing grounds and had to pay close attention to camouflage.

Below A close-up photograph of a Henschel Hs 293 rocket-powered, radio-controlled glider bomb under the starboard wing of its launch aircraft. There were hopes that this weapon would play a major part in defeating the expected Allied invasion of northern-western Europe.

Top right An Hs 293 mounted under the wing of a Dornier Do 217 of *Kampfgeschwader 100*.

Centre right The Fritz X, an unpowered radio-guided bomb, used a similar control system to that fitted to the Hs 293. Released from high altitude, the weapon achieved an impact velocity sufficient to penetrate the deck armour of heavy cruisers and even battleships.

Bottom right The Messerschmitt Me 262 began operations over France in July 1944, flying as a fighter-bomber with *Kampfgeschwader 51*; in this photograph two of the unit's aircraft are seen taking off, each with a pair of SC-250 bombs under the nose. (Via Dierich)

FIRST JET RECONNAISSANCE OPERATIONS

Above Arado Ar 234 reconnaissance aircraft of *Kommando Sperling*, pictured at Rheine in western Germany in the autumn of 1944.

Below Because of the shortage of fuel during the final stages of the war, and to enable them to take off with full tanks, aircraft had to be towed to the take-off point before a mission.

Above right Ground crewmen removing the film magazine from one of the cameras in the rear fuselage, after a mission.

Above far right *Leutnant* Erich Sommer flew the world's first jet reconnaissance mission, over the Allied lodgement area in Normandy, on 2 August 1944. (Sommer)

Below right The 'Mulberry' harbour off the coast of Normandy, photographed by Erich Sommer during his mission on 2 August 1944.

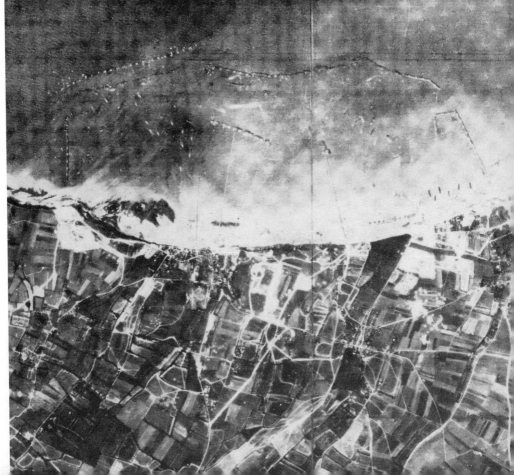

ATTACK AIRCRAFT ON THE EASTERN FRONT

Top left By mid-1944 the Focke Wulf Fw 190 had replaced the Ju 87 in most ground-attack units. This example, an F-8 fitted with additional armour on the underside of the fuselage, belonged to *Schlachtgeschwader 10* based in Hungary during the final winter of the war. It is loaded with a 550lb bomb. (Via Obert)

Centre left A Junkers Ju 87 modified for the anti-tank role, fitted with two 3.7cm high-velocity automatic cannon under the wings.

Bottom left A Henschel Hs 129 fitted with a 7.5cm anti-tank gun with electro-mechanical loading. About 25 aircraft were modified in this way and served on the Eastern Front with *Schlachtgeschwader 9* during the winter of 1944–45. (Via Schliephake)

Above and below The night attack units (*Nachtschlachtgruppen*) were an important part of the ground-attack forces on the Eastern and Southern Fronts. Operating slow-flying biplanes with open cockpits, these patrolled over enemy rear areas and attacked anything that moved with machine-gun fire and small bombs. Some of the aircraft used, like the Arado Ar 66 (above), were converted trainers. Others were foreign types. The Fokker CV aircraft operated by *NSGr 11* and pictured below were of Dutch prewar design; they were built under licence in Denmark and seized when that country was overrun in 1940.

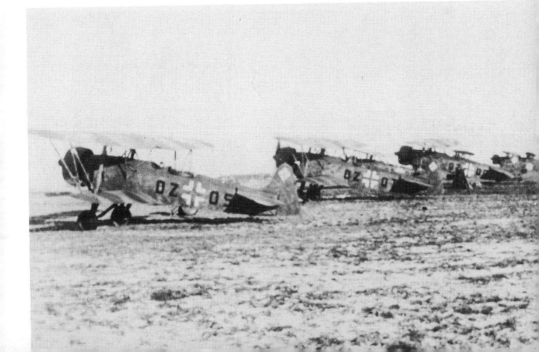

LUFTWAFFE COMBAT LEADERS

Above left *Oberstleutnant* Helmut Lent, the commander of *NJG 3*, was the top-scoring night-fighter ace during much of 1944 after amassing 102 night and 8 day victories.

Above right *Oberst* Werner Baumbach commanded *Kampfgeschwader 200*, the élite unit charged with carrying out a range of clandestine activities including the dropping of spies and saboteurs behind the enemy lines. It also operated the *Mistel* attack weapon in action. (Cescotti)

Below Göring raises his baton in final salute at the funeral of Lent, who was killed in a flying accident in October 1944.

Above left *Oberst* Hans-Ulrich Rudel, commander of *Sturzkampfgeschwader 2*, was the most successful dive-bomber pilot. He flew 2,530 operational missions and was credited with the destruction of more than seven hundred Soviet tanks and armoured vehicles.

Above right *Oberst* Hajo Herrmann was the leading proponent of Operation 'Wehrwolf', in which lightly armed fighters conducted ramming tactics on enemy bombers during the closing stages of the war. (Herrmann)

Below left In September 1944 *Major* Walter Nowotny, a leading fighter ace with 250 victories, led the first operational Me 262 fighter unit, *Kommando Nowotny*, into action. The introduction of the type into full service was premature, however. Nowotny was killed in action on 8 November 1944 and the *Kommando* was withdrawn from operations.

Below right *Leutnant* Werner Gail, a Focke Wulf Fw 190 ground-attack pilot of *III./SG 3*, whose account of operations on the Eastern Front is given in Chapter 5.

THE NIGHT FIGHTER FORCE

Left A Junkers Ju 88G fitted with the SN-2 airborne interception radar, which had replaced the early 'Lichtenstein' equipment early in 1944.

Right From the middle of 1944, Royal Air Force Mosquitos became a serious threat to German night fighters. This Ju 88 carries a rear-looking radar to provide warning of enemy aircraft approaching from behind.

Right A close-up view of a Ju 88G fitted with 'Neptun' airborne interception radar, which entered service early in 1945.

Left This Junkers Ju 88G was one of several night fighters fitted with the so-called 'Schrägemusik' installation, a pair of 2cm cannon fixed to fired obliquely upwards. The aircraft also carries the 'Naxos' homing device, its aerial in the blister above the cockpit.

Right One of the small number of Me 262 two-seat trainers that were fitted with radar and served in the night fighter role with NJG 11.

MISCELLANY

Top left Although it was intended to replace the Junkers Ju 52, the plans failed to materialize and the type continued as the workhorse of the *Luftwaffe* transport fleet throughout the final year of the war. (Via Schliephake)

Centre left The Arado Ar 232 transport was designed for operations from unprepared fields and a few were used by *KG 200* during clandestine missions. (Via Schliephake)

Bottom left The Junkers Ju 188D formed the backbone of the long-range reconnaissance force on the Eastern Front during the final year of the war. (Roosenbrom)

Above A Dornier Do 217 of *Aufklärungsgruppe Nacht*, a unit specializing in night reconnaissance missions using flares.

Below A rare photograph of a Messerschmitt Me 262 that had been operating in the tactical reconnaissance role, pictured at Lechfeld following the collapse of the nose wheel. The armament had been removed and a pair of vertical cameras mounted in the nose, with bulges to cover the film magazines.

LATE — AND TOO LATE

Top left An Me 262 of *III./JG 7* fitted with racks for twenty-four R4M unguided rockets under the outer wings. (Via Schliephake)

Centre left The Focke Wulf (Tank) Ta 152, the definitive development of the Fw 190 design, had a maximum speed of 472mph at 41,000ft. These examples went into action with *Jagdgeschwader 301* but too few were deployed for the type to have any impact on events.

Bottom left A Heinkel He 162 jet fighter of *Jagdgeschwader 1*, which was on the point of beginning operations with this type when the war ended. (Demuth)

Above Underground production of He 162 fuselages, in a disused salt mine at Tarthun near Magdeburg.

Below, left and right The rocket-propelled Bachem 349 *Natter* point-defence interceptor took off vertically from a special railed launcher. The first of these aircraft were deployed for action when the war ended.

THE END

Above Messerschmitt Bf 110 night fighters of *III./NJG 1* pictured at Fritzlar shortly after the airfield was overrun by US ground forces. Some of the planes have been blown up by the retreating Germans while others, captured intact, have one or both mainwheel tyres shot through to prevent unauthorized flights. (USAF)

Below An Arado Ar 234 and two Ju 88 night fighters in a damaged hangar at Manching after its capture by US forces.

CHAPTER 8

PAUSE IN THE AUTUMN

Autumn 1944

DURING SEPTEMBER AND OCTOBER the Allied advances in the west and in the east juddered to a halt, as the armies outran their supplies and were forced to stop and consolidate their gains. After the huge losses suffered in the summer, the German Army was allowed a breathing space in which to reorganize itself before the next major exertion.

The slow-down in the land fighting meant that the *Luftwaffe* could reduce its air operations to a bare minimum, except for those in defence of the homeland. Also during the autumn the focus of the Allied bomber attack had shifted to the German transport system, as a means of supporting the land operations. This provided welcome relief for the German oil industry and enabled repairs to be completed at several plants. As a result, monthly production of aviation fuel increased from 18,000 tons in October to 39,000 tons in November. This increase in production, coupled with the reduction in consumption, ended the precipitous fall in stocks of aviation fuels which from the end of September were stabilized at around 180,000 tons.

At the same time, the German aircraft industry was emerging from its large-scale reorganization and in September it delivered 3,821 new combat aircraft. This was the highest monthly total it would ever achieve, and was nearly one-third greater than in May. Almost four-fifths of these aircraft were Messerschmitt Bf 109s and Fw 190s, the two types emerging in very large numbers from the dispersed production facilities. There were just under five hundred Messerschmitt Bf 110s and Junkers Ju 88s, almost all destined for the night fighter force. Only 144 were jet-propelled types, Messerschmitt Me 163s, Me 262s, and Arado Ar 234s. To achieve this dramatic increase in fighter production, however, with the exception of the Arado Ar 234 and the Junkers Ju 388 all non-fighter types had been culled from the manufacturing programme.

The increase resulted in a sudden glut of aircraft for the front-line units. Fifteen fighter *Gruppen* that had suffered heavy losses during the fighting in France were completely re-equipped. Then came a large-scale expansion of the single-engined day fighter force, from 1,900 aircraft at the beginning of September to 3,300 aircraft in the middle of November – an increase of nearly 70 per cent. Each day fighter *Gruppe* in the west was expanded from three to four *Staffeln*, each of 10–15 aircraft. The additional pilots came from training schools or from bomber and other units that

Acceptances of combat aircraft by the *Luftwaffe*, September 1944

The table shows the new aircraft accepted by the *Luftwaffe* from the manufacturers during September 1944. The total number of new combat aircraft received was 3,821, nearly one-third more than in May. However, to achieve this increase in numbers the production of non-fighter types had been cut drastically. Since May the Heinkel He 177, the Junkers Ju 52, the Ju 290, the Arado Ar 196, the DFS 230 and the Gotha Go 242 had passed out of production. During September the last Messerschmitt Me 410s, Junkers Ju 87s and Ju 352s, Heinkel He 111s, Dornier Do 24s and Henschel Hs 129s left the lines and these types also went out of production. Production of most obsolescent types had now ceased, with the notable exception of the Messerschmitt Bf 110 night fighter which was being built in greater numbers than ever. The Junkers Ju 88 was now being built mainly for the night fighter role.

The only new types to enter production during the period were the Arado Ar 234 and the Junkers Ju 388. Factories were tooling up to mass-produce the Dornier Do 335 heavy fighter but the first production aircraft had not yet flown.

Aircraft	No	Remarks
Fighters		
Messerschmitt Bf 109	1,605	Includes tactical reconnaissance version
Focke Wulf Fw 190	1,391	Includes tac. recce. and ground-attack versions
Messerschmitt Bf 110	188	Night fighter
Messerschmitt Me 410	40	End of production
Messerschmitt Me 163	35	
Messerschmitt Me 262	91	
Heinkel He 219	28	
Junkers Ju 88	292	Night fighter, reconnaissance
Bombers		
Junkers Ju 188	74	Includes reconnaissance version
Heinkel He 111	2	End of production
Junkers Ju 87	21	End of production
Arado Ar 234	18	
Junkers Ju 388	3	Initial production batch
Transports		
Junkers Ju 352	2	End of production
Fieseler Fi 156	11	
Miscellaneous types		
Henschel Hs 129	17	End of production
Dornier Do 24	3	End of production
Total	**3,821**	

had been disbanded. Also at this time the re-engined D version of the Focke Wulf Fw 190 entered service, with a performance comparable to that of the American P-51C Mustang and the British Tempest and Spitfire XIV and superior to that of the latest Soviet fighters.

Taken together, these moves would make possible an extraordinarily rapid recovery by the *Luftwaffe* fighter force and one that would come as a surprise to its enemies.

Even as the recovery was in progress, the representation and influence of the *Luftwaffe* at Hitler's headquarters fell to rock-bottom. It will be remembered that, following the death of *General* Korten after injuries suffered in the assassination attempt on Hitler on 20 July, *Generalleutnant* Werner Kreipe had been appointed Chief of Staff. From the time he assumed office Kreipe had increasingly frequent clashes with the *Führer*. Göring made little attempt to support his subordinate: that summer, on the pretext of a throat infection, the *Reichsmarschall* withdrew from his headquarters for several weeks.

For the unfortunate Kreipe, matters came to a head at a war conference at Hitler's headquarters at Rastenburg on 18 September. A couple of days earlier the Allied airborne landings at Nijmegen and Arnhem in Holland had taken place without interference from the *Luftwaffe*, and Hitler used the occasion to deliver a savage condemnation of that service's recent failures. Kreipe attempted to reply to the criticisms in detail, but the conversation became increasingly heated until finally Hitler dismissed him from the room. Later that day the *General* was informed that the *Führer* had banished him from the headquarters.

Despite his rejection, Kreipe remained Chief of Staff of the *Luftwaffe*, at least nominally, until *General* Karl Koller succeeded him in November. During the hiatus Göring did not replace him, nor did he attempt to fill the void with his own ample frame. After recovering from his illness, the *Reichsmarschall* visited the *Führer*'s headquarters only when specifically summoned. In the interim the sole *Luftwaffe* representative at the *Führer*'s planning conferences was usually *General* Eckhard Christian. Christian's post was that of assistant to *General* Jodl commanding the *Oberkommando der Wehrmacht*; he was a relatively junior general holding no executive post within the *Luftwaffe*, and as a result there was little input from that service to the plans for major operations then in the course of preparation.

Following the end of the Battle of France, Hitler rescinded his earlier decree that new Messerschmitt 262s be delivered only to fighter-bomber units. At last the way was open for the aircraft to enter service with the fighter force.

Major Walter Nowotny, a leading ace credited with 250 victories, had been appointed commander of *Erprobungskommando 262* in July and the unit was re-designated *Kommando Nowotny*. The jet-fighter trials unit expanded slowly and by mid-August it possessed fifteen aircraft; engine serviceability remained poor, however, and rarely were more than four Me 262s available for flying. Despite these problems the unit had some successes against high-flying Allied reconnaissance aircraft, and during August it claimed the destruction of four of these.

In September the Jumo 004 engine was at last ready for mass production. That month ninety-one Me 262s were delivered to the

Luftwaffe – more than four times as many as in August. By the 30th of the month *Kommando Nowotny* had built up almost to *Gruppe* strength, with twenty-three Me 262s, and was declared ready for operations. Four days later the unit moved to the airfields at Achmer and Hesepe in north-west Germany, to position it nearer the battle front. *Kommando Nowotny*'s primary task would be to engage American fighters escorting deep-penetration attacks by heavy bombers; if the former could be forced to jettison their drop tanks, the bombers would be denied fighter protection at the target and so be placed at the mercy of German conventional fighters.

Several factors combined to prevent *Kommando Nowotny* achieving any immediate impact, however. The serviceability of the jet engines continued to be poor, and many aircraft were confined to the ground for engine changes. The jet fighter landed at speeds around 120mph, much faster than piston-engined types and too fast for the tyres made from synthetic and reclaimed rubber, which often burst. Furthermore, the links joining the hefty 3cm ammunition rounds were not strong enough and tended to break if the guns were fired during a high-G turn.

Added to these problems were those caused by the Allied air forces, whose fighter pilots quickly discovered the Achilles' heel of the new jet fighter – its vulnerability to attack while flying at low speed immediately after take-off or on the approach for landing. A factor contributing to this vulnerability was the difficulty of concealing the airfields used by jet aircraft. On standard *Luftwaffe* airfields the runways were made of asphalt, but during operations by jet aircraft this material was liable to catch fire. The concrete runways at airfields earmarked for jet operations showed up clearly on photographs taken by the omniscient Allied reconnaissance aircraft. Once discovered, these airfields were the subject of repeated bombing attacks and Allied fighters mounted standing patrols overhead in the hope of catching jet aircraft taking off or landing.

On 7 October *Kommando Nowotny* scrambled five Me 262s – the largest number it had yet put up for an engagement – to intercept formations of American bombers heading for oil targets in central Germany. The Mustangs were active over the jet fighter airfields that day, however, and, from his vantage point 15,000ft over Achmer, Lieutenant Urban Drew of the 361st Fighter Group watched a couple of the jets start their take-off runs. He waited until both enemy fighters were airborne, then rolled his P-51 on its back and pulled into a high-speed dive and plummeted down on the jets. He rapidly caught up with the Me 262s and shot down both before they could accelerate to fighting speed. A third jet fighter was lost in a separate action with escorting fighters. The first multi-aircraft action by *Kommando Nowotny* had cost three Me 262s destroyed and one pilot killed, in return for three American bombers shot down. It was an inauspicious start for operations by the new jet fighter.

During its first month of operations on the Western Front

Kommando Nowotny claimed the destruction of four American heavy bombers, twelve fighters and three reconnaissance aircraft, for the loss of six Me 262s in combat and seven more destroyed and nine damaged in accidents. Then, on 8 November, the jet-fighter unit suffered its most grievous blow of all: Nowotny himself was shot down and killed in action. As it happened, *Generalmajor* Galland was at Achmer that day, on an inspection visit to determine why the jet fighter unit had not achieved more positive results. Galland saw enough to realize that Nowotny had been given an almost impossible task, and despite his best efforts the unit was barely effective. Nowotny had been charged with introducing into operational service a completely new type of fighter, though many pilots had not received proper conversion training and aircraft serviceability was poor. The unit was based at airfields close to the front line in an area where the enemy air forces had a massive numerical superiority, and it came under frequent air attack. Galland ordered the jet fighter *Kommando* to withdraw to Lechfeld, where it was to re-form and its pilots were to receive further training. At the same time the aircraft were to undergo modifications to overcome some of the defects.

Throughout the autumn the Me 262 fighter-bomber unit, *I. Gruppe* of *KG 51*, mounted regular pin-prick attacks on Allied airfields and troop positions in France, Holland and Belgium. In this role the aircraft suffered from the same teething troubles as had those in *Kommando Nowotny*, with one significant exception. Because of their different role the fighter-bomber pilots needed to work the throttles far less often than their fighter counterparts, and as a result their jet engines lasted longer and suffered fewer failures.

For the *Luftwaffe*, the one outstanding success during the Battle of France had been the deployment of the two Arado Ar 234As modified for the reconnaissance role. The speed and altitude performance of the jet aircraft enabled them to range over Allied territory at will, restoring to the *Luftwaffe* in the west a capability denied to it since 1942. In the autumn the first Ar 234B reconnaissance aircraft entered service, fitted with a normal wheeled undercarriage. (It will be remembered that the pre-production 'A' version took off from a jettisonable trolley, a factor which limited the number of airfields it could use.) The first Ar 234Bs were issued to *Kommando Sperling*, a *Staffel*-sized reconnaissance unit based at Rheine. In the months that followed, the unit conducted regular photographic missions over Holland, Belgium, eastern France and south-east England. Later a second Ar 234B unit, *Kommando Specht*, became operational in northern Italy to perform a similarly valuable task in that theatre.

Also during the autumn of 1944, the highly secret *Kampfgeschwader 200* was reorganized to undertake a range of new missions and placed under the command of the famous bomber ace *Oberstleutnant* Werner Baumbach. *I. Gruppe* continued its task of transporting agents and saboteurs to their destinations behind enemy lines, while *II. Gruppe* was assigned to the *Mistel* attack role, its establishment including several Junkers Ju 88s and Ju 188s which were to serve as pathfinders and illuminate targets during night operations. *III. Gruppe*, about to form, was to be equipped with Fw 190 fighter bombers modified to carry torpedoes and other new types of anti-shipping weapons then being developed, and *IV. Gruppe* was responsible for the training of aircrew for the rest of the *Geschwader*, also serving as a holding unit for the so-called '*Totaleinsatz*' personnel, volunteers for suicide missions. In the months to follow *KG 200* would become 'an air force within an air force', exploiting its close relationship with the SS and the *Abwehr* military intelligence and its direct subordination to the *Luftwaffe* High Command to obtain resources not available to other units.

With production of the Arado Ar 234 building up, the first bomber unit earmarked to receive the type began its conversion. Based at Burg-bei-Magdeburg, *III. Gruppe* of *Kampfgeschwader 76* took delivery of the first jet bombers. A few pilots had received conversion training on the aircraft at the test establishment at Rechlin and now served as instructors. Many of the ground crews had 'hands-on' experience on the aircraft, having been detached to work on the production lines and assist in preparing the aircraft for flight testing.

Following the recent disbandment of so many bomber *Gruppen*, *III./KG 76* had the pick of the bomber pilots in the *Luftwaffe. Major* Hans-Georg Bätcher, appointed to command the *Gruppe*, was one of the best-known bomber aces, holding the *Ritterkreuz* with Oakleaves and with some 620 operational missions to his credit. *Hauptmann* Diether Lukesch, commander of *9. Staffel*, also held the *Ritterkreuz* with Oakleaves and had flown 372 operational missions. *Hauptmann* Regler had flown 279 missions; five other pilots had flown more than a hundred missions; and everyone on the unit had flown at least ten operational missions.

The Arado required several modifications before it was ready for operations, however, which kept many of the aircraft on the ground until the work was complete and slowed the pace of training. Hitler expected great things from the new jet bomber and pressed Göring to bring the aircraft into action as soon as possible. Rather than wait until the *Gruppe* had its full complement of operational jet bombers and trained pilots, it was decided to concentrate the available resources into a single *Staffel*, the 9th, and bring that one to operational status. We shall examine the initial operations conducted by this *Staffel* later, in Chapter 10.

Tests with the new tank-busting version of the Henschel Hs 129, fitted with the BK 7.5cm high-velocity cannon, demonstrated that the weapon was effective against the side and rear armour of the heaviest Soviet tanks. As a result, a crash programme was ordered to modify all Hs 129s on the production line to B-3 standard, able to carry the weapon. Shortly after this decision was taken, however, it was superseded by another to terminate Hs 129 production altogether. Less than thirty Hs 129 were produced with the 7.5cm cannon. These aircraft were delivered to *IV./SG 9* on the Eastern Front, and were found to be even slower and more unwieldy than previous versions of the Hs 129. Since it was vulnerable to fighter attack, the new 'tank buster' was unsuitable for operations against tanks in enemy territory. It could engage only those enemy armoured vehicles that had broken through the Front and were without fighter cover. As Hs 129s fitted with heavy cannon were lost in action they could not be replaced, and after a brief and undistinguished career the tank-buster disappeared from service.

In the autumn of 1944 Germany's military position was considerably worse than it had been in May. In the west, the east and the south enemy troops were close to and in some cases over her borders. Faced with the sole alternative of unconditional surrender, a course made the more hideous by imaginative propaganda, the German armed forces resolved to fight to the bitter end. As one oft-repeated saying of the period ran, 'Enjoy the war, because the peace will be dreadful'.

None of the new weapons introduced into the *Luftwaffe* made even a dent in the all-pervading air superiority established by the Allies. Yet, following the depradations of the summer, the *Luftwaffe* fighter force had staged a remarkable recovery. By concentrating forces it was once again in a position to deliver one or more spectacular blows against the enemy. In the next chapter we shall examine some of its 'white hopes' for the future.

CHAPTER 9

THE WHITE HOPES (2)

Autumn 1944

DURING THE AUTUMN of 1944 a new jet fighter type was added to the German fighter production programme and ordered 'off the drawing board' – the '*Volksjäger*' or 'People's Fighter'. It was conceived in the summer of 1944 as an unsophisticated, simple and cheap lightweight machine that could be designed and built rapidly and in large numbers from readily available materials by semi-skilled and unskilled labour. The operational take-off weight of the new fighter would be around 6,000lb, less than half that of the Me 262 and considerably less than that of any of the Western fighter types it might meet in combat. One of the requirements of the '*Volksjäger*' was that it would be easy to fly in combat, and there was even a quaint idea that pilots with only glider-flying training would be able to convert directly on to the jet fighter.

From the start *General* Galland and other senior officers in the fighter force expressed vehement opposition to the '*Volksjäger*' project, regarding it as a diversion of resources away from the Me 262 and other more effective programmes. But the light-weight fighter had the support of Göring, Armament Minister Albert Speer and *Jägerstab* leader Otto Saur, and it was inserted into the production programme as a high-priority item.

Several aircraft companies submitted design proposals for the '*Volksjäger*', and that by Heinkel was selected for mass production under the designation Heinkel He 162. The small single-seat fighter was to be powered by a single BMW 003 turbojet mounted above the fuselage, and in its initial production version it would be armed with two 2cm cannon. The aircraft was intended solely for use a short-range day fighter, and it had no provision to carry drop tanks or other external stores.

Work on the new fighter advanced rapidly and it was planned

The Heinkel He 162A-2 '*Volksjäger*'

Role: Single-seat jet fighter.
Powerplant: One 2,028lb thrust BMW 003 jet engine.
Armament: Two MG 151 20mm cannon.
Performance (at 19,500ft): Maximum speed 562mph. Maximum range 385 miles.
Weights: Empty equipped 3,875lb. Normal operational take-off weight 6,184lb.
Dimensions: Span 23ft 7½in. Length 29ft 8¼in. Wing area 120 sq ft.

that the prototype would fly early in December 1944. Simultaneously, preparations were in train to produce the aircraft in large
numbers, with a target figure of one thousand completed by the
end of April 1945.

As in any air force in time of war, the *Luftwaffe* had numerous
plans for future operations under consideration although, as
mentioned earlier, few of these survived the general destruction
of *Luftwaffe* documents during the final days of the war. On the
pages that follow are details of two plans that came close to
fruition in the autumn of 1944, which show that the *Luftwaffe*
had lost none of its penchant for imagination in planning
operations.

Following the failure of the fighter force to blunt the enemy
daylight attacks on the homeland, *Generalmajor* Galland drew up
plans for a radically different defence operation. Exploiting the
lull in operations and the current expansion of the fighter force,
he withdrew several units from action and moved them to
airfields in central Germany to re-form and retrain. He thus
assembled a large force of fighters for the operation he termed
'*Der Grosse Schlag*' ('The Great Blow'), a single crushing attack
on the US bombers to be delivered at a time and place of his
choosing.

In his book *The First and the Last*, Galland outlined his plan.
No fewer than 2,000 fighters were to engage the enemy bombers
on their way to the target. Many of the fighters that had
intercepted were then to land, refuel and rearm, and it was
expected that about 500 would then take off to engage the
bombers again during their withdrawal. While this was happening, about 100 night fighters were to move into position to
intercept damaged bombers attempting to escape to Switzerland
or Sweden. The intention was to shoot down between 400 and 500
bombers in a single day, at an expected cost of about 400 German
fighters and 100 to 150 German pilots.

Galland went on to describe the detailed preparations made for
the operation:

> This was going to be the largest and most decisive air battle of the war.
> On November 12th 1944 the entire fighter arm was ready for action:
> eighteen fighter groups with 3,700 aircraft and pilots, a fighting force
> such as the *Luftwaffe* had never possessed before. More than 3,000 of
> these were waiting for 'The Great Blow'.
>
> Now it was a question of awaiting favourable weather, as good
> weather was one of the essentials for this mass action. It was a difficult
> decision to hold back the defensive fighters, which were standing by
> in the face of the air armadas dropping gigantic bomb-loads daily, but
> contrary to my previous experience the leaders [i.e. the High Com-
> mand] kept calm and did not insist on vain and costly forced action.
>
> The enemy began to sense the strong German fighter potential in
> those days, but the main object of these combats was to train the units
> intended for 'The Great Blow'.

To make up for the shortage of experienced formation leaders,
individual *Gruppen* earmarked for the operation had been ex-

panded, in some cases to twice their normal establishment in pilots and aircraft. With limited supplies of fuel available for training, Galland used this to prepare his new pilots for the set-piece air defence operation he had in mind, which would be mounted from well-equipped airfields in central Germany. The fate of the fighters that Galland had husbanded so carefully will be described in the next chapter.

When the *Mistel* combination aircraft had first become available for operations, in the late spring of 1944, *Luftwaffe* staff officers had prepared a paper discussing operations that were possible with the new weapon. The *Mistel* was designed for use against high-value naval targets, and attacks on three major fleet anchorages, Gibraltar, Leningrad and Scapa Flow, were considered.

Gibraltar lay 850 miles from the nearest German base in France and was considered the most difficult to hit. The Bf 109 component of the *Mistel* carried insufficient fuel to reach France after the attack, which meant that pilots would have to bail out into in the sea or over Spanish territory. Even if this proviso were accepted, the attack was judged impracticable unless the aircraft were allowed to cross Spanish territory on the way to the target. The paper noted that 'the *Führer* has always refused to give permission for this'. An attack on Leningrad was ruled out because of the difficulty of achieving surprise after a long approach flight over enemy territory. Moreover, the Soviet warships in the port were effectively bottled up in the Baltic and did not pose much of a threat.

That left the attack on the Royal Navy fleet anchorage at Scapa Flow in the Orkneys as the most likely of the three to achieve significant results. The airfield at Grove in central Denmark, 480 miles from the Royal Navy base, was well within *Mistel* range. The paper warned, however, that

In the target area the very strongest defences may be expected. Exactly how strong is not known, for our radio monitoring service is not effective north of The Wash. However, Department Ic [Intelligence] estimates that on the airfields between the Firth of Forth and the North of Scotland there are 160 to 200 aircraft of the types Spitfire, Hurricane, Mosquito and Beaufighter. In addition, there is a belt of radar stations giving gap-free cover out to sea . . .

If the operation were to have any chance of success, surprise was essential. Since only one attack could be made, it had to be with sufficient force to inflict the required damage at one go. For that a minimum of forty *Mistel* combinations would be necessary. The nearest *Luftwaffe* airfield to the anchorage, at Stavanger in Norway, was 350 miles from the target and that ruled out the possibility of fighter cover over the target. It was thought that dusk was the best time to launch the strike. The combinations were to cross the North Sea at low altitude, keeping below the British radar cover, and at the last moment they were to climb to 3,000ft and go straight into their attack runs.

There were two prerequisites for such a straight-in attack – accurate and uptodate intelligence on the positions of capital ships at anchor, and accurate navigation to the pull-up point. The paper stressed the need for the most careful reconnaissance prior to the attack. Faced with those powerful defences, *Mistel* pilots would not be able to orbit over the anchorage to seek their targets. Each pilot would need an aerial photograph of the anchorage with the exact position of his main and alternative targets marked on it. To assist the pilots to navigate to the target, pathfinder aircraft were to lay down a line of '*Schwan*' floating radio beacons along the route.

The effectiveness of the attack on Scapa would, of course, depend on there being major naval units in the anchorage at the time. In fact, there were frequent comings and goings. During June and July 1944, for example, the Royal Navy fleet carriers *Victorious, Indomitable, Implacable, Indefatigable, Formidable* and *Furious* all put in appearances there, as did the battleships *Duke of York* and *Howe*. The feasibility of the attack was accepted, and during the autumn of 1944 forces began to concentrate at Grove and nearby airfields for the attack on Scapa Flow.

In the next chapter we shall examine the increasingly desperate actions being mounted by the *Luftwaffe* against the Western Allies.

CHAPTER 10

DESPERATE TIMES, DESPERATE MEASURES

1 November 1944 to 10 January 1945

REINVIGORATED DURING the autumn respite, the *Luftwaffe* fighter force was once again sufficiently strong to deliver a concentrated blow against the enemy. Its next major defensive effort was on 2 November, when 490 fighters from ten *Gruppen* took off to engage more than a thousand heavy bombers escorted by 873 fighters fanning out across Germany to attack the Leuna-Merseburg oil refinery and rail targets.

On that day *Gefechtsverbande* were able to press home two separate attacks. The *Sturmbock* Fw 190s of *IV.(Sturm)/JG 3* got through to the Flying Fortresses of the 91st Bomb Group and knocked down thirteen of them, including two by ramming. Later, *II./JG 4* attacked the Fortresses of the 457th Bomb Group and destroyed nine. Then, in each case, Mustangs arrived on the scene in force and suddenly the predators became the prey. Thirty-one of the 61 *Sturmbock* aircraft taking part in the actions were shot down, seventeen of their pilots being killed and seven wounded.

Five Messerschmitt Me 163s of *JG 400* were scrambled from Brandis, but this part of the operation was a complete failure. One of the rocket fighters crashed on take-off, and as the remainder were moving into position to attack the bombers they were hotly engaged by the escorting fighters which shot down three of them. The unit lost four aircraft and three pilots killed, without shooting down a single enemy aircraft.

Of the conventional fighter units, the hardest hit was *JG 27*. All four of its Bf 109 *Gruppen* became embroiled with American escorts and suffered heavy losses in the series of swirling dog-fights that followed. The *Geschwader* claimed the destruction of seven American fighters. Records of its own losses in aircraft appear not to have survived, though certainly they were heavy: pilot casualties totalled 27 killed or missing and eleven wounded.

That day the *Luftwaffe* exhibited the façade of air power without its substance. Altogether it lost 120 fighters shot down during the various engagements, with 70 pilots killed or missing and 28 wounded. The loss of 98 difficult-to-replace fighter pilots in a single day constituted a devastating blow. In return, what had the defenders achieved? From all causes that day, the Eighth Air Force lost 40 bombers (3.6 per cent of the force) and sixteen fighters (1.8 per cent). The Americans would take such losses in their stride, and within a day or two replacement aircraft and crews had arrived to restore the afflicted units to their original

---

On the receiving end of a *'Sturmbock'* attack

Attack by twenty-two Sturmbock *Fw 190s of* II.(Sturm.)/ JG 4 *on 2 November 1944, as observed by Staff Sergeant Bernard Sitek, ball turret gunner in a B-17 of the 457th Bomb Group:*

Everything happened pretty fast, as it usually does when the Germans offer any opposition. We had been off the bomb run about ten minutes when vapour trails from fighters started to fill the sky. Friendly or enemy, was the question on everybody's mind. We soon learned the answer. They were Fw 190s and Me 109s forming up for one of those wolfpack attacks. At first it appeared that they were on the same level as our Box, the High Box, but as they came closer they lowered themselves for an attack on the Low and the Lead Boxes. Every one of them followed this pattern to hit those other two Boxes except the leader, who must have liked the looks of one of the B-17s straggling in our Box.

I got my gunsights on him from about 600 or 700 yards as he made his attack from seven o'clock. I could almost see the bullets hit home. As he got closer I could feel his 20mm bursts around me. At about 200 yards distance he seemed to stop dead. He rolled over and the pilot came out. In a split second the plane burst into flames and broke into several pieces. The pilot didn't wait long to open his chute. Watching his chute drift down, I could see other aircraft burning and exploding beneath me.

---

strengths. For the *Luftwaffe* day fighter force, the defeat on 2 November would have consequences that ran far beyond the actual losses it had suffered.

The 2 November action was discussed at length at the *Führer* Conference at Rastenburg four days later. The defenders claimed to have shot down 82 US aircraft (the real figure was 56), of which about 50 were credited to fighters and about 30 to flak. It will be remembered that the Chief of Staff of the *Luftwaffe*, *General* Kreipe, was still banished from Hitler's headquarters. So it was left to the relatively junior *General* Christian from the OKW staff, and the even more junior *Major* Herbert Büchs, a *Luftwaffe* adjutant, to explain to the *Führer* what had gone wrong.

BÜCHS: There were two *Sturmgruppen.*
HITLER: With altogether . . . ?
BÜCHS: With altogether 63 aircraft, of which 61 made contact.
HITLER: Right, 61.
BÜCHS: They shot down 30 heavy bombers.
HITLER: That leaves 20 over. If you take away these 60 machines from the 305, then that leaves 240 [sic]. So 240 machines made 20 kills in all, and themselves lost . . . 30 in the *Sturmgruppen*?
BÜCHS: Yes, 30 in the *Sturmgruppen.*
HITLER: And the rest lost 90. Then we have 240 sorties with 90 lost and 20 kills altogether.
CHRISTIAN: One point, the *Sturmgruppen* has another *Gruppe* with it to provide cover.
HITLER: I don't give a damn about that. The covering *Gruppe* must shoot [at the bombers] too. It wasn't just bombers that were shot down – some [escort] fighters were too.

BÜCHS: Yes, that's clear.
HITLER: Then the result is thoroughly unsatisfactory.

As he examined the results of this attack on enemy bomber formations by a sizeable German fighter force, the *Führer*'s mind was focused on the still larger attack in an advanced stage of preparation – 'The Great Blow', with three times as many fighters. The failure to achieve worthwhile results on 2 November did not bode well for the success of such a venture.

> HITLER: That's a miserable result. I put in 260 [sic] fighters and get 20 kills. So if I put in 2,000 I would get 200 kills. That means I just can't count on those machines producing any . . . and they're pouring out of the factories at the devil's own pace. They're just eating up labour and materials.

On the evidence available it seemed to Hitler that in executing 'The Great Blow', the German fighter force might suffer heavy losses without securing decisive results. If that were the case, he had another use for the large force of fighters that *General* Galland had so painstakingly assembled – to support the counter-offensive he was planning in the west. We shall examine the *Luftwaffe*'s part in this operation later in this chapter.

The pilot losses on 2 November were the worst yet suffered by the *Luftwaffe* on a single day, but it was only one of four black days for the fighter force that month: on the 21st, sixty-two German fighter pilots were killed or wounded; on the 26th, eighty-seven; and on the 27th, fifty-one. In the course of those actions the force lost 348 pilots killed, wounded, missing or taken prisoner. *Oberstleutnant* Dahl, the commander of *Jagdgeschwader 300*, summed up the month's actions:

> The flying in November 1944 was the toughest I encountered during the entire war. The odds against us were 20 to 1 and sometimes even 30 to 1. Every day we were taking casualties. Our replacement pilots had not received sufficient training and were of low quality. And more and more the fuel shortage was making itself felt.

By this time the preparations for the *Mistel* attack on Scapa Flow were well advanced. But now an attack by Royal Air Force bombers neutralized the carefully laid German plan. On 11 November a force of Lancasters delivered a successful attack on the battleship *Tirpitz* in Tromsø Fjord, causing her to capsize. The warship had been the last surviving major unit of the Germany Navy, and following her demise there was no reason for the Royal Navy to retain capital ships in the Atlantic; within a week the majority of the larger ships that had been using Scapa Flow were on their way to join the Royal Navy's Pacific Fleet. German reconnaissance aircraft soon detected the change in the British dispositions and, with no worthwhile targets remaining in the anchorage, the planned attack was abandoned.

Although it had suffered enormous losses during the battles that summer, the German Army also made a remarkable recovery in the autumn of 1944. It was still a sizeable force, and by concentrating resources it was able to hurl a mighty blow at a time and place of its choosing. Hitler had his generals draw up plans for a large-scale counter-offensive in the west involving 200,000 men, including seven *Panzer* divisions. These were to smash through the weakly held Ardennes sector of the US front and thrust towards the port of Antwerp. The operation was code-named '*Wacht am Rhein*' ('Watch on the Rhine'). Hitler believed that such an attack, delivered at a time when they thought her militarily exhausted, was likely to catch Germany's enemies off balance. Above all, the *Führer* sought to buy time – time to introduce the advanced new aircraft and weapons into the *Luftwaffe* and bring the potent new U-boat types into service in the Navy. And in time he believed that the irreconcilable political systems of the Western Allies and the Soviet Union would lead to their falling out and even perhaps start fighting among themselves (an oft-recurring theme in the German propaganda at this time).

Under 'Watch on the Rhine' the *Luftwaffe* would have four tasks to perform. First, it was to deliver a large-scale attack to put several of the Allied forward airfields out of action; second, it was to establish an air umbrella over the battle zone to prevent Allied aircraft from interfering with German troop movements; third, it was to fly close air support and interdiction missions to assist the advancing troops; and fourth, it was to mount a small-scale airborne assault operation to secure the important road junction near Malmédy, through which American reinforcements would pass on their way to the Front.

The *Luftwaffe*'s fighter force was at peak numerical strength, in preparation for 'The Great Blow'. Now, to the chagrin of its commanders, Hitler cancelled the planned operation. In his book, Adolf Galland wrote:

> In the middle of November I received an alarming order, the whole impact of which I could not foresee. The fighter reserves were to be prepared for action on the front where a great land battle was expected in the west. This was incredible!
>
> On November 20th the transfer to the west was ordered, regardless of my scruples and objections . . . I must admit that even now, as I took part in the discussions for the mobilisation of the fighters in the west, it had not occurred to me that all these preparations were for our own counter-offensive. Until the very last I was kept in the dark, and only a few days before the start of the offensive in the Ardennes was I informed of the plan. Only now did I realise that the High Command from the beginning had understood something quite different by 'The Great Blow'.

Galland and other *Luftwaffe* officers pointed out that the air defence training the new pilots had received was quite different from that required for rough-and-tumble operations from small airfields close to the battle front in the west, but these injunctions fell on deaf ears.

To support the counter-offensive, the *Luftwaffe* assembled a force of 2,460 combat aircraft, comprising 1,770 single-engined fighters, 140 twin-engined fighters, 55 bombers, 40 jet bombers, 390 ground-attack aircraft and 65 reconnaissance aircraft. Following careful husbanding of stocks, and the resumption of deliveries from the newly repaired refineries, there was sufficient fuel to sustain this force in action at high sortie rates.

Under the original German plan the large-scale attack on the Allied airfields, code-named Operation *Bodenplatte* ('Baseplate'), was to be launched on the same morning as the ground offensive. To preserve secrecy, flying units moved to their advanced bases in the west at low altitude, maintaining radio silence. On their arrival radio silence was preserved, and radio operators at the bases previously used maintained the previous pattern of transmissions.

By mid-December the units assigned to 'Baseplate' had moved forward, and on the 14th the commanders of the fighter and ground-attack *Gruppen* were summoned to *Jagdkorps II* headquarters near Altenkirchen. *Generalmajor* Dietrich Peltz, in overall charge of the operation, informed his audience that simultaneous attacks were to be delivered against sixteen of the more important airfields used by Allied fighters and fighter-bombers in France, Holland and Belgium. More than a thousand aircraft were to take part in the operation.

Two days later, during the early morning darkness on 16 December, a massive artillery bombardment heralded the opening of 'Watch on the Rhine'. But the executive code-words for Operation 'Baseplate' were not transmitted and the aircraft earmarked for the attack stayed on the ground. German weather forecasters had predicted several days of low cloud over the battle area, and this presented the attacking troops with a heaven-sent opportunity: if the weather prevented both sides' air forces from taking part in the land battle, the German cause would be greatly assisted.

The night paratroop drop on Malmédy was still to have gone ahead, but owing to an administrative hitch the German paratroops failed to reach their dispatch airfield in time. This operation had to be postponed 24 hours. However, as forecast, dawn on the 16th brought a thick fog over the battle area and this persisted throughout the day. Protected by the swirling mists, the German armoured units thrust deeply into the American forward positions.

On the evening of the 16th the cloud lifted sufficiently for the planned drop by German paratroops to go ahead. Sixty-eight Junkers Ju 52s from *II. Gruppe Transportgeschwader 3* and *Transportgruppe Brambach* took off from Paderborn and Lipp-springe, carrying the 870 paratroops and their equipment. Many of the Ju 52 pilots had insufficient training in blind flying, however, with the result that one transport crashed shortly after take off and ten others became lost and either dropped their paratroops outside the dropping zone or returned with them still on board. At the dropping zone the wind had risen to over 30mph, nearly twice the safe maximum speed for such an operation.

Luftwaffe personnel strength, 15 December 1944			
Aircrew, administrative and ground staff	596,250	Works units	9,100
		Civil Defence personnel	63,250
Flak	816,200	Paratroops	200,100
Signals	305,000	Miscellaneous	163,000
Supply	109,100		
Medical and veterinary	42,500	**TOTAL**	2,304,500

Paratroops were scattered over a wide area and several suffered injuries on landing. In some cases severely wounded men lay where they landed on the snow-swept hillsides until they died of exposure, or were taken prisoner.

When *Oberst* von der Heydte, the paratroop commander, assembled his force and began moving on his objective he had only about a quarter of his men and no weapons larger than small mortars and machine pistols. The postponement had denied the operation any advantage of surprise, and the area was swarming with American troops. Instead of seizing the vital cross-roads, establishing a perimeter and fighting a defensive action on his terms, von der Heydte could mount only harassing operations aimed at slowing the movement of enemy troops forwards.

Despite poor visibility on the 17th, German ground-attack units flew some 600 sorties. In a series of scrappy air combats the *Luftwaffe* fighter force lost 55 pilots killed and 24 wounded. After dark, German bombers, night ground-attack aircraft and night fighters flew some 300 sorties against Allied troops moving towards the battle area. Thereafter the weather again closed in, and for the next six days there was little air activity over the Ardennes. Meanwhile the German advance started to lose its momentum, as battle-hardened American units from other areas moved into blocking positions. By 20 December the German spearheads, which in places had advanced forty miles since the start of the offensive, had all been halted. Also on that day von der Heydte's surviving paratroopers, having exhausted almost all their food and ammunition, split into small units which headed east, trying to fight their way back to the German lines. Few would succeed. Thus ended the last airborne assault operation mounted by the *Luftwaffe*, an inglorious end to its part in a form of warfare that it had pioneered.

On Christmas Eve the fog and low cloud over the battle area finally lifted and German fighters and fighter-bombers were hurled into the fray over the salient. Jet bombers also joined in the fighting – Me 262s of *Kampfgeschwader 51*, and the 'white hope' of the *Luftwaffe* bomber force, the Arado 234, on its first operational mission in this role. That morning *Hauptmann* Diether Lukesch, commander of *9. Staffel Kampfgeschwader 76*, led nine Arado 234s out from Münster/Handorf. Each aircraft carried a single 1,100lb bomb under the fuselage. The jet bombers climbed to 13,000ft and levelled out. With little to fear from enemy fighters, the Arados flew in loose trail with no attempt to assemble formation. At the target, a factory complex and the rail yards at Liège in Belgium, the aircraft released their bombs from altitudes of around 6,500ft in shallow dives. Then they headed straight for base without attempting to regain altitude. The German pilots observed Spitfires and Thunderbolts patrolling in the target area, but no Allied fighter made a serious attempt to engage the jet bombers. As he came off the target Lukesch found himself closing rapidly on a Spitfire that chanced to be in his path. With no way of knowing that the enemy plane bearing down on him carried no weapon other than the pilot's pistol, the pilot turned away sharply and dived clear. All the jet bombers returned safely, though one suffered minor damage when its undercarriage collapsed on landing. In a similar operation that afternoon, Lukesch led eight Arados against the same target. Again all of the jets returned safely.

Elsewhere that day, other *Luftwaffe* units suffered heavy losses in the renewed bout of air fighting that came with the clear skies. Eleven of the more important *Luftwaffe* airfields supporting the offensive were bombed and suffered serious damage. In air combats the German fighter force lost 85 pilots killed and 21 wounded.

On the following day, Christmas, the regrouped American troops went on to the offensive and started to squeeze the Germans out of 'The Bulge'. In the air there was no let-up in the fighting, with a further rash of combats over western Germany. The Arados flew two 8-aircraft operations against Liège. One of the jet bombers was attacked by an RAF Tempest and forced to crash-land, and two more suffered minor damage on landing.

Jagdkorps II War Diary, 26 December 1944

Very cold. Limited operations by the Americans and British, and the intensity of our own operations was reduced accordingly.

II./JG 1 had the heaviest losses of the day. Eight pilots failed to return and are reported missing following dog-fights in the Bastogne area.

Fifteen 'long noses' [Fw 190Ds] of *I./JG 26* led by *Oblt.* Hartigs were airborne at 10.58 and engaged Mustangs over Belgium. *Oblt.* Hartigs and *Fw.* Schöndorf taken prisoner near Carlsbourg. *Flieger* Bergmeier and *Feldwebeln* Grad and Sattler were killed in action. *Stabsfeldwebel* Schwarz reported one victory.

JG 27 lost six pilots killed during action near Liège.

In the south-west, *II./JG 53* engaged an American incursion in the Stuttgart area. *Hptm.* Meimberg, the *Gruppe* commander, was shot down and baled out over Schaichhof. *Oblt.* Ludolf was killed near Rutesheim; he was too low when he baled out and the parachute did not have time to open fully. *Gefr.* Rutland was wounded and made a wheels-up landing near Flacht. *Gefr.* Meermann was shot down and killed east of Wimsheim.

SG4 lost four pilots, including two *Staffel* leaders. *Hptm.* Jungelausen and *Hptm.* Schürmer were killed in action in map reference LK. *Ofw.* Weinrich and *Ofw.* Zumkeller missing.

Outside the battle area, the Christmas period brought no relief for the beleaguered German fighter force: on the 25th, 62 pilots were killed or wounded, and on the 31st, 41. Whenever the weather allowed, single Arado Ar 234s and Me 262 fighter-bombers flew nuisance attacks on American troop positions in the Ardennes. To meet these incursions, Allied fighters flew standing patrols at various altitudes. Whenever a German jet aircraft appeared, there would be chaotic scenes as the fighters attempted to dive into firing positions. Few jet aircraft were shot down in these actions. The bombs they dropped caused little damage, but at least the 'decoy duck' tactics kept Allied fighters busy when they might otherwise have been strafing the hard-pressed German troops. At this stage of the war, it was the nearest thing to air cover the latter would receive.

During the two weeks following the Altenkirchen briefing the 'Baseplate' operation had faded into the background as the units allocated to the attack were used to support the offensive in other ways. Many commanders assumed that the airfield attack plan, like so many before it, had been quietly shelved. Their surprise was all the greater when, on the afternoon of 31 December, the preliminary signal triggering the execution of the operation clattered out on the teleprinters at their headquarters. The attack was to be launched soon after first light the following morning.

During briefings at their airfields that evening the German pilots learned about the operation and of the part they were to play in it. They saw their routes laid out on the wall charts, their turning points, and the compass headings to the targets. The approach flights were to be made at tree-top height to avoid detection by enemy radar, and the pilots were to observe strict radio silence even if forced to bail out or crash-land. The main briefings over, the 'Baseplate' pilots were ordered to bed for an early night. The date of the operation had been determined by a forecast of clear skies over the target airfields the following morning. But if the enemy's New Year's Day hangovers left him that much less alert than usual, so much the better.

During the early morning darkness Diether Lukesch led the first-ever jet night bombing mission, though the bombs were a diversion and any damage caused was incidental to the aim of the operation. Four Arado Ar 234s climbed to high altitude and flew a circular route over Rotterdam, Antwerp, Brussels and Liège, their pilots noting that the skies were clear for the attack to be launched in a few hours. To allay enemy suspicions if they were watched on radar, the planes released their bombs in the Brussels and Liège areas.

At 05.00hrs the pilots assigned to 'Baseplate' were roused, received final briefings and changed into flying kit; by 09.00hrs the first aircraft were airborne and heading for their rendezvous points. In all, about 900 fighters and fighter-bombers took off, most of them Bf 109s and Fw 190s. The previous week's battles had taken their toll, and although the force was not so large as the one originally planned, it remained sizeable by any standard.

Operation 'Baseplate'

Leutnant *Georg Füreder, a Bf 109 pilot with* II./JG 11, *described his attack on the RAF airfield at Asch in Belgium:*

Because of mist patches we took off later than planned, and I think that this did a lot to impair the success of the mission. The *Gruppe* joined the formation and set course for the target led by a couple of Ju 188 pathfinders . . .

I did not notice whether any aircraft were hit by our own or enemy flak on the way in, but as we neared the target I remember hearing on the radio that someone had been hit. Just short of the target we pulled up and fanned out to left and right to look over the airfield, then we went into our firing runs. I pulled up and went straight into my attack. My approach was too steep to engage the Thunderbolts on the east side of the airfield, so I aimed at four or five twin-engined planes in the north-west corner. I started a sharp 180-degree turn to go for the Thunderbolts on the east side, when tracer rounds streaked past me. At first I thought it was flak, then to my surprise I saw two Thunderbolts behind me. One was firing at me with everything but his aim was wild. I pulled sharply to port and his rounds passed astern of me. My pursuer and his No 2 gave up the chase and headed off west. I started after them, then broke away for a final run over the airfield heading south. At this time I saw no other aircraft over or near the airfield. A pall of black smoke rose from the southern half of the airfield, coming from several burning aircraft. I made my firing run somewhat higher because of the smoke, but I still had to fly through the pall over the southern half of the airfield.

When the raiders reached the Allied airfields they achieved complete surprise everywhere. One of the most successful attacks was that on the airfield at Eindhoven, carried out by *I., II.* and *IV. Gruppen JG 3*. The first two operated Bf 109s and were based at Paderborn and Lippspringe respectively; *IV./JG 3* was a *Sturmgruppe* equipped with Fw 190s based at Gütersloh. The aircraft took off in sections of four, and section followed section in line astern. The individual *Gruppen* linked up over Lippstadt and from there the eighteen four-plane sections, 72 aircraft in all, flew at low altitude on an almost straight track for 140 miles to their target. The penultimate leg to the target brought the force to a prominent feature to the north-east of Eindhoven airfield, and there the fighters pulled up and turned in to deliver their attacks.

The German force arrived over Eindhoven as Typhoon fighter-bombers of Nos 438 and 439 (RCAF) Squadrons were taxiing out for an operation. The attackers raked the Typhoons with cannon and machine-gun fire, pulled round, then ran in to deliver further strafing runs. Canadian records noted that the Messerschmitts and Focke Wulfs 'attacked the field in a well-organized manner, being persistent and well-led'. Within minutes most of the aircraft in the two Canadian squadrons were destroyed or seriously damaged, and other units at Eindhoven suffered heavily too. Similarly effective attacks were mounted on the

117

airfields at Brussels/Evère, Brussels/Melsbroek, St-Denis-Westrem and Maldegem. At other airfields, however, the raiders were far less effective. In some cases the German formations failed to locate their targets, in others there was great confusion over the objective and attacking aircraft got in each other's way. As a result, at Volkel, Antwerp/Deurne and Le Culot, the attacks were in each case conspicuous failures.

The New Year's Day attack cost the Allies 144 aircraft destroyed and a further sixty-two damaged beyond unit repair. To the Americans and British units, the losses inflicted by 'Baseplate' were serious but within a couple of weeks the aircraft would all be replaced. The Allies suffered minimal losses in pilots in the action. For the *Luftwaffe* fighter force, 'Baseplate' was by far the largest single calamity it would ever suffer. No official figure for *Luftwaffe* aircraft losses during the operation appears to have survived, but it probably amounted to about 300 planes or about one-third of those taking part. From surviving records we know that 237 German pilots were killed, went missing or were taken prisoner, and eighteen were wounded. Several of those lost were experienced leaders, including three *Geschwader* commanders, six *Gruppe* commanders and eleven *Staffel* commanders. Those men would be quite irreplaceable. The disaster was an object lesson in what happens if airmen are forced to do battle in a manner quite different from that for which their training has prepared them.

'Baseplate' left the German piston-engined day fighter force worse off than ever, bereft of several of its most capable leaders and combat pilots. In the next chapter we shall observe how the *Luftwaffe* faced up to its new situation and how the Messerschmitt Me 262 jet fighters fared when, at last, they joined the battle in numbers.

WAR DIARY, *III. GRUPPE KAMPFGESCHWADER 76*

During the autumn of 1944 this unit converted on to the Arado Ar 234 jet bomber at Burg-bei-Magdeburg in central Germany. By mid-December the unit possessed sixteen serviceable Ar 234s and on the 19th one of its Staffeln, the 9th, was declared operational and moved to Münster-Handorf. The unit was soon committed to supporting German troops engaged in the Ardennes salient – 'The Battle of the Bulge'.

22.12.44
For operational orders see Appendix C, Teleprinter message 11a,12a/44, Secret, 21.12.44. Owing to bad weather the operation which had been ordered could not be carried out. The *Staffel* continued to improve operational readiness by getting the available aircraft serviceable and improving the ground organization.

23.12.44
For operational orders see Appendix C, Teleprinter message 15a, 1944, Secret, 22.12.44. Owing to bad weather the operation which had been ordered could not be carried out. *Staffel* personnel were employed to improve the ground organization and for technical services.

24.12.44
For operational orders see Appendix C, Teleprinter message 17a/44, Secret, 23.12.44.

1st operation: Operation by nine Arado 234s, take-off time 10.14–10.25hrs.
Flight route: Base – radio beacon Iburg at low altitude [to conceal the location of their base from the enemy, the jet bomber pilots were to commence their climbs only when they were well clear of the airfield] – climb to 4,000 metres [13,000ft] heading towards Cologne – flight to the target at Liège from out of the sun – return flight over Cologne or Bonn, thence to base.
Landed: 11.22–11.48hrs.
Attack: The cities of Liège and Namur were attacked in shallow dive, 10.50–11.00hrs. Bomb release altitude 2,000 metres [6,500ft]. Nine SC 500 bombs (Trialen) [1,100lb bombs fitted with Trialen, a powerful new explosive] released on railway and factory facilities which were operating, and large complex of buildings in the centre of the city. Five hits observed.
Defences: Weak ground defences observed, medium flak. Spitfires and Thunderbolts observed flying defensive patrols in the target area. No interceptions, because obviously the Arado 234 is not yet known to the enemy.
Losses: Undercarriage of aircraft F1+PT collapsed on landing, causing damage to the wing. The pilot, *Uffz.* Winguth, was uninjured.
2nd operation: Operation by eight Arado 234s, take-off time 14.52–1520.
Flight route: As during 1st operation.
Landed: 16.00–15.25hrs.
Attack: Attack carried out on the same target as during the 1st operation, with shallow-dive attacks at 15.31–16.00hrs from release altitudes between 2,000 and 2,400 metres [6,500 and 7,800ft]. There were eight SC 500 bombs (Trialen) but due to a technical failure one SC 500 could not be released and had to be brought back. Result of the attack on Liège North railway station was not observed by any of the pilots.
Defences: Ground defences were not observed. In the target area [our aircraft] had to fly through strong formations of [enemy] fighters and bombers, and this hindered accurate bombing. No fighter attacks were observed.
Losses: Nil.
During both missions the [ground along the] route and the target could be clearly seen, and the mission was a complete success. The railway stations at Liège and Namur were seen to be working. The airfield north of the city was observed to be in use by fighters.
Remarks: Arrival of the remaining six Arado 234s at the operational base, from Burg.

25.12.44
For operational orders see Appendix C Nr 20a/44, Secret 24.12.44.

1st operation: Operation by eight Arado 234s, take-off 08.25–08.48hrs.
Flight route: As during 1st operation on 24.12.44, landed 09.17–09.48hrs.
Attack: Shallow-dive attack on the city of Liège from altitudes of 5,000 to 2,000 metres [16,250 to 6,800ft], between 08.46 and 09.24hrs. The target was on the railway station west of the junction of the [Rivers] Maas and Ourthe and the factory area south-west of the station. Five hits were observed on railway lines and sheds in the station area, one on a block of houses east of the station which started a large fire, and one hit the factory area to the southwest of the station.
Defences: Strong medium flak was observed coming from the ground. Thunderbolts operated in 4–6-aircraft patrols in the target area. On one occasion an unsuccessful gun attack was observed. It must now be taken into account that the enemy has identified the Arado 234.
Losses: *Leutnant* Frank in F1+DT crash-landed near Teuge in Holland. Pilot

uninjured [this aircraft had been hit during an attack by a Tempest of No 80 Squadron RAF].

Despite the failure of one engine *Oberfeldwebel* Dierks carried out his orders and returned to base in F1+NT. On landing the aircraft was damaged. Pilot uninjured.

The railway installations to the south and north of Liège are still in full use. Reconnaissance reports that as a result of the attacks rail traffic has halted in the northern part of the town.

2nd operation: Attack by eight Arado 234s, take-off 14.00–14.03hrs.

Flight route: Base – Datteln (canal junction) at low altitude, then climb to 500 metres [1,625ft] on course Bonn – Laacher Lake – Bastogne. Approach Liège out of the sun in a shallow dive at 2,000 metres [6,500ft]. Returned to base via Bonn and Dortmund. Landed 15.03–15.18hrs.

Attack: On the railway station in the north-western part of Liège, traversing the entire battle area in order to intimidate enemy forces. The attack was carried out in a shallow dive from 5,000 to 1,500 metres [16,250 to 4,875ft], 14.35–14.45hrs. Eight SC 500 bombs (Trialen) were released. Seven hits were observed in the station area (three hits on lines in use, one hit on the south-east corner of a large transhipment shed, one hit on a block of houses north of the station). One hit close to the railway lines at the south-west corner of the station; one hit on the factory area to the south of the station started a fierce fire.

Defences: Powerful medium flak defences were observed in the target area. Formations of Spitfires flew barrier patrols in the Liège–Bastogne area. It appears that the enemy is trying to use fighters to seal off the entire area of our breakthrough on the Western Front.

Losses: Aircraft F1+FT, pilot *Oblt.* Fendrich, burst a tyre on landing. Damage to the canopy. Both operations can be stated to have been successful. The results of the shallow-dive attacks could be assessed as average, even though the aircraft reached speeds up to 900kph [560mph]. Pilots must familiarize themselves with details of new targets and the new attack procedures. Our aircraft type is now recognized by the enemy and we are liable to come under fighter attack. Attacks have come mostly from ahead and above, so far without success. Because of the high speed of our aircraft, attacks from behind have not been successful.

Because of the powerful fighter defences, so far horizontal attacks using the Lotfe [high altitude horizontal bombsight] have not been possible.

26.12.44

For operational orders see Appendix C Nr 21a/44, Secret 25.12.44.

1st operation: Operation by six Arado 234s, take-off 10.40–11.05hrs.

Flight route: Base – Datteln at low altitude – Bonn, then climb to 5,000m – shallow-dive attack on target, the town of Verviers. Return flight over Cologne-Datteln to base. Landing 11.32–12.07hrs.

Attack: Shallow-dive attack on the town of Verviers from 5,000m altitude, release of six SC 500 (Trialen) from 1,200m between 11.10 and 11.32hrs. Three hits on the east part of the town, one hit seen in the middle of the town, two hits not observed.

Defences: Ground defences, moderate flak. Enemy fighters flying standing patrols in the Liège area.

In general the attack can be considered to have been satisfactory. The station in the eastern part of the town was empty. There was little activity at that in the west. No movement seen on the ground.

2nd operation: Operational orders see Appendix C Nr 22a/44, Secret, 25.12.44. Operation by six Arado 234s, take-off 14.29–14.31hrs.

Flight route: Base – Dortmund at low altitude – climb to 5,000m on course Bonn – Trier – attack on Libramont (descending to 2,000m altitude). Return flight via Cologne to base. Landing 15.37–15.44hrs.

Attack: Shallow-dive attack at 15.11 on the station at Libramont from 2,000m altitude. Four hits on the rail centre, two hits in the vicinity of the station (on houses). Six SC 500 (Trialen) released.
Defences: Ground defences, light flak. Heavy flak, with moderate accuracy, encountered in the Bastogne area. Strong formations of enemy fighters (Mustangs and Spitfires) flying standing patrols in the Monschau-Dueren area.
Losses: Nil.

On roads in the Aachen area columns of trucks were moving south. No movement seen on roads in the Neufchateau and Libramont areas.

During this operation, for the first time, six aircraft took off in two minutes and flew in close formation to the target. All aircraft attacked simultaneously.

TOTALS OF SERVICEABLE AIRCRAFT, 10 JANUARY 1945

Luftflotte	Reich	1	2	3	4	5	6	Total
Fighters (single-engined)	254	90	–	770	78	82	153	1,427
Fighters (twin-engined)	–	–	–	–	–	35	–	35
Night fighters	723	–	–	–	–	9	76	808
Bombers	32	–	–	196	56	–	10	294
Anti-shipping	–	–	–	–	–	83	–	83
Ground-attack	–	35	–	101	199	–	278	613
Night ground-attack	–	26	14	84	101	30	47	302
Strategic reconnaissance	7	–	13	5	38	45	88	196
Tactical reconnaissance	23	22	23	49	67	6	143	333
Transports	–	42	–	99	49	52	27	269
KG 200	206	–	–	–	–	–	–	206
Totals	**1,245**	**215**	**50**	**1,304**	**588**	**342**	**822**	**4,566**

DEPLOYMENT OF COMBAT FLYING UNITS, 10 JANUARY 1945

At this time the total number of serviceable aircraft deployed in combat units, 4,566, was slightly greater than at the end of May 1944. However, during the previous seven months the composition of the *Luftwaffe* had changed greatly. The fuel shortage had imposed sharp cutbacks in flying by all units except those engaged in day fighting. A majority of bomber *Gruppen* had been disbanded and those that remained played little further part in the fighting. The force now stood at just under 300 aircraft and was a shadow of its former strength; within a week there would be a further significant reduction, with the disbanding of the three He 111 *Gruppen* that had been conducting operations with air-launched flying bombs. Meanwhile the single-engined day fighter and the night fighter forces had been strengthened greatly.

Although three types of jet aircraft were now in service with front-line units – the Messerschmitt Me 163 and Me 262 and the Arado Ar 234 – there were fewer than a hundred of these advanced machines available for operations.

Since May two major formations, *Luftwaffenkommando Südost* and *Fliegerkorps XIV*, had been disbanded and those units that survived were shared out among the various *Luftflotten*.

Luftflotte Reich
Compared with the situation at the end of May *Luftflotte Reich* was considerably weaker, having transferred several day fighter *Gruppen* to

Luftflotte 3. With the transfer of those units, however, *Luftflotte Reich* was relieved of the responsibility for the air defence of a large strip of western Germany by day. The night fighter *Gruppen* that had belonged to *Luftflotte 3* had been transferred to *Luftflotte Reich*, and these now comprised the bulk of its fighting strength.

Luftflotte 3

Now based in western Germany, *Luftflotte 3* had received several single-engined fighter *Gruppen* from *Luftflotte Reich* during the preparations for the Ardennes counter-offensive in the autumn of 1944. Despite the heavy losses suffered during the land battle and in the 'Baseplate' attack on Allied airfields, *Luftflotte 3* still had more than twice as many aircraft as at the time of the D-Day invasion. With the additional fighter strength had come the responsibility for the defence of a large strip of Germany against air attack, however. Since May the *Luftflotte* had received two *Gruppen* of jet bombers, a *Geschwader* of Heinkel 111s modified to launch Fi 103 flying bombs and three small jet reconnaissance units.

Luftflotten 1, 4, 5 and 6

Taken together, the four *Luftflotten* on the Eastern Front had been restored to their previous strength following the heavy losses suffered during the Soviet summer offensive. They now possessed a total of 1,967 serviceable combat aircraft, slightly more than at the end of May. As in the west, the composition of the force had been greatly changed and the bomber force was down to a mere 66 aircraft. To compensate for this reduction, the *Luftflotten* in the east had received additional day fighter, night fighter and tactical reconnaissance *Gruppen*.

The number of available aircraft belied other weaknesses. *Luftflotte 1* was cut off in the Courland peninsula pocket in Lithuania, and would play little further part in the fighting. *Luftflotte 4* had been pushed back into Hungary and Yugoslavia, and had taken over the tasks previously carried out by *Luftwaffenkommando Südost*. Its bomber force, comprising three *Gruppen* of Heinkel 111 medium bombers, was employed mainly in night operations to supply German troops holding out in pockets cut off by the rapid Soviet advance. *Luftflotte 5* had been pushed out of the USSR and Finland and was now based in Norway. It was numerically slightly stronger than in May, following the transfer of three *Gruppen* of Junkers Ju 88 torpedo-bombers for attacks on Allied convoys carrying supplies to the Soviet Union. Because of the fuel shortage this potentially powerful striking force saw little use, however. *Luftflotte 6*, now based in East Prussia and western Poland, remained the strongest of the *Luftflotten* in the east.

Luftflotte 2

Luftflotte 2, based in northern Italy, had been drained of its last vestiges of strength during the previous seven months, to reinforce other areas. Now in even more dire straits than in May, it had lost all fighter and bomber units and was down to just 50 serviceable combat aircraft.

LUFTFLOTTE REICH

Geschwader	Unit	Aircraft	Total	Serviceable
Day fighter units				
JG 300	Stab	Fw 190	6	4
	I. Gruppe	Bf 109	57	37
	II.(Sturm)	Fw 190	41	28
	III. Gruppe	Bf 109	44	38
	IV. Gruppe	Bf 109	53	39

JG 301	*Stab*	Fw 190	5	5
	I. Gruppe	Fw 190	38	26
	II. Gruppe	Fw 190	40	38
	III. Gruppe	Fw 190	26	20
JG 400	*I. Gruppe*	Me 163	46	19

Night fighter units

NJG 1	*Stab*	Bf 110	20	18
		He 219		
	I. Gruppe	He 219	64	45
	II. Gruppe	Bf 110	37	24
	III. Gruppe	Bf 110	37	31
	IV. Gruppe	Bf 110	33	24
NJG 2	*Stab*	Ju 88	8	7
	I. Gruppe	Ju 88	41	26
	II. Gruppe	Ju 88	28	20
	III. Gruppe	Ju 88	49	26
	IV. Gruppe	Ju 88	36	29
NJG 3	*Stab*	Ju 88	6	3
	I. Gruppe	Bf 110	48	40
	II. Gruppe	Ju 88	30	23
	III. Gruppe	Ju 88	37	22
	IV. Gruppe	Ju 88	37	19
NJG 4	*Stab*	Bf 110	5	5
		Ju 88		
	I. Gruppe	Ju 88	34	17
	II. Gruppe	Ju 88	23	18
	III. Gruppe	Ju 88	28	19
NJG 5	*Stab*	Ju 88	10	8
	I. Gruppe	Bf 110	43	29
		Ju 88		
	III. Gruppe	Bf 110	66	60
		Ju 88		
	IV. Gruppe	Bf 110	51	24
		Ju 88		
NJG 6	*Stab*	Bf 110	29	23
		Ju 88		
	I. Gruppe	Bf 110	26	12
		Ju 88		
	II. Gruppe	Ju 88	26	18
	III. Gruppe	Bf 110	23	19
		Ju 88		
	IV. Gruppe	Bf 110	37	29
		Ju 88		
NJG 11	*I. Gruppe*	Bf 109	43	30
		Ju 88		
	II. Gruppe	Bf 109	41	23
		Me 262		
NJG 100	*II. Gruppe*	Ju 88	25	18
–	*Nachtjagdgruppe 10*	Ju 88	17	14

Bomber unit

KG 100	*II. Gruppe*	He 177	44	32

Reconnaissance units

–	*Bordfliegergruppe 196*	Ar 196	25	23
–	*AGr. 122*	Ju 188	9	7

Special unit

–	*Kampfgeschwader 200*	Various types	295	206[1]

LUFTFLOTTE 3

Day fighter units

JG 1	Stab	Fw 190	5	4
	I. Gruppe	Fw 190	27	22
	II. Gruppe	Fw 190	40	30
	III. Gruppe	Fw 190	40	35
JG 2	Stab	Fw 190	4	3
	I. Gruppe	Fw 190	28	23
	II. Gruppe	Fw 190	3	2
	III. Gruppe	Fw 190	19	6
JG 3	I. Gruppe	Bf 109	31	22
	III. Gruppe	Bf 109	32	26
	IV.(Sturm) Gruppe	Fw 190	35	24
JG 4	Stab	Fw 190	2	1
	I. Gruppe	Bf 109	41	33
	II.(Sturm) Gruppe	Fw 190	25	18
	III. Gruppe	Bf 109	13	10
	IV. Gruppe	Bf 109	26	17
JG 11	Stab	Fw 190	7	6
	I. Gruppe	Fw 190	23	20
	II. Gruppe	Bf 109	37	31
	III. Gruppe	Fw 190	42	26
JG 26	Stab	Fw 190	3	3
	I. Gruppe	Fw 190	60	36
	II. Gruppe	Fw 190	64	42
	III. Gruppe	Fw 190	56	28
JG 27	Stab	Fw 190	2	2
	I. Gruppe	Bf 109	33	24
	II. Gruppe	Bf 109	25	20
	III. Gruppe	Bf 109	28	23
	IV. Gruppe	Bf 109	24	22
JG 53	Stab	Bf 109	4	1
	II. Gruppe	Bf 109	46	29
	III. Gruppe	Bf 109	39	25
	IV. Gruppe	Bf 109	46	34
JG 54	III. Gruppe	Fw 190	47	31
	IV. Gruppe	Fw 190	50	39
JG 77	Stab	Bf 109	2	1
	I. Gruppe	Bf 109	43	24
	II. Gruppe	Bf 109	32	20
	III. Gruppe	Bf 109	10	7

Bomber units

LG 1	Stab	Ju 88	1	1
	I. Gruppe	Ju 88	29	25
	II. Gruppe	Ju 88	34	26
KG 51	Stab	Me 262	1	0
	I. Gruppe	Me 262	51	37
KG 66	I. Gruppe	Ju 88	29	17
KG 76	III. Gruppe	Ar 234	12	11

Air-launched missile units

KG 53	Stab	He 111/Fi 103	1	1
	I. Gruppe	He 111/Fi 103	37	25
	II. Gruppe	He 111/Fi 103	33	29
	III. Gruppe	He 111/Fi 103	30	24

Ground-attack units

SG 4	Stab	Fw 190	49	17
	I. Gruppe	Fw 190	29	24

	II. Gruppe	Fw 190	40	36
	III. Gruppe	Fw 190	34	24
Night ground-attack units				
–	*NSGr. 1*	Ju 87	44	37
–	*NSGr. 2*	Ju 87	39	26
–	*NSGr. 20*	Fw 190	28	21
Strategic reconnaissance units				
–	*Kommando Sperling*	Ar 234	4	4
–	*Kommando Hecht*	Ar 234	1	1
Tactical reconnaissance units				
–	*NAGr. 1*	Bf 109	15	8
–	*NAGr. 13*	Bf 109	51	39
		Fw 190		
–	*Kommando Braunegg*	Me 262	5	2
Transport units				
TG 3	*II. Gruppe*	Ju 52	50	48
TG 4	*III. Gruppe*	Ju 52	51	46
–	*Transportgruppe 30*	He 111	10	5

LUFTFLOTTEN 1, 4, 5 AND 6 IN THE EAST

Luftflotte 1

Day fighter units				
JG 51	*Stab*	Bf 109	20	16
		Fw 190		
JG 54	*Stab*	Fw 190	1	1
	I. Gruppe	Fw 190	35	32
	II. Gruppe	Bf 190	40	41
Ground-attack unit				
SG 3	*III. Gruppe*	Fw 190	39	35
Night ground-attack unit				
–	*NSGr. 3*	Go 145	34	26
		Ar 66		
Tactical reconnaissance unit				
–	*NAGr. 5*	Bf 109	29	22
		Fw 189		
Transport unit				
TG 1	*I. Gruppe*	Ju 52	45	42

Luftflotte 4

Day fighter units				
JG 51	*II. Gruppe*	Bf 109	36	26
JG 52	*II. Gruppe*	Bf 109	34	30
JG 53	*I. Gruppe*	Bf 109	19	18
JG 76	*Stab*	Bf 109	4	4
Bomber units				
KG 4	*Stab*	He 111	1	1
	I. Gruppe	He 111	25	22
	II. Gruppe	He 111	23	12
	III. Gruppe	He 111	24	11
	IV. Gruppe	He 111	14	10

125

Ground-attack units

SG 2	Stab	Fw 190	10	7
		Ju 87		
	I. Gruppe	Fw 190	32	23
	II. Gruppe	Fw 190	34	29
	III. Gruppe	Ju 87	35	29
	10. Staffel[2]	Ju 87	10	9
SG 9	IV. Gruppe[2]	Hs 129	59	45
SG 10	Stab	Fw 190	3	1
	I. Gruppe	Fw 190	22	17
–	II. Gruppe	Fw 190	23	19
	III. Gruppe	Fw 190	21	20

Night ground-attack units

–	NSGr. 5	Go 145	47	39
		Ar 66		
–	NSGr. 7	Hs 126	54	37
		Fiat CR 42		
–	NSGr. 10	Ju 87	30	25

Strategic reconnaissance units

–	FAGr. 2	Ju 88	25	17
		Ju 188		
–	AGr. 33	Ju 88	13	10
–	AGr. 121	Ju 188	8	5
–	FAGr. Nacht	Do 217	7	6
		Ju 88		

Tactical reconnaissance units

–	NAGr. 12	Bf 109	23	16
		Ju 88		
–	NAGr. 14	Bf 109	46	35
		Fw 189		
–	NA Staffel Kroatien	Bf 109	24	16
		Hs 126		

Transport unit

TG 2	II. Gruppe	Ju 52	11	11
	III. Gruppe	Ju 52	28	16
TG 3	III. Gruppe	Ju 52	31	22

Luftflotte 5

Day fighter units

JG 5	Stab	Bf 109	4	4
	III. Gruppe	Bf 109	55	43
	IV. Gruppe	Bf 109	45	35
		Fw 190		
ZG 26	IV. Gruppe	Me 410	41	35

Night fighter unit

–	Nachtjagdsta. Norwegen	Bf 110	10	9
		Ju 88		
		He 219		

Torpedo-bomber units

KG 26	Stab	Ju 88	11	4
	I. Gruppe	Ju 88	30	22
	II. Gruppe	Ju 88	37	32
	III. Gruppe	Ju 88	37	25

Night ground-attack unit

–	NSGr. 8	Ju 87	33	30

Strategic reconnaissance units

–	AGr. 32	Fw 190	9	6
		Bf 109		
–	AGr. 120	Ju 88	19	17
		Ju 188		
–	AGr. 124	Ju 88	12	8
		Ju 188		

Maritime reconnaissance unit

–	SAGr. 130	Bv 222	2	1
		Bv 138	21	19

Transport unit

–	Transportgr. 20	Ju 52	50	47
–	Seetransportst. 2	Ju 52	7	5

Luftflotte 6

Day fighter units

JG 51	I. Gruppe	Bf 109	36	26
	III. Gruppe	Bf 109	38	28
	IV. Gruppe	Bf 109	34	24
JG 52	Stab	Bf 109	10	5
		Fw 190		
	I. Gruppe	Bf 109	34	30
	III. Gruppe	Bf 109	42	40

Night fighter units

NJG 5	I. Gruppe	Bf 109	43	35
		Ju 88		
NJG 100	I. Gruppe	Bf 109	51	41
		Ju 88		

Bomber unit

KG 55	IV. Gruppe	He 111	14	10

Ground-attack units

SG 1	Stab	Fw 190	5	5
	II. Gruppe	Fw 190	39	38
	III. Gruppe	Fw 190	38	36
SG 3	Stab	Fw 190	9	8
	I. Gruppe	Fw 190	47	43
	II. Gruppe	Fw 190	34	31
SG 77	Stab	Fw 190	6	6
	I. Gruppe	Fw 190	40	34
	II. Gruppe	Fw 190	38	31
	III. Gruppe	Fw 190	38	30
	10. Staffel	Ju 87	19	16

Night ground-attack unit

–	NSGr. 4	Ju 87	60	47
		Si 204		

Maritime reconnaissance unit

–	SAGr. 126	Ar 196	21	11
		Bv 138	9	6

Strategic reconnaissance units

–	FAGr. 1	Ju 188	25	17
		Me 410		
–	FAGr. 3	Ju 188	22	15
		Me 410		
–	AGr. 22	Ju 188	13	10

–	*AGr. Nacht*	Ju 88	36	23
		Ju 188		
		Do 217		
–	*AGr. 122*	Ju 88	28	23
		Me 410		
Tactical reconnaissance units				
–	*NAGr. 2*	Bf 109	35	30
		Fw 189		
–	*NAGr. 3*	Bf 109	57	46
		Fw 189		
–	*NAGr. 4*	Bf 109	23	21
		Fw 189		
–	*NAGr. 8*	Bf 109	24	16
		Fw 189		
–	*NAGr. 15*	Bf 109	20	13
		Fw 189		
Transport unit				
TG 3	*I. Gruppe*	Ju 52	36	27
	LUFTFLOTTE 2			
Night ground-attack unit				
–	*NSGr. 3*	Ju 87	23	14
Long-range reconnaissance unit				
–	*AGr. 122*	Me 410	16	13
		Ju 88, Ju 188		
Tactical reconnaissance unit				
–	*NAGr. 11*	Bf 109	29	23
		Fw 190		

[1]KG 200 operated under the direct control of the *Luftwaffe* High Command and flew many different types, including captured aircraft used for clandestine missions.
[2]Anti-tank unit.
[3]Floatplane transports.

CHAPTER 11

FIGHTING A LOSING BATTLE

11 January to 10 April 1945

EVEN BEFORE 'BASEPLATE' was launched against the Allied forward airfields, the German ground offensive in the Ardennes had been fought to a standstill and from then on the salient was inexorably squeezed out of existence. Although Hitler still thought in terms of holding back the enemy at both the eastern and western frontiers of Germany, he was compelled to give priority to the Eastern Front where Soviet forces now threatened to advance on Berlin itself. More than half the *Panzer* divisions that had fought in 'Watch on the Rhine' were transferred to the Eastern Front in readiness to meet the expected Soviet attack.

In the air, 'Baseplate' had impressed on the Allies the dangers of believing that the *Luftwaffe* could no longer hit back hard, though after the attack on the airfields that was virtually true. Its first large-scale air-defence operation in the New Year took place on 14 January when it scrambled 189 aircraft – including half a dozen Me 262s – to meet a force of over nine hundred B-17s and B-24s with fighter escort making for a spread of targets in central Germany. The only noteworthy success by the defenders was achieved by *II.(Sturm)/JG 300*, which delivered a sharp attack on B-17s of the 390th Bomb Group and shot down all eight aircraft in the formation. Elsewhere the escorts beat off most of the attempts by German fighters to get through to the bombers, and altogether the raiding force lost only seventeen bombers and eleven fighters. Outnumbered and outfought, during that and a series of smaller-scale actions over western and central Germany the defending fighter force lost more than 140 aircraft, with 107 pilots killed and 32 wounded.

Coming on top of the severe losses incurred during 'Baseplate', the action brought a virtual end to large-scale operations by the German piston-engined day fighter units. During December 1944 a total of 2,953 brand new combat aircraft, the lion's share of them fighters, had been delivered to the *Luftwaffe*. Yet during the air operations in support of 'Watch on the Rhine' a large part of the fuel stocks accumulated by the *Luftwaffe* had been used up. At the same time, the air attacks on the refineries had resumed at their earlier intensity and for the remainder of the war these establishments would produce no more than a trickle of fuel. With the exception of the jet aircraft, which would always comprise a relatively small part of the force, most of the new planes would sit out the war in aircraft parks.

Leutnant Hans-Ulrich Flade, a Bf 109 pilot with *II./JG 27*,

The paralysing effect of the fuel famine

Hauptmann *Roderich Cescotti, an Fw 190D pilot and* Gruppe *maintenance officer with* II./JG 301, *described the difficulty of obtaining aviation fuel for his aircraft during the early months of 1945:*

Getting fuel for the fighters was not so much a logistics operation, more an intelligence battle. We would send tankers on circuitous journeys, picking up 5,000 litres in one place, 2,500 litres at another; sometimes it might take as long as a week to collect the twenty tons of fuel needed for a single fighter operation.

---

recalled that if a fighter were damaged it was simpler to get a new one than to make repairs:

We simply went to the depot nearby, where they had hundreds of brand new 109s – G-10s, G-14s and even the very latest K models. There was no proper organization any more: the depot staff just said, 'There are the aircraft, take what you want and go away'. But getting fuel – that was more difficult . . .

Flade's *Gruppe* had a strength of about twenty pilots, it was losing two or three each day and morale was low:

Each morning we pilots had breakfast together, and the replacements would come in. The older pilots regarded the young newcomers as though they had only days to live – and with reason, for the standard of fighter conversion training was now so low that most of the new pilots flew only two or three missions before they were shot down. I remember many conversations along these lines – not exactly a cheerful subject for a young man who had just joined his first operational unit!

The *Gruppe* operated in the top-cover role, to keep the American escort fighters busy while other German fighters went for the bombers:

We followed the old rules: dive as a pair or a four out of the sun, make a quick attack to break up their formation and make them drop their tanks, then climb out of danger and assess the situation. If conditions were favourable, we would go down for a second attack. Always the escorts were so numerous that it would have been foolish to get into a dog-fight.

The clear inability of the day fighter force to provide adequate defence for German industry, in part stemming from the heavy losses suffered during 'Baseplate', led to loud recriminations and counter-recriminations within the higher echelons of the *Luftwaffe* on the way the force was being handled. In many cases, these criticisms developed into personal attacks on Göring and his failures as Commander-in-Chief. *Generalmajor* Galland was particularly disparaging of the *Reichsmarschall*, and his verbal abuse became so blatant that it could no longer be ignored. As a result, during January, he was sacked from his post of Inspector General of Fighters. *Oberst* Gordon Gollob, an ace fighter pilot who had been closely involved in bringing the new jet types into service, replaced him.

The move caused consternation in the fighter force. A few days later a deputation of senior leaders, led by *Oberst* Lützow and including *Oberst* Graf (commander of *JG 52*), *Oberst* Rödel (commander of the 2nd Fighter Division), *Oberst* Steinhoff (commander of *JG 7*) and *Oberst* Trautloft (Inspector of Fighters on the Eastern Front), asked for and received an audience with Göring. There they presented a memorandum proposing changes in the way the fighter force was being run, and requesting that Galland be reinstated and that certain named officers (most of them the *Reichsmarchall*'s appointees) be removed from command positions in the fighter force. After reading the memorandum Göring recognized it as a thinly veiled attack on himself. He flew into a rage, accused the officers of what amounted to mutiny, threatened to have them shot and stormed out of the room.

The upshot of the meeting was that Lützow was banished to a minor post in Italy and Trautloft was sent to command a training unit. The rest of the officers remained in their posts and, for the time being, Adolf Galland remained in limbo.

Much of the political in-fighting in and around the fighter force stammed from the failure to get the Messerschmitt Me 262 into service with combat units in anything approaching the expected numbers. By the first week in January about six hundred had been delivered to the *Luftwaffe*, and production was running at about 36 per week. Yet the Quartermaster General's records for 10 January show that only about sixty of these aircraft (about 10 per cent of those built) were in service with operational units – and none of them was with an operational day fighter unit. *I.* and *II./KG 51* (fighter-bombers) had 52, *10./NJG 11* (night fighters) about four and *Kommando Braunegg* (short-range recce) five – this, four months after Hitler had agreed to release the Me 262 for service in the fighter role. What had gone wrong?

In fact a substantial force of Me 262s was being prepared for action, though this was taking somewhat longer than expected. *III./JG 7* was at full strength, but the unit was still working up at airfields in the Berlin area. *I./JG 7* was in the process of forming at Kaltenkirchen near Hamburg, as was *II./JG 7* at Brandenburg/Briest.

Also at this time, several pilots from *Kampfgeschwader 54*, a bomber unit, were converting on to the Me 262 and undergoing training to operate the aircraft in the *fighter* role. The unit was redesignated *KG(J) 54*, and this diversion of Me 262s away from 'pure' fighter units sparked a lively controversy. In several postwar accounts this move has been linked with Hitler's earlier insistence that these aircraft should initially be used as bombers, though by the early part of 1945 the issues were quite different.

Since before the war, as a matter of policy to shorten the training time and save resources, pilots assigned to *Luftwaffe* day fighter units had not received training in instrument flying (though many of the more experienced fighter pilots received

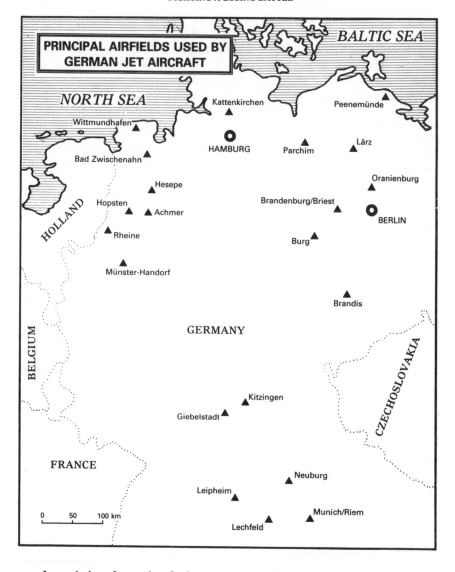

PRINCIPAL AIRFIELDS USED BY GERMAN JET AIRCRAFT

such training later in their careers). Pilots assigned to bomber, reconnaissance and night fighter units all received blind-flying training as a matter of course. American heavy bombers carried radar and regularly conducted attacks on targets covered by cloud; this meant that, to engage them, the German fighters had often to climb through cloud, and after the action they descended through cloud to return to their airfields. In the relatively slow piston-engined fighters, this climb and descent through cloud presented few problems, but for a pilot untrained in instrument flying a rapid descent through cloud in an Me 262 was an operation fraught with danger. If the aircraft descended too steeply it was liable to exceed its limiting Mach number and an inexperienced pilot might lose control and be unable to regain it before the aircraft plunged into the ground. Several jet fighters were lost in otherwise inexplicable circumstances.

Göring, *General* Koller and other senior officers, including some of those in the fighter force, accepted the argument that it was easier and quicker to re-train bomber pilots to fly fighters than it was to re-train fighter pilots to fly on instruments. Probably they were right. But *Generalmajor* Galland and other fighter leaders were resolutely opposed to the idea, and the request that it be dropped had been one of the items in the memorandum that Lützow had presented to Göring. In spite of these objections, the issue of Me 262s to selected bomber units was to continue.

As we have seen, by this time there were about 60 Messerschmitt 262s operational with fighter-bomber, night fighter and reconnaissance units. A further 150 or so were flying with day fighter units working up for action or training pilots: the three *Gruppen* of *Jagdgeschwader 7*, *KG(J) 54*, and the operational training unit *EJG 2*. About thirty Me 262s were with the various test centres. To date about 150 Me 262s had been destroyed by enemy action in the air or on the ground, or in flying accidents. That accounts for just under four hundred Me 262s and those figures are, if anything, on the high side. What had befallen the remaining two hundred or so aircraft, amounting to one-third of the total built? Strangely, a large number were tied up in the German rail system. After their acceptance test-flights, most Me 262s were dismantled and transported to the operational units by rail, thereby saving precious aviation fuel, but with Allied bomber attacks systematically pounding the German rail network many Me 262s simply got 'lost in the post'.

The new phase of jet fighter operations began on 9 February when *I. Gruppe KG(J) 54* put up about ten Me 262s against a multi-pronged attack by 1,500 American heavy bombers against Magdeburg, Weimar, Lutzkendorf, Bielefeld, Paderborn, Arnsberg and Dulmen. The action ended in utter defeat for the German ex-bomber pilots, who had received only a sketchy training in air-to-air combat. The jet fighters caused damage to one B-17, but then escorting Mustangs counter-attacked and shot down six Me 262s in rapid succession. The *Geschwader* commander, bomber ace *Oberstleutnant* Volprecht von Riedesel, was one of those killed.

Just over two weeks later *KG(J) 54* had another bad day. On the morning of the 25th, as four Me 262s of *II. Gruppe* took off on a training flight from Kitzingen, Mustangs pounced and shot down three of them. That day the *Gruppe* lost no fewer than twelve Me 262s, six in air combat, four during a strafing attack on the airfield and two in flying accidents resulting from technical failures.

Following these disasters *Major* Hans-Georg Bätcher was posted from *Kampfgeschwader 76* to take command of *KG(J) 54*. He told the author:

KG(J) 54 had been declared ready for operations prematurely. The first thing I did was to order further training. The main problem was to get

133

the ex-bomber pilots used to the much greater speed – the 262 cruised two or three times faster than the Ju 88s or He 111s the pilots had flown previously. Also we had only single-seat Me 262s, no two-seaters.

In spite of the difficulties experienced by the ex-bomber pilots, Bätcher felt that in the circumstances the decision to use pilots with blind-flying training to fly the Me 262 in the fighter role was correct. It was still winter, and on several days cloud prevented the normal jet-fighter units from operating. 'The biggest error,' he believed, 'was that German fighter pilots had not been trained in blind-flying in the first place.' But it was far too late in the war to correct that mistake.

Not until the third week in February was *III. Gruppe Jagd-geschwader* 7 again considered ready for action. Following its spell of extra training, the unit re-entered the fray considerably the more effective. On 21 February Mustangs of the 479th Fighter Group on patrol in the Berlin area encountered about fifteen Me 262s and, as the American leader afterwards reported, these jets behaved differently from any seen previously:

> Bounce was directed at Red Flight, as squadron was making a shallow turn to the left from an easterly direction. Bounce came from 3 o'clock position at our level by four Me 262s flying the usual American combat formation, looking like P-51s with drop tanks. Our Red Flight broke into jets but they crossed in front of our flight up and away. A second flight of four Me 262 flying in American combat formation then made a bounce from the rear, 6 o'clock high. Our Flight turned into this second Me 262 flight and the Me 262s broke climbing up and away. At this time the first flight of Me 262s came back on us again from above and to the rear. We broke into this flight and this kept up for three or four breaks, neither ourselves nor Jerry being able to get set or close in for a shot. Each time we would break they would climb straight ahead, outdistancing us. Within the Jerry flight the Number 4 man, while turning, would fall behind and slightly above, so that it was necessary to take on this Number 4 man or he would slice in on our tail if our Flight would take on the rest of the Jerry flight.

The American pilots noted that their German counterparts 'were aggressive and experienced. They were not caught in a turn, and if they were caught in such a position would roll out and climb up and away. It was impossible to catch or climb with them.'

The report exemplified the sort of inconclusive action likely to result when well-handled jets confronted well-handled Mustangs. Unless it had the advantage of surprise, the Me 262 was no real threat to the latter. But there was no doubt that the jet fighter posed a considerable threat to the American bombers, for with its high speed it could pierce the screens of escorting Mustangs with relative ease.

During February the most successful German jet fighter pilot was *Leutnant* Rudolf Rademacher of *III./JG* 7. After shooting down a Spitfire reconnaissance aircraft near Brunswick on the 1st, he was credited with a B-17 on the 4th, two more on the 8th and one on the 14th, a P-51 on the 16th, a further B-17 on the 23rd and a B-24 on the 25th, making his score for the month eight 'kills'.

Order for formation of *Jagdverband 44*

24 February 1945
JV 44 is established at Brandenburg-Briest with immediate effect. Ground personnel are to be drawn from *16./JG 54*, Factory Protection Unit 1 and *III./Erg JG 2*. The commander of this unit receives the disciplinary powers of a Divisional Commander as laid down in *Luftwaffe* Order 3/9.17. It is subordinated to *Luftflotte Reich* and comes under *Luftgaukommando III (Berlin)*. *Verband 'Galland'* is to have a provisional strength of sixteen operational Me 262s and fifteen pilots.

[signed] *Generalleutnant* Karl Koller
Chief of the General Staff of the *Luftwaffe*

Towards the end of February a new and remarkable Me 262 fighter unit was formed: *Jagdverband 44*. That it was commanded by a *Generalmajor* – Adolf Galland, who had recently been dismissed from the post of Inspector of Fighters – was only one of its unique features (no doubt Göring hoped that by sending Galland back into action the Allies might rid him of his turbulent but well-connected foe). With many of the German piston-engined day fighter units now grounded for want of fuel, Galland was able to draw into his unit several of the most experienced and successful fighter pilots in the *Luftwaffe*. As he later commented, 'The *Ritterkreuz* was, so to speak, the badge of our unit'. In addition to Galland himself, other holders of this coveted decoration to join the unit were *Oberst* Johannes Steinhoff, *Oberst* Günther Lützow and *Oberstleutnant* Heinz Bär, as well as Gerhard Barkhorn, Erich Hohagen, Karl-Heinz Schnell, Willi Herget, *Hauptmann* Walter Krupinski, Hans Grünberg, Klaus Neumann and Heinz Sachsenberg. During and after the war there was much loose talk about 'crack *Luftwaffe* fighter units'. The term implies a unit with more than its share of ace pilots and able to draw these in from other units. In the nature of things, such units are rare for the fighting power of the depleted units is reduced by the loss of such key individuals. Since most other units had been grounded for want of fuel that did not matter, and *JV 44* was the sole 'crack *Luftwaffe* fighter unit'. However, even with this level of expertise, it would take some weeks to prepare the new unit for action. In the meantime, the fighting would be left to the longer-established *Gruppen*.

During March, for the first time, Me 262 fighter units began to deliver large-scale attacks on American bomber formations. The 3rd of the month saw the largest response by jets so far – twenty-nine Me 262 sorties, mainly by *III./JG 7*, to counter USAAF attacks on Magdeburg, Brunswick, Hannover, Chemnitz and other targets. Twenty of the German pilots reported making contact with the enemy, and they claimed the destruction of six bombers and two fighters. One Me 262 was lost and its pilot killed. American records list nine bombers and eight fighters lost on that day and claim no Me 262 destroyed.

For the next two weeks the Me 262 fighters saw little action. Then, on 18 March, 37 jet fighters were sent up to engage a force of 1,221 American heavy bombers escorted by 632 fighters making for Berlin. During this action the jet fighters used the new R4M air-to-air rocket for the first time; twenty-four of these 5.5cm impact-fused missiles were carried on wooden racks under the wings of the Me 262 and ripple-fired at a bomber in a single attack. *Oberleutnant* Günther Wegmann of *III./JG 7* led six of the jet fighters in an attack with R4Ms against one of the American formations, and the German pilots loosed off their rockets against the B-17s from 1,000yd. The victims were B-17s of the 100th Bomb Group ('The Bloody Hundredth'), two of which went down immediately while a third suffered serious damage. During a subsequent firing run the jet fighters finished off the bomber damaged in the first attack and shot down another B-17. Then the jets had to dive clear to avoid a counter-attack by Mustangs.

During the 18 March action 28 German jet fighter pilots reported making contact with the enemy, claiming the destruction of twelve bombers and one fighter (all except two of the bombers were claimed by *JG 7*); from American records it appears likely that only eight heavy bombers fell to the Me 262s. *III./JG 7* lost two jet fighters. On the following day, the 19th, the Me 262 fighter units put up 45 sorties; 28 made contact with the enemy and six bombers were claimed shot down for the loss of two Me 262s and their pilots. On the 20th there were 29 jet fighter missions, of which 24 made contact; nine heavy bombers were claimed for the loss of four Me 262s.

Training to fly the Me 262

In March 1945 Leutnant *Walther Hagenah, an experienced fighter pilot who earlier had flown with a* Sturmgruppe JG 3, *was posted to* III./JG 7 *at Lärz. He described the cursory conversion training he received before flying the Me 262:*

Our 'ground school' lasted one afternoon. We were told of the peculiarities of the jet engine, the dangers of flaming out at high altitude, and their poor acceleration at low speeds. The vital importance of handling the throttles carefully was impressed upon us, lest the engines catch fire. But we were not permitted to look inside the cowling of the jet engine – we were told it was very secret and we did not need to know about it!

By the time I reached *III./JG 7* there were insufficient spare parts and insufficient spare engines; there were even occasional shortages of J-2 [jet] fuel. I am sure all of these things existed and that production was sufficient, but by that stage of the war the transport system was so chaotic that things often failed to arrive at the front-line units.

In our unit, flying the Me 262, we had some pilots with only about a hundred hours' total flying time. They were able to take off and land the aircraft, but I had the definite impression that they were of little use in combat. It was almost a crime to send them into action with so little training. Those young men did their best, but they had to pay a heavy price for their lack of experience.

On 21 March the Me 262 units put up 31 sorties against more than a thousand American heavy bombers attacking the airfields at Handorf, Hesepe, Vorden, Zwischenahn, Marx, Wittmundhafen, Ahlhorn, Achmer, Hopsten, Rheine and Essen/Mülheim, most of them used by German jet aircraft. Twenty-five Me 262 pilots reported making contact with the enemy. One of them was *Leutnant* Firtz Müller of *III./JG 7*:

I took off with my *Rotte* [pair] on 21-3-45 against the major enemy incursion in the Leipzig-Dresden area. On this day our radio traffic was especially heavily jammed by the enemy. At 7,500m, while south of Dresden, I came upon a B-17 flying east at the same altitude as the main bomber force but about 10km to one side and about 4km behind it, with four Mustangs above it flying escort. It seemed to me that this machine was on some sort of special mission, and I resolved to attack it. The enemy radio-jamming was so powerful that communication was impossible. I flew close underneath the four Mustangs, which were now following my *Rotte*, trailing black smoke [indicating that they were flying at full throttle]; but a glance at my airspeed indicator showed that I would not have to worry about them. The Boeing was now ahead of me in a left-hand turn, so that I was flying about 10 degrees to the left and about 5 degrees above it. At about 1,000m the rear gunner opened up a harassing fire. It was all over in seconds. At a range of about 300m my wingman and I opened up with our cannon and gave it short bursts allowing slight lead. We saw a dozen rounds exploding against the fuselage and between the engines. Then we were past him. Curving round in a wide circle (with the Mustangs behind us, still trailing smoke but getting smaller the whole time) we observed the end of the bomber. It spun down through about 2,000m, with several large bits falling from the fuselage and wings, then exploded.

From an examination of the US records it appears that five heavy bombers were shot down by Me 262s during this action, compared with a German claim of thirteen. USAAF fighters claimed the destruction of nine Me 262s, but *JG 7* lost only two pilots on that day and *I./KG(J) 54* lost one more.

After the action on 21 March there were further pitched battles between Me 262s and American formations daily until the 25th, after which there was a lull of four days. The next great exertion was on the 30th, when 31 jet fighters took off to engage Eighth Air Force units attacking Hamburg, Bremen and Wilhelmshaven. As always, the jet fighters were vulnerable when they were taking off or landing. Captain Robert Sargent of the 330th Fighter Group was leading a pair of P-51s escorting bombers running in to attack Hamburg:

I saw two enemy aircraft taking off from Kaltenkirchen airfield. I called them in and we 'split-S'd' down on them. Unfortunately, due to their camouflage, we lost them for a second and when we got down to their level I was able to pick up just one of them. From here on it was easy. My air speed was 430mph and I estimated his as being about 230mph. As we closed I gave him a long burst and noticed strikes immediately – the left unit began to pour white smoke and large pieces of the canopy came off. The pilot baled out. We were at 300ft at this time and the plane dove into the ground and exploded, causing a large oil-like fire which went out almost at once. The pilot's chute did not open fully and the last I saw of him was on the ground near the plane with the chute streaming out behind him. Lt Kunz did a splendid job of covering my tail and after the encounter we pulled up and looked for the second jet. But when we sighted him he was going balls out for central Germany and we couldn't overtake him.

The pilot of the Me 262, *Leutnant* Erich Schulte of *I./JG 7*, was killed. That day the jet fighters claimed the destruction of three enemy bombers and three fighters, for the loss of three of their number.

The B-17s and B-24s of the USAAF were the main victims of the attacks by Me 262s, but they were not the only ones. During the closing months of the war Royal Air Force Bomber Command had been mounting powerful daylight attacks on targets in Germany. On 31 March a force of 460 Lancasters and Halifaxes set out to attack the U-boat assembly yards at Hamburg. The bombers should have picked up their escorts – twelve squadrons of Royal Air Force Mustangs – over Holland. In the event, however, the third wave of bombers drawn from No 6 (Canadian) Group was late at the rendezvous point and had no escort.

At the target the Mustangs warded off several attempts by Me 262s to engage the first two waves of bombers. For the third wave there was no such protection, and during the sharp encounter that followed three Halifaxes and four Lancasters fell in rapid succession. The jet fighter attacks were new to most RAF bomber crews and afterwards the official report of the action stated:

> The usual technique of the jet-propelled fighters appears to be an approach from astern or the fine quarters, possibly with a preference for slightly above, opening fire at 800–900 yards and closing rapidly to close range. In a few cases, however, fire was not opened until 300–400 yards. Combat reports stated that the closing speed of these fighters is so great that they frequently do not have time to fire more than one burst. More than one rear gunner reports that although he had opened fire at 900–1,000 yards he had only time to fire 200 rounds before the fighter broke away 3–4 seconds later at 30–50 yards, and one stated he was unable to rotate his turret fast enough to obtain strikes on the fighter at this close range though he had opened fire at it at 900 yards . . .

Almost certainly the reference to the jet fighters 'opening fire at 800–900 yards' related to attacks with R4M rockets, which were made from such ranges. The RAF heavy bomber crews, who flew in 'vics' of threes in a loose gaggle rather than the serried formations of the American counterparts, went into their famous 'corkscrew' evasive manoeuvre when threatened with fighter attack. This countermeasure, which was new to the Me 262 pilots, probably prevented the bomber losses from being much higher than they were.

At the same time as the RAF bombers were striking at Hamburg, over a thousand American heavy bombers were attacking Zeitz, Brandenburg, Brunswick and Halle. Altogether *JG 7* flew 38 sorties that day, and on the available evidence it appears that they shot down a total of about fourteen enemy bombers and two fighters, making this probably the most successful day's action for the Me 262. Four of the jet fighters were shot down.

At the end of 1944 the *Luftwaffe* night fighter force had introduced a new type of airborne radar, '*Neptun*', which operated on frequencies in the 170MHz range. It enjoyed a couple of months of unhindered use before the RAF learned of its existence and it too was jammed. Not that the new equipment made much difference, for beset by pressures from all sides there was little the defenders could do to stem the powerful night attacks. During January 1945, for example, in the course of 6,572 night sorties by heavy bombers against targets in Germany, only 99 aircraft were lost from all causes – 1.4 per cent of the total. Losses would remain at this very low rate for the remainder of the war.

The most devastating attack during this period was on the night of 13 February, when the centre of Dresden was burned to the ground in two terrible attacks mounted in rapid succession. Backed by the cacophony of radio and radar jamming that supported night attacks at this stage of the war, the raiders were able to complete their tasks with little interference from defending night fighters. *Feldwebel* Hermann Kinder, a Ju 88 pilot with *NJG 100*, was on the ground at Radeber airfield just outside the city throughout the attack. His diary account illustrates the chaos that reigned that night:

13 February 1945
My saddest day as a night fighter – SN-2 adjusted. Evening, first scramble, naturally for A-crews only. Take-off too late. Huge firework display over the city. Jockenhoffer shot down by our own anti-aircraft guns. Then second scramble, rather before 2 a.m. No communications with divisional headquarters. Apparently *Division* was in the dark . . . Result: major attack on Dresden, in which the city was smashed to smithereens – and we were standing by and looking on. How can such a thing be possible? One's mind turns more and more to sabotage, or at least a certain irresponsible defeatism among the 'gentlemen' up there. Feeling that things are approaching an end with giant strides. What then? Poor Germany!

That night only 27 night fighters took off to meet the assault by 1,406 aircraft against Dresden, Böhlen and other targets. Nine of the raiders (0.6 per cent) were lost but the defenders played no part in the destruction of two of those, one being brought down near the target by bombs falling from another aircraft and a second crashing after a mid-air collision with another bomber.

During this period *10. Staffel Nachtjagdgeschwader 11* operated a small number of Me 262 two-seat trainers modified to carry radar. Flying from Burg near Berlin and operating under close control from ground stations, the Me 262 night fighters flew interception missions against RAF Mosquito high-speed bombers. The jets probably accounted for most of the thirteen Mosquitos lost in the Berlin area during the first three months of 1945.

Like the day fighter force, the night fighter arm had drawn up plans for an all-out attack on the enemy where it was least expected. During the early morning darkness of 4 March a force of 450 Lancasters, Halifaxes and Mosquitos raided Kamen and Ladbergen in western Germany. After completing their attacks for the loss of seven aircraft, the bombers turned for home. And as they did so a large force of German night fighters roared into the air and headed west in pursuit. This was Operation 'Gisella', the long-planned intruder operation against Bomber Command bases. During previous weeks individual German night fighters had followed the bombers back to their bases, their crews with strict orders to note the enemy approach and landing procedures but on no account were they to engage. Now the constraints were lifted and more than a hundred Junkers Ju 88 and Heinkel He 219 night fighters swept over the North Sea making for the Bomber Command airfields in Norfolk, Suffolk, Lincolnshire and Yorkshire. Twenty-seven of the bases came under attack from cannon and machine-gun fire, and from small bombs. As well as the bombers returning from Germany, the intruders caught several aircraft on training flights. Twenty bombers were shot down over England, bringing Bomber Command's total loss that night to 27 – the heaviest for a long time. German losses are not known, but were probably between three and six aircraft.

From the *Luftwaffe*'s point of view 'Gisella' was a success, but the operation would never be repeated on the same scale. Two weeks later, on the night of the 17 March, eighteen Junkers Ju 88s took off from Holland for a follow-up attack. But the RAF bombers were not operating in force that night and the intruders shot down only one Lancaster that had been on a training flight. The action was of historical significance, however, for it was to be the last offensive action by the *Luftwaffe* over Britain.

By this time the fuel famine had grounded virtually all German bomber units equipped with piston-engined aircraft. Only the two jet bomber units, *KG 76* equipped with Ar 234s and *KG 51* with Me 262 fighter-bombers, continued regular operations. Both *Geschwader* were well below their established strengths, however, and their operations had only a nuisance effect against the advancing Allied ground troops.

For most of January poor weather kept the jet bombers on the ground. The Arados of *9./KG 76* flew only five operations that month: on the 1st against Gilze Rijen aircraft as part of 'Baseplate'; during the early morning darkness on the 2nd against targets in the Brussels and Antwerp areas (nine sorties); on the 14th against US troop positions at Bastogne (five sorties); and on the 20th (eight sorties) and again on the 24th (four) against port installations at Antwerp.

By the third week in January the rest of *III./KG 76* had completed its conversion and the *Gruppe* was brought to full operational strength. On the 23rd, eighteen Arados from *7.* and *8. Staffeln* flew to Achmer near Osnabrück, but as the bombers arrived over their new base two squadrons of Spitfires pounced on them and during a hectic action three Arados were shot down and two damaged. Two German pilots were killed.

February was a better month for the jet bombers, and when fuel was available they were able to exploit their new-found operational strength. On the 8th the Arados mounted a seven-aircraft attack on targets near Brussels. Me 262 fighter-bombers of *Kampfgeschwader 51* were also active, and on the 14th these aircraft mounted one of their most powerful attacks, with 55 sorties against British forces advancing near Clève. Three Me 262s were shot down by fighters. On the 16th *III./KG 76* put in two attacks each with sixteen jet bombers against British troops near Clève. On 21 February the *Gruppe* flew what was to be its largest number of sorties in a single day, 37, against advancing British forces in the same area, and on the following day the *Gruppe* flew 23 sorties against British troop positions near Aachen. Operations continued at this rate throughout the rest of February and into March.

On 7 March the German defensive strategy in the west was plunged into crisis when American troops seized the Ludendorf Bridge over the Rhine at Remargen. Damaged but usable, the bridge breached the last major natural defensive obstacle in the west. Göring designated the bridge a target of the highest priority and hurled against it his few remaining bomber and fighter-bomber units in the west. The *Reichsmarschall* even called for volunteers willing to dive their aircraft into the bridge and blow themselves up with their bombs. Several men came forward, but the idea was dropped when it was made clear that the fuse safety interlocks would prevent the bombs from detonating until they were safely clear of the bomb racks, rendering such an operation pointless.

For most of the week following its capture, the bridge at Remargen was shielded by low cloud, preventing accurate low-altitude attacks. Nevertheless, Me 262 and Fw 190 fighter-bombers made several determined but unsuccessful attempts to bomb the bridge, which by then was surrounded by anti-aircraft guns of all calibres. On the 9th three Ar 234s attacked the bridge and one was shot down. That attack failed to cause significant damage, as did another by a pair of Arados on the 11th. On the 12th *III./KG 76* tried a different tactic. Eighteen Arados were sent to make horizontal bombing attacks from altitudes of between 16,000 and 26,000ft, using the '*Egon*' blind-bombing system. This attack, and a similar one by nineteen aircraft the following day, also failed to dislodge the bridge.

On the next day, the 14th, the cloud cleared to reveal clear skies over Remargen – and immediately those skies were filled with large numbers of British and American fighters flying standing patrols at all levels. As well as fighter-bombers, eleven Arados took off to attack the bridge. As the jet bombers ran in to deliver their shallow-dive attacks the Allied fighters pounced, and in the series of high-speed engagements that followed four of the Arados were shot down. Still the bridge remained standing.

Flying the Fw 190 *'Dora'* on the Eastern Front

Oberleutnant *Oskar-Walter Romm commanded* 15. Staffel *of* JG 3, *which re-equipped with the Fw 190D early in 1945. His was one of the fighter units that transferred to the Eastern Front following the opening of the Soviet winter offensive:*

As an air superiority and interceptor fighter the Fw 190D-9 handled better than the Fw 190A; it was faster and had a superior rate of climb. During dog-fights at altitudes of between about 10,000 and 24,000ft, usual when engaging the Russians, I found that I could pull the Fw 190D into a tight turn and still retain my speed advantage. In the descent the *'Dora-9'* picked up speed much more rapidly than the A type; in the dive it could leave the Russian Yak-3 and Yak-9 fighter standing.

By now the battle to prevent American troops crossing the Rhine in force had been lost: their bridgehead on the east bank of the river was secure, and pontoon bridges were in position to speed the flow of traffic eastwards. Ten days after its capture the Remargen bridge succumbed to the cumulative damage inflicted on it, and it collapsed. But the crossing had survived long enough to leave its mark on history. With an end to the air attacks on Remargen, the jet bombers resumed their previous attacks on enemy troop positions and vehicles whenever the weather permitted.

On 12 January the Soviet Army opened its winter offensive with a series of powerful thrusts over the River Vistula on either

Operations by *Jagdgeschwader 4* on the Eastern Front

In January this home air defence unit was transferred to the Eastern Front and pitchforked into action in the ground-attack role, for which it was ill-equipped and its pilots untrained.

26.1.45: *I./JG 4, II./JG 4, III./JG 4, IV./JG 4* – 82 aircraft, reconnaissance and low-altitude attacks in Scharnikau-Wollstein area.

27.1.45: *I./JG 4, II./JG 4, III./JG 4, IV./JG 4* – 72 aircraft, operations as on 21.1.45.

28.1.45: *I./JG 4, II./JG 4, III./JG 4, IV./JG 4* – 36 aircraft, operations as on 21.1.45.

29.1.45: *I./JG 4, II./JG 4, III./JG 4, IV./JG 4* – 104 aircraft, reconnaissance and low-altitude attacks in Scharnikau-Wollstein area and to the west.

30.1.45: *I./JG 4, II./JG 4, III./JG 4, IV./JG 4* – 121 aircraft, reconnaissance and low-altitude attacks in Scharnikau-Wollstein-Zuellichau-Mesertiz area.

30.1.45: *I./JG 4, II./JG 4, III./JG 4, IV./JG 4* – 22 aircraft, reconnaissance and low-altitude attacks Küstrin area.

Claims, set on fire or destroyed: 395 motorized or towed vehicles, one tank, three rocket launchers, one multi-barrelled gun, three aircraft on the ground.

Losses (for whole of January, including those in the West): 26 pilots killed or missing, 14 wounded; 20 Fw 190s destroyed or missing, 14 damaged; 37 Bf 109s destroyed or missing, 25 damaged.

side of Warsaw. After a week of hard fighting withdrawals the German front crumbled, and during the next seven days the Soviet forces plunged deep into western Poland. Simultaneously, armoured forces thrust deep into East Prussia from the south and the east. By the end of the month virtually the whole of Poland and East Prussia were in Soviet hands, and the westwards rush had taken them into Silesia to the River Oder and within 50 miles of Berlin itself. At the beginning of February further Soviet thrusts in the north seized most of the Baltic coastline to the east of the Oder, while in the south advancing troops occupied almost the whole of the Silesian industrial area and entered northern Czechoslovakia.

Fighting almost alone against the might of the Red Air Force, *Luftflotte 6* was able to do little to block the Soviet armoured thrusts. Reinforcing units were transferred from the Western Front, but for the most part they were air-defence fighter units (about eighteen *Gruppen*) when the crying need was for ground-attack units (of which only three *Gruppen* were transferred).

One unit involved in the transfer was *Jagdgeschwader 4*, a home-defence squadron that had taken part in Operation 'Base-plate'. Its *Stab* and *I., III.* and *IV. Gruppen* were equipped with Bf 109s while *II. Gruppe* was equipped with *Sturmbock* Fw 190s. On 21 January the *Geschwader* received orders to move from its airfields in the Frankfurt-am-Main area to new bases in Silesia. Even before the move commenced, the Soviet forward elements were menacing the Breslau area, and the destination airfields were changed to Neuhausen, Guben, Drewitz and Heppen further to the west.

By the 26th the *Geschwader* was established in its new bases and resumed action. But the type of operation now demanded of it was not the air-defence mission, for which it was equipped and which lay just within the grasp of many of its newer pilots, but the more demanding and specialized battlefield ground-attack role for which its pilots had neither training nor experience. During the final five days of January the *Geschwader* flew just over 400 ground-support sorties, in the course of which it claimed the destruction of a similar number of enemy vehicles. Even if the unit's reports are given full credence – and claims by inexperienced pilots flying ground-attack missions are usually over-optimistic – such attacks would have had only a pin-prick effect on the enormously powerful Soviet forces.

As the Soviet forces plunged ever more deeply into East Prussia, Silesia and Pomerania, several aircraft plants and storage parks had to be evacuated. As many aircraft and as much equipment as possible were withdrawn, everything else being blown up to prevent it falling into enemy hands. *Feldwebel* Adolf Dilg, a delivery pilot, took part in the evacuation of Fw 190s from Kolberg (now Kolobrzeg in Poland), carrying, on occasion, unusual loads:

> In the middle of March 1945 we received orders to evacuate all aircraft from Kolberg. I flew out a Focke Wulf 190 with the armour plate behind

my seat removed and in its place there crouched a twelve-year-old girl; the radio had been removed from the rear fuselage and there was huddled her mother, who had first to remove all metal objects from her clothing so as not to interfere with the master compass beside her. Another of the ferry pilots, *Gefreiter* Herzmann, flew an Fw 190 out of Kolberg with a young child on each knee and the mother in the rear fuselage.

At the beginning of April the Western Allies were well established in Germany and advancing rapidly, while Soviet forces consolidated their gains in the east. What remained of the *Luftwaffe* was squeezed into a dwindling strip of territory in the middle of the country, yet even at this desperate time it still nursed plans to mount spectacular attacks on its enemies. These will be described in the next chapter.

CHAPTER 12

THE WHITE HOPES (3)

Spring 1945

BY THE END of 1944 the Henschel Hs 117 *Schmetterling* surface-to-air missile system had satisfactorily completed its firing trials, and the weapon was ordered into full production. The target figure was the production of 150 missiles a month by the end of March 1945, leading to the establishment of three operational missile batteries during late spring. However, it soon become clear that in the current industrial climate these plans were over-optimistic and the weapon would not enter service until some-what later.

The development of the *Wasserfall* surface-to-air missile was some way behind that of *Schmetterling*, and production of this more complex weapon was scheduled to start in October 1945. Production of the Ruhrstahl X-4 air-to-air missile had begun in January 1945, but although more than a thousand missile airframes were completed at the company's plant at Brackwede, the manufacture of the all-important rocket motors was halted when the BMW works at Stargard was destroyed in a bombing attack. There was no time to repair the plant or to relocate the production line before Soviet troops overran the area in February.

By the middle of February it was clear that none of the anti-aircraft guided missiles would be ready to go into action within the next four months. That deficiency gave impetus to the development of a novel type of weapon that was, in effect, a manned missile: the Bachem *Natter*.

The Bachem Ba 349 *Natter* (Adder) semi-expendable inter-ceptor was quite unlike any fighter built before (or since!). Intended solely for the defence of point targets, it was designed

---

The Bachem Ba 349B *Natter*

Role: Single-seat, semi-expendable, vertical take-off, target-defence interceptor.

Powerplant: One Walter HWK 509 bi-fuel rocket motor developing a maximum of 4,400lb thrust. Four solid-fuel booster rockets to assist take-off, each developing 1,100lb thrust.

Armament (initial production version): Thirty-three R4M fin-stabilized unguided rockets.

Weights: 4,920lb at take-off, 1,940lb with fuel expended and take-off boosters jettisoned.

Dimensions: Span 13ft 11½in. Length 19ft 9in. Wing area 50 sq ft.

---

to take off vertically from an 80ft railed launcher and climb rapidly to its engagement altitude. When the pilot manoeuvred into an attacking position he ripple-fired the battery of unguided rockets at a single aircraft. He then dived away, and once clear of the enemy he was to shut down the rocket motor. When the aircraft slowed sufficiently he was to release his seat harness and also the catches holding the nose section in place, allowing the latter to fall way. The pilot then jumped clear and descended on his own parachute, while a larger parachute brought the main part of the aircraft slowly to earth. After each sortie the rocket motor and other expensive items were to be removed from the airframe and re-used. The rest of the machine was made of wood and other non-strategic materials, and was scrapped after the flight.

The Ba 349 was the world's first practical design for a fighter capable of vertical take-off (under rocket power) and vertical landing (using a parachute). During February and March the novel interceptor type made more than a score of test flights and production of the armed operational version began.

As mentioned in earlier chapters, the *Luftwaffe*'s operations staffs drew up numerous plans for attacks on the enemy, but few of them have survived. Early in 1945 two large-scale operations were in an advanced stage of preparation, a major defensive action to take place in the west and an offensive action in the east.

Confined to the ground for much of the time because of the fuel famine, most of the German day fighter units equipped with piston-engined aircraft could do nothing to slow the powerful air attacks on the homeland. Against this background of near-despair, *Oberst* Hajo Herrmann submitted a revolutionary proposal for the defence of the Reich. Herrmann, a bomber ace earlier in the war, had come to prominence in 1943 when he devised the so-called '*Wilde Sau*' ('Wild Boar') tactics used successfully by German single-seat fighters against the night bombers. In 1944 he had been appointed commander of the 1st Fighter Division responsible for the air defence of central Germany, including the area around Berlin. Herrmann now proposed the formation of special units, manned by volunteer pilots, that were to destroy American heavy bombers in large numbers by ramming. During an interview he told the author:

> I did not have a *Sturmgruppe* in my *Division*, but I knew about them of course. I knew they were not effective in the long run, on account of the losses they suffered from the escort fighters. It was clear to me that no system of destroying the enemy bombers would work unless some way could be found of avoiding the escorts. The long-term answer was to use the Me 262 jet fighter. But its introduction into service would take time, and we desperately needed some means of inflicting an unacceptably high loss rate on one or two American raiding formations, so that we would gain a breathing space to get the jet fighters into service in large numbers.

Herrmann's proposed tactical scheme differed in almost every significant respect from that used earlier, and with no lasting success, by the *Sturmgruppen*. The latter flew the unwieldy *Sturmbock* version of the Fw 190, which required its own fighter escort if it were to reach an attacking position behind a bomber formation. The pilots employed ramming only as a last resort, if their heavy cannon jammed or ran out of ammunition, and in the event there had been few instances of the tactic having been used.

For his new plan Herrmann wanted to use a completely different type of aircraft: a high-altitude fighter version of the Messerschmitt Bf 109, the G-10 or the K-1, stripped of armour and all unnecessary equipment and carrying only a single 13mm machine gun for self-defence. Thus lightened, the fighter could outclimb and outrun the American escort fighters and so would not require an escort. When an enemy bomber formation was tracked approaching central Germany, the lightweight fighters were to take off individually and climb as rapidly as possible to altitudes of around 36,000ft. Keeping out of reach of the enemy escorts, the Messerschmitts would be directed by radio into an attacking position over a formation of bombers. Each German pilot was then to select a bomber and dive on it from almost vertically above, aiming to hit the structure at its weakest part immediately in front of the tail unit. Thus, in contrast to the earlier *Sturmgruppen* attacks, ramming would be the *sole means* available to the Messerschmitt pilots to destroy enemy bombers.

In his paper Herrmann proposed that several ramming *Gruppen* be formed, to be employed in a single large-scale operation by up to 800 aircraft. If half of the attempts succeeded, as many as four hundred American heavy bombers would be destroyed in a single day. After one successful operation of this type, Herrmann argued, the Americans would take several weeks to recover and during that time the heavy bombers would cease their large-scale daylight attacks on Germany.

Herrmann did not minimize the risk to the men involved in the operation: probably half those who rammed enemy bombers would bail out safely but the other half – about 200 German pilots – were likely to be killed or suffer serious injuries. That was a high price to pay and at first sight might appear to be a callous way to use men, even if they were volunteers. But war is a callous business, and if Herrmann's scheme was implemented in full it stood a good chance of halting the destructive daylight attacks that were tearing the guts out of German industry.

In war the correct tactics are those that achieve the aim for the lowest cost in men and materials. During its attempts to stop the American attacks using conventional or near-conventional fighter tactics, the German fighter force had been losing pilots at a rate of more than two hundred per month – and in doing so it had achieved no worthwhile results against the enemy. In return for the same loss of pilots as would be suffered in a couple of months' normal operations, Herrmann's tactical scheme promised to bring a far more tangible result.

Herrmann had submitted his paper at the end of 1944, and the document sparked a lively discussion within the *Luftwaffe* High Command. Göring saw the merits of the scheme but was against the use of fully trained fighter pilots – he needed them for his expanding force of jet fighters. The *Reichsmarschall* ruled that only student pilots at fighter training schools be allowed to volunteer for the ramming units. There remained one further hurdle – getting Hitler's permission for the operation. When his views were sought, the *Führer* said that he would not *demand* such a sacrifice from any German; but if sufficient volunteers came forward who were willing to ram the enemy heavy bombers, the scheme had his approval.

During February 1945 a secret Order of the Day signed by Göring was posted at fighter training schools, calling for trainee pilots to volunteer for 'special and dangerous' duties whose nature was not divulged. Although there was no coercion on individuals to volunteer, about half the trainee pilots did so. Early in March the volunteers assembled at the fighter airfield at Stendahl near Berlin where they were told the nature of the operation for which they had offered themselves. Even at this stage any that wished to recant were allowed to do so; some did, and they left the unit immediately with no recriminations.

The special training for the operation, code-named '*Wehrwolf*', lasted about two weeks. As well as instruction in flying and tactics, the pilots flew the lightweight Bf 109 and practised handling the aircraft at high altitude and in high-speed dives. There was intensive indoctrination on the current political situation, with stress on how Germany's military position would improve if the operation were successful.

By this stage of the war the rapidly worsening situation meant that even relatively simple operations were the subject of frustrating delays. Thus although the formation of the ramming units was pushed through with considerable energy and at the highest priority, it was the third week in March before the first 250 pilots were trained and ready to go into action – and by then only about 150 Bf 109s had been modified. The first operational ramming unit, *Sonderkommando Elbe*, was established at *Geschwader* strength with three *Gruppen* each with 45 pilots.

Herrmann was placed in overall command of the '*Wehrwolf*' units and immediately came under pressure to throw his units into action as they became available. At the end of March he complained to Göring:

Regardless of the scale on which the [ramming] operation is carried out, it is the most effective course open to us under present conditions. It is in no way more expensive in personnel than are ordinary operations. It will consume only one-third as many aircraft, and one-fifth to one-tenth as much fuel, as would normal operations . . . [however,] with only 150 or 250 pilots ready for '*Wehrwolf*' only limited objectives can be achieved. This will not serve our purpose and it is important that we aim higher. The operation should be carried through with a minimum of 650 pilots. The time until the Me 262 can be brought into large-scale service must be bridged, before the fighter arm is wiped out in normal operations and on the ground. We have to achieve such a massive success that the enemy will be forced to alter his methods and the frequency of his attack.

Yet the time was past when such fine arguments could carry the day. By the beginning of April British and American troops had crossed the Rhine in strength and were thrusting deep into Germany, and in the east the Soviet forces, in places within 50 miles of Berlin itself, were gathering for the final assault to take the capital. Operation *'Wehrwolf'* was to be mounted almost immediately with the available resources.

Like the earlier plan to attack Scapa Flow, the main offensive action now planned by the *Luftwaffe* centred on the use of a large force of *Mistel* combinations. Operation *'Eisenhammer'* ('Iron Hammer'), a powerful air attack aimed at forcing a large part of the Soviet armament industry to cease production, had first been considered late in 1943. The weak point of the armament production factories in the Moscow and Gorky areas was the electricity generation system. The USSR was short of manufacturing capacity to produce turbines for the steam and hydro-electric generating stations. Indeed, much of the equipment in use had originally been bought from Germany before the war. If the power stations could be put out of action, large sections of Soviet industry would be forced to cease work until the turbines could be replaced or repaired. Originally the attack was to have been carried out in the spring of 1944, but before preparations were complete the airfields in western Russia were lost and the targets lay beyond the operational radius of action of the Heinkel He 111.

In December 1944 Operation *'Eisenhammer'* was revived, expanded in scope and re-scheduled for the following spring. The commander of *Kampfgeschwader 200, Oberstleutnant* Werner Baumbach, was appointed to head the operation. This time an extended-range version of the *Mistel* was to be used, employing as its upper component a Focke Wulf Fw 190 with the armament removed and carrying two drop tanks to give it a flying range of 760 miles after the Ju 88 was released.

Under the revised plan the targets were the dozen steam and hydro-electric power stations around Moscow, including those at Tula, Stalinogorsk and Gorky. Also to be attacked were the dam and turbine installations at Rybinsk to the north-east of Moscow; if that dam were breached it was estimated that the level of the River Volga would rise by several feet and cause severe flooding of the Volga basin.

Although a long flight over enemy territory was necessary to reach the targets, *Luftwaffe* staff officers felt that the operation stood a good chance of success. For several months there had been little German bomber activity over the Soviet rear areas. The sole *Luftwaffe* unit flying regular missions deep into the USSR, *Kampfgeschwader 200*, sent single aircraft at night to drop agents and keep them supplied. These aircraft carried radar listening receivers, and from their indications it was clear that radar cover was poor in the areas around the 'Iron Hammer' targets.

Under the revised plan, the *Mistel* combinations were to take off from airfields in East Prussia soon after dark and attack their targets simultaneously at first light the following morning. Junkers Ju 88s and Ju 188s from the pathfinder unit *I./KG 66* were to fly ahead of the *Misteln*, dropping flares to mark the route to target. Four-engined Junkers 90s and Ju 290s were to drop flares to illuminate the targets for attack. After the mission the Fw 190s were to land at airfields in the Courland pocket in Lithuania.

By the time sufficient *Mistel* combinations had been made ready for the operation, there were other pressing tasks for which they could have been used. By March Soviet troops were streaming across bridges over the Vistula. One can sense the dilemma facing the German High Command, from this excerpt from the minutes of the *Führer* conference on 26 March 1945:

> GENERAL KARL KOLLER (Chief of Staff of the *Luftwaffe*): Altogether there are 82 *Mistel* combinations ready for use. If the urgent attacks on the Vistula bridges are carried out as you, my *Führer*, have commanded *Oberstleutnant* Baumbach, there will remain 56 combinations for '*Eisenhammer*'. Since the report from *General* Christian, would you not prefer that we carry through a smaller '*Eisenhammer*' with these 56 *Misteln*? I wish to propose that as well as the urgent Vistula bridge attacks, '*Eisenhammer*' be carried through with these 56 *Mistel* combinations. The attack on the Gorky group of targets would then have to be omitted. We should then knock out 80 per cent of their electrical generating capacity. Of their 1,094 million kilowatts, the reduction would be only 378 million kilowatts. I ask therefore that the proposed '*Eisenhammer*' operation be approved. Technically we can be completely ready by the 28th/29th [March] provided that the weather conditions are favourable.
>
> HITLER: I do not wish to divide the effort, because when we do it a second time the enemy will be ready, and will reply with strong defensive measures.
>
> KOLLER: Naturally it would be a shame if the complete '*Eisenhammer*' operation could not be flown, but I do not know when we could ever do it again. The earliest that it could be done again is during the next [full] moon period. I should also like to believe that the range of the targets is such that strong defences will not be met, because presumably the enemy will not expect us to attack over such great distances.
>
> HITLER: Nevertheless, one knows how significant it would have been if the enemy had attacked our power stations simultaneously. It is exactly the same with the enemy. For the present I prefer to give up the Vistula bridge attacks. That can be done later.
>
> KOLLER: So '*Eisenhammer*' can be carried out in full, with no diversion of effort for the Vistula bridge attacks?

The transcript concluded: 'The *Führer* agreed with this.'

At the end of March the crews earmarked for 'Iron Hammer' received their detailed briefings, and during each of the next few afternoons they stood-to each evening, awaiting the executive order to launch the operation. On each day the weather was unfavourable, then, without explanation, the operation was cancelled. The *Misteln* would be used against the bridges after all.

Short of fuel and pilots and, increasingly, of munitions and aircraft also, the surviving *Luftwaffe* combat units battled to give whatever support they could to the beleaguered German Army as the land battle entered its final phase. In the next chapter we shall observe the final collapse of the force that, such a short time earlier, had made Europe tremble.

TOTALS OF SERVICEABLE AIRCRAFT, 9 APRIL 1945

Note: In several cases the figures given are approximate.

Luftflotte	Reich	LF 4	LF 6	LK West	LK E.Pr.	LFG Den	LK Cour.	LFG Italy	LFG Nor.	Total
Fighters (day)	389	62	641	76	26	–	76	–	40	1,310
Fighters (night)	480	–	–	–	–	–	–	–	–	480
Bombers	–	–	20	17	–	–	–	–	–	37
Ground-attack	21	93	533	–	24	–	41	–	–	712
Night ground-attack	17	61	86	–	–	–	16	35	–	215
Strategic recce	–	44	59	8	–	8	–	14	20	153
Tactical recce	16	68	185	26	17	–	18	14	–	344
Transports	–	–	–	–	–	–	–	–	10	10
KG 200	70	–	–	–	–	–	–	–	–	70
Totals	**993**	**328**	**1,524**	**127**	**67**	**8**	**151**	**63**	**70**	**3,331**

DEPLOYMENT OF COMBAT FLYING UNITS, 9 APRIL 1945

On this date *Luftwaffe* combat units possessed a total of about 3,330 serviceable combat aircraft, more than one-quarter less than in January. The rundown of parts of the force had by now been completed, and its once-mighty bomber arm was reduced to a mere 37 aircraft; there were few transport and heavy fighter (*Zerstörer*) units, and all the anti-shipping units had been disbanded. Only the ground-attack arm had expanded significantly since the previous May, and now stood at 712 aircraft.

Given the rapidly deteriorating position within the *Luftwaffe*, with several aircraft production centres and storage parks having been overrun by enemy ground forces and others now under threat and being hastily evacuated, it is perhaps remarkable that the strength of its combat units had not fallen even further. Two factors contributed to the maintenance of their strength, on paper at least. First, there was the huge number of aircraft held in storage parks and available for immediate issue to replace losses as they occurred; second, the fuel shortage confined units equipped with piston-engined aircraft to the ground for much of the time, and these machines sat out the

151

war in relative safety in camouflaged and dispersed blast pens some distance from their airfields and defended with light flak.

Luftflotte Reich
With some 389 serviceable fighters, of which just over a hundred were jet-propelled, *Luftflotte Reich* was poorly prepared to meet the almost daily incursions by American heavy bombers. During any one action the American escort forces might outnumber the defending fighters by as many as five to one. Against this background, it is not surprising that even the Me 262 units made scarcely any impression on the enemy. Its night fighter units possessed 480 serviceable aircraft, but the fuel shortage had severely curtailed flying and the number of aircraft suggested an operational capability far greater than was the case.

Luftflotte 4
Luftflotte 4, based in the south-east of Germany and in Hungary and Yugoslavia, had transferred several units to *Luftflotte 6* and was now down to only 328 serviceable aircraft.

Luftflotte 6
Since January there had been a large-scale transfer of fighting units from the Western Front and elsewhere, to bolster *Luftflotte 6* in readiness to meet the anticipated Soviet offensive against Berlin. With 1,524 serviceable aircraft, that moderately powerful formation was now the strongest in the *Luftwaffe*.

Other fighting formations
Elsewhere, revisions to the *Luftwaffe* command structure provided evidence aplenty of the collapse in fighting strength in several areas. Four once-mighty *Luftflotten* had been downgraded to minor formations. *Luftwaffenkommando West*, previously *Luftflotte 3*, was reduced to just 127 serviceable aircraft – less than one-tenth the number it had in January. *Lufwaffenkommando Courland*, previously *Luftflotte 1* and now bypassed in Lithuania by the Soviet advance, was down to 151 serviceable aircraft. *Luftwaffe General* Norway, previously *Luftflotte 5*, possessed only about 70 serviceable aircraft, while *Luftwaffe General* Italy, previously *Luftflotte 2*, had a paltry 63.

LUFTFLOTTE REICH

Geschwader	Unit	Aircraft	Total	Serviceable
Day fighter units				
JG 2	I. Gruppe	Fw 190	5	3
	II. Gruppe	Fw 190	8	4
	III. Gruppe	Fw 190	12	9
JG 4	Stab	Fw 190	6	4
	II. Gruppe	Fw 190	50	34
	III. Gruppe	Bf 109	61	56
JG 7	Stab	Me 262	5	4
	I. Gruppe	Me 262	41	26
	II. Gruppe	Me 262	30	23
JG 26	Stab	Fw 190	4	3
	I. Gruppe	Fw 190	44	16
	II. Gruppe	Fw 190	57	29
	III. Gruppe	Fw 190	35	15
JG 27	I. Gruppe	Bf 109	29	13
	II. Gruppe	Bf 109	48	27
	III. Gruppe	Bf 109	19	15
KG(J) 54	I. Gruppe	Me 262	37	21
JG 301	Stab	Ta 152	3	2

	I. Gruppe	Fw 190	35	24
	II. Gruppe	Fw 190	32	15
JG 400	II. Gruppe	Me 163	38	22
–	Jagdgruppe 10	Fw 190	15	9
–	Jagdverband 44	Me 262	30[1]	15[1]

Night fighter units

NJG 1	Stab	He 219	29	25
		Bf 110		
	1. Staffel	He 219	22	19
	4. Staffel	Bf 110	16	15
	7. Staffel	Bf 110	16	14
	10. Staffel	Bf 110	17	15
NJG 2	Stab	Ju 88	2	2
	I. Gruppe	Ju 88	25	22
	II. Gruppe	Ju 88	24	21
	III. Gruppe	Ju 88	29	27
NJG 3	Stab	Ju 88	4	4
	1. Staffel	Ju 88	14	12
	7. Staffel	Ju 88	19	16
	10. Staffel	Ju 88	20	17
NJG 4	Stab	Ju 88	4	4
		Bf 110		
	1. Staffel	Ju 88	17	9
	4. Staffel	Ju 88	28	23
	7. Staffel	Ju 88	14	11
NJG 5	Stab	Ju 88	16	10
		Bf 110		
	1. Staffel	Ju 88	17	10
	4. Staffel	Ju 88	28	25
		Bf 110		
	7. Staffel	He 219	34	32
		Ju 88		
		Bf 110		
	10. Staffel	Ju 88	12	11
NJG 6	Stab	Ju 88	17	17
		Bf 110		
	1. Staffel	Ju 88	17	17
	4. Staffel	Ju 88	14	11
	7. Staffel	Bf 110	15	12
	10. Staffel	Ju 88	15	8
NJG 11	1. Staffel	Bf 109	16	15
	4. Staffel	Bf 109	14	9
	7. Staffel	Bf 109	21	19
	10. Staffel	Me 262	9	7
NJG 100	I. Gruppe	Ju 88	23	20
		Fw 58		
–	Kommando Bonow	Ar 234	2	1

Night ground-attack units

–	NSGr. 1	Ju 87	8	1
–	NSGr. 2	Ju 87	5	5
–	NSGr. 20	Fw 190	27	11

Tactical reconnaissance units

–	NAGr. 1	Bf 109	16	9
–	NAGr. 6	Me 262	7	3
–	NAGr. 14	Fw 189	4	4

Special unit[2]

KG 200	I. Gruppe	Various transport types		
	II. Gruppe	Misteln, Ju 88, Ju 188		
	III. Gruppe	Fw 190	31	21

LUFTFLOTTE 4

Day fighter units

JG 51	II. Gruppe	Bf 109	7	5
JG 52	II. Gruppe	Bf 109	43	29
JG 53	I. Gruppe	Bf 109	27	27
JG 76	Stab	Bf 109	1	1

Ground-attack units

SG 2	I. Gruppe	Fw 190	33	21
SG 9	10. Staffel	Hs 129	6	6
	14. Staffel	Hs 129	13	9
SG 10	Stab	Fw 190	6	4
	I. Gruppe	Fw 190	23	21
	II. Gruppe	Fw 190	24	15
	III. Gruppe	Fw 190	30	17

Night ground-attack units

–	NSGr. 5	Go 145 Ar 66	69	52
–	NSGr. 10	Ju 87	14	9

Strategic reconnaissance units

–	AGr. 11	Ju 88	12	12
–	AGr. 33	Ju 188 Ju 88	10	10
–	AGr. 121	Ju 188	12	12
–	Nacht Aufkl. Gr.[3]	Do 217	11	10

Tactical reconnaissance units

–	NAGr. 12	Bf 109 Hs 126	30	26
–	NAGr. 14	Bf 109 Bf 110	42	19
–	NAGr. 16	Fw 189	10	7
	NAStaffel Croatian	Bf 109 Hs 126	17	16

LUFTFLOTTE 6

Day fighter units

JG 3	Stab	Fw 190	4	4
	II. Gruppe	Bf 109	51	49
	III. Gruppe	Bf 109	47	46
	IV. Gruppe	Fw 190	61	56
JG 6	Stab	Fw 190 Bf 109	4	4
	I. Gruppe	Fw 190	72	59
	II. Gruppe	Fw 190	48	45
	III. Gruppe	Bf 109	21	17
JG 11	Stab	Fw 190	4	4
	I. Gruppe	Fw 190	55	53
	II. Gruppe	Fw 190	54	51
JG 52	Stab	Bf 109	8	7
	I. Gruppe	Bf 109	40	37

	III. Gruppe	Bf 109	32	30
JG 77	*Stab*	Bf 109	1	1
	I. Gruppe	Bf 109	30	26
	II. Gruppe	Bf 109	36	30
	III. Gruppe	Bf 109	34	25
Ergänzungs				
JG 1	–	Bf 109	109	97

Bomber units

KG 4	*Stab*	He 111		1
	I. Gruppe	He 111	27	17
	8. Staffel	He 111	5	1
KG 53	*7. Staffel*	He 111	4	1

Ground-attack units

SG 1	*Stab*	Fw 190	3	2
	I. Gruppe	Fw 190	40	39
	II. Gruppe	Fw 190	44	38
	III. Gruppe	Fw 190	42	36
SG 2	*Stab*	Fw 190	6	6
	II. Gruppe	Fw 190	44	38
	III. Gruppe	Ju 87	30	25
	10. Staffel	Ju 87	21	21
SG 3	*Stab*	Fw 190	8	4
	II. Gruppe	Fw 190	47	43
SG 4	*I. Gruppe*	Fw 190	30	24
	II. Gruppe	Fw 190	39	39
	III. Gruppe	Fw 190	24	20
SG 9	*I. Gruppe*	Fw 190	59	54
SG 77	*Stab*	Fw 190	8	8
	I. Gruppe	Fw 190	34	34
	II. Gruppe	Fw 190	34	27
SG 77	*III. Gruppe*	Fw 190	47	46
SG 77	*10. Staffel*	Ju 87	14	12
SG 151	*13. Staffel*	Fw 190	18	17

Night ground-attack units

–	*NSGr. 4*	Ju 87	45	36
		Si 204		
–	*NSGr. 5*	Ar 66	16	11
		Go 145		
–	*NSGr. 8*	Ar 66	48	39
		Go 145, Ju 87		

Strategic reconnaissance units

–	*FAGr. 2*[3]	Ju 188	1	0
–	*FAGr. 3*[3]	Me 410	2	2
–	*AGr. 11*	Ju 88	10	10
–	*AGr. 22*	Me 410	26	12
		Ju 88, Ju 188, Si 204		
–	*FAGr. 100*	Ju 188	8	5
–	*FAGr. 121*	Me 410	13	4
–	*FAGr. 122*	Me 410	23	16
–	*Nacht Aufkl. Gr.*[3]	Do 217	25	10
		Ju 88, Ju 188		

Tactical reconnaissance units

–	*NAGr. 2*	Bf 109	30	20
–	*NAGr. 3*	Bf 109	37	22

155

–	*NAGr. 4*[3]	Bf 109	2	2
–	*NAGr. 8*	Bf 109	35	21
–	*NAGr. 11*[3]	Fw 189	10	8
–	*NAGr. 13*[3]	Bf 110	13	8
		Fw 189, Si 204		
–	*NAGr. 15*	Bf 109	31	26
–	*NAGr. 31*	Fw 190	15	12
		Si 204		
–	*Panzer* reconnaissance units	Fi 156	33	26
Maritime reconnaissance units				
–	*SAGr. 126*	Ar 196	18	11
		Bv 138		
	BFGr.	Ar 196	29	29

LUFTWAFFENKOMMANDO WEST

Day fighter units

JG 53	*Stab*	Bf 109	1	1
	II. Gruppe	Bf 109	39	24
	III. Gruppe	Bf 109	40	24
	IV. Gruppe	Bf 109	54	27

Bomber units

KG 51	*I. Gruppe*	Me 262	15	11
	II. Gruppe	Me 262	6	2
KG 76	*Stab*	Ar 234	2	2
	II. Gruppe	Ar 234	5	1
	III. Gruppe	Ar 234	5	1

Strategic reconnaissance units

–	*FAGr. 100*	Ar 234	6	1
–	*FAGr. 123*	Ar 234	12	7
		Ju 188		

Tactical reconnaissance units

–	*NAGr. 13*	Bf 109	39	26

LUFTFLOTTENKOMMANDO EAST PRUSSIA

Day fighter unit

JG 51	*Stab*	Fw 190	20	11
	I. Gruppe	Bf 109	10	8
	III. Gruppe	Bf 109	23	7

Ground-attack unit

SG 3	*I. Gruppe*	Fw 190	27	24

Tactical reconnaissance unit

–	*NAGr. 4*	Bf 109	26	17
		Fw 189		

LUFTWAFFE GENERAL DENMARK

Strategic reconnaissance unit

–	*AGr. 33*	Ar 234	13	8
		Ju 188		

LUFTWAFFE GENERAL NORWAY[4]

Day fighter units

JG 5	*Stab*	Bf 109
	II. Gruppe	Me 410

III. Gruppe		Bf 109		
IV. Gruppe		Bf 109, Fw 190		

Night fighter unit
–	*Nachtjagdstaffel*	Bf 110, Ju 88		
	Norwegen	He 219		

Reconnaissance units
–	*AGr. 32*	Fw 190, Bf 109		
–	*AGr. 124*	Ju 88, Ju 188		

Maritime reconnaissance unit
–	*SAGr. 130*	Bv 222, Bv 138		

Transport unit
–	*Transportgr. 20*	Ju 52		
–	*Seetransportst. 2*	Ju 52		

LUFTWAFFENKOMMANDO COURLAND

Day fighter units
JG 54	*Stab*	Fw 190	5	5
	I. Gruppe	Fw 190	38	33
	II. Gruppe	Fw 190	41	38

Ground-attack unit
SG 3	*III. Gruppe*	Fw 190	43	41

Night ground-attack unit
–	*NSGr. 3*	Go 145	18	16

Tactical reconnaissance unit
–	*NAGr. 5*	Bf 109	25	18
		Fw 190		

LUFTWAFFE GENERAL ITALY

Night ground-attack unit
–	*NSGr. 9*	Fw 190	38	35
		Ju 87		

Strategic reconnaissance unit
–	*FAGr. 122*	Ju 88	14	12
–	*Kommando Sommer*	Ar 234	3	2

Tactical reconnaissance units
–	*NAGr. 11*	Fw 190	24	14
		Bf 109		

[1]Approximate figure.
[2]The total strength of *KG 200* was about 100 aircraft, of which some 60 were serviceable.
[3]Part unit.
[4]The total strength of *Luftwaffe General* Norway was approximately 140 aircraft, with about 100 of these serviceable.

CHAPTER 13

THE FINAL COLLAPSE

1 April to 8 May 1945

BY THE BEGINNING of April the end of the war was clearly in sight. The position of the *Luftwaffe* was akin to that of a tug-of-war team some of whose members have lost their footing after a hard but unequal struggle and all of whom are unwillingly but inexorably being dragged forwards.

By now Allied ground forces had seized large tracts of German territory, and troops were advancing rapidly into the country from the west. Several aircraft factories had been overrun and others were threatened, bringing production to an abrupt end. At the Focke Wulf plant at Cottbus, for example, production of the Ta 152 high-altitude fighter had just got into its stride, and just over a hundred of these aircraft had been delivered, when Soviet ground forces neared the area and the factories were blown up to prevent their capture. The Ta 152 went into action, but only in very limited numbers. Three other aircraft types that had been 'white hopes' for the *Luftwaffe* – the Heinkel He 162 '*Volksjäger*', the Bachem Ba 349 *Natter* and the Dornier Do 335 heavy fighter – were swallowed up in the general chaos and saw no action.

By April *I.* and *II. Gruppen Jagdgeschwader 1* had received virtually their full complement of He 162s and conversion training was well advanced. Pilots found the new fighter to be fast and manoeuvrable, but it was not without vices and it could be merciless to those who mishandled it. Certainly it was no aircraft for the novice, and the idea of giving it to semi-trained pilots had to be dropped; that Göring ever gave his support to such a notion provides an insight into the fantasy world in which he was then living. Nearly two hundred He 162s were delivered to the *Luftwaffe* in the closing weeks of the war, but the new jet fighter saw no operational service.

Following successful manned tests of the Bachem Ba 349 *Natter* vertical take-off interceptor, the first operational site with ten launchers was set up at Kircheim near Stuttgart and the diminutive planes were 'loaded' in readiness to meet the next heavy-bomber attack to come within range. In the event American tanks arrived in the area before the bombers, and the aircraft and their ramps were blown up to prevent capture.

The programme to mass-produce the Dornier Do 335 twin-engined fighter-bomber encountered severe technical and supply problems, and when construction work ended in April less than a dozen production aircraft had flown. This type, also, failed to enter operational service.

At the beginning of April *Jagdverband 44*, the élite Me 262 unit commanded by *General* Adolf Galland, was established at Munich/Riem and ready for action. The unit flew its first interception mission on the 5th, when five fighters were scrambled and claimed the destruction of two enemy bombers. By now the *Luftwaffe* fighter control organization was in tatters and even with its unique collection of talented pilots *JV 44* was unable to operate effectively. Later Galland wrote in his biography:

> Our last operation was anything but jolly, light-hearted hunting, for we not only had to battle against technical, tactical and supply difficulties, but also lacked a clear [radar] picture in the air of the floods coming from the west – a picture which was absolutely necessary for the success of an operation. Every day the fronts moved in closer from three sides, but, worst of all, our field was under continuous observation by an overwhelming majority of American fighters. During one raid we were hit three times very heavily. Thousands of workers had to be mobilised to keep open a landing strip between the bomb-craters . . .
>
> Operations from Riem started, despite all resistance and difficulties. Naturally we were able to send up only small units. On landing, the aircraft had to be towed immediately off the field. They were dispersed over the countryside and had to be completely camouflaged. Bringing the aircraft on to the field and the take-off became more and more difficult; eventually it was a matter of luck. One raid followed another.

With so much going against *JV 44*, only rarely was the unit able to fly more than half a dozen sorties or shoot down more than a couple of enemy aircraft in a single day. The 'crack fighter unit' achieved so little that its entry into battle passed unnoticed by the Allied air forces.

Meanwhile, what of Operation '*Wehrwolf*', the planned large-scale ramming operation against one of the American bomber attacks? '*Wehrwolf*' was launched on 7 April as a force of more than 1,300 B-17s and B-24s with a strong fighter escort was heading into central Germany to attack marshalling yards, airfields and other targets. About 120 Bf 109s of *Sonderkommando Elbe* were scrambled, supported by conventional fighter units and 59 sorties by Me 262 fighter units (the largest number of Me 262 fighter sorties that would be flown on a single day).

Mounted using far fewer aircraft than Herrmann had proposed, the ramming operation was a failure. From American records it appears that only eight heavy bombers were destroyed by ramming, while a further fifteen suffered damage but were able to regain friendly territory. The bombers and their escorts claimed the destruction of 59 German piston-engined fighters, and it is likely that most were from the ramming unit.

What had gone wrong? There is evidence that difficult icing conditions had prevented some German pilots from reaching positions from which to begin their attack dives (it will be remembered that their training had been sketchy, even by the meagre Luftwaffe standards of 1945). Others were caught by the escorts, which were able to pick off the Bf 109s in the climb far more easily than would have been the case had the operation been mounted in full strength. There was no attempt to repeat the operation.

At the end of the second week in April the remaining German forces were being squeezed into two separate enclaves – in the area around Bavaria in the south of the country and in that around Schleswig-Holstein in the north. In recognition of this, the command structure of the *Luftwaffe* had to be changed yet again. Units in northern Germany, East Prussia, Denmark, Norway and Courland were placed under *Luftflotte Reich*, commanded by *Generaloberst* Stumpff. Units in southern Germany, Hungary, Czechoslovakia and northern Italy were placed under *Luftflotte 6*, commanded by *Generaloberst* von Greim.

Shortly before dawn on 16 April, heralded by a tempestuous artillery bombardment, the units of Soviet Army stormed over the Rivers Oder and Neisse and began to develop salients on the west banks. After first light some 7,000 Soviet combat aircraft joined in the battle. Outnumbered by more than two to one in men, four to one in guns and tanks and more than five to one in aircraft, the Germans fought a series of skilful actions and initially the defensive line held. At some places the Soviets moved across bridges that had been captured intact, at others the reinforcements passed over pontoon bridges hastily erected by Army engineers.

That day every *Luftwaffe* combat unit that could be brought to bear was thrown into action in an attempt to destroy the crossings and slow the enemy advance. Escorted by a *Gruppe* of Bf 109s from *III./JG 4*, a dozen *Mistel* combinations from *Kampfgeschwader 200* took off to attack the crossings. With the ungainly combinations went ten Bf 109s flown by volunteer pilots of *Schlachtgeschwader 104*, making a '*Totaleinsatz*' (suicide) attack on the bridges. In previous hazardous operations by the *Luftwaffe* – the ramming attacks by individuals from *Sturmgruppen* and by *Sonderkommando Elbe* – the pilot had a fifty-fifty chance of escaping from his aircraft after the collision. This time there was no such escape route: the pilots dived their aircraft into the targets in kamikaze style, and blew themselves up when the specially rigged bombs detonated. Although the idea of '*Totaleinsatz*' missions was discussed several times during the closing stages of the war, it is believed that this was the only time such an operation was mounted by the *Luftwaffe*.

The extent of the damage inflicted on the bridges by these attacks is not known. If it was significant, either it was quickly repaired or replacement pontoon bridges were thrown across the rivers. There appeared to be little or no let-up in the rate at which Soviet troops streamed westwards.

During the small hours of the 17th Soviet tanks and artillery were moved over the river. Shortly after dawn there was a further sharp artillery bombardment on the German positions lasting half an hour, backed by attacks by 800 bombers and ground-attack aircraft. Then the Soviet tanks and infantry moved forward, and slowly but inevitably the defences started to buckle in the face of superior numbers and firepower.

Meanwhile, a longer-running drama was approaching its climax at Hitler's headquarters bunker, situated beside the Reichs Chancery building in the centre of Berlin. The machinations taking place there have been described in other works, and this account concerns itself only with those that impinged directly on the *Luftwaffe*. Fortunately for history, *General* Karl Koller, the *Luftwaffe* Chief of Staff and one of the chief players, kept a daily chronicle of what he saw and heard during his frequent visits to the *Führerbunker*. The document provides a fascinating insight into a headquarters that was inexorably losing touch with reality.

17 April
Führer Briefing.
1. [Attacks to be launched] against the motor-road from the south-east, towards Cottbus, where the Russians are continually sending in reinforcements! Also Messerschmitt 262! *Führer*'s orders!
The *Führer* says: The Russians will suffer the bloodiest defeat imaginable in front of Berlin.
[Koller's comment: The Russians will probably be repulsed on the Oder during the first few days, but they have such an amount of troops and equipment that they can keep sending in reinforcements, where as we have no reserve at our disposal to the rear . . .]
2. The [German] bridgehead [on the east side of the Oder] at Frankfurt/ Oder is to be reduced by four battalions and will then probably be given up.
3. The *Führer* demands a sufficient supply of fuel for the Courland pocket and for the *Luftwaffe* units [there].
[Koller: Only moderate quantities of fuel are available. It would be madness to send more units there because there would be no way to supply them.]
4. *Führer*: All the jet fighter-bombers are to be given to [*Oberst* Hans-Ulrich] Rudel, who is to concentrate them under his command. The *Führer* asks whether Rudel has already taken over his new duties. He (the *Führer*) has ordered that Rudel should take command of all the jet fighters.

Koller and other *Luftwaffe* officers tried to talk Hitler out of the idea. They said Rudel was an extremely brave and capable *Stuka* and ground attack-leader, but he knew little about the new types of aircraft:

Rudel will have difficulty in taking over the jet planes, because he is not familiar with them at all yet, he has never flown them, their flight technique is unknown to him, and precise knowledge is essential in order to maintain the operational efficiency. Rudel's ability and efficiency lie in an entirely different field.
Führer: Makes no difference. During the First World War there wasn't a pilot at the head of the Flying Corps, but a General of the Infantry. The *Luftwaffe* has no general better qualified. Which general can fly the Me 262? None of the generals will go to the front line. Rudel is a fine fellow, the others in the *Luftwaffe* are clowns, Galland the actor and many of the others are just showmen.
[Koller: There is nothing I can say to this, because this all came out

162

with a great deal of heat. The *Führer* then ordered Rudel to come to him . . .]

20 April

Catastrophic situation: LübbenBaruth, south of Berlin. The last road to the south is in danger of being cut.

A transfer to the south is planned and being prepared, but since Keitel continually spoke of transfer by air, I emphatically reminded the *Reichsmarschall, Generalfeldmarschall* Keitel, *Generaloberst* Jodl, *General* Winter and *Oberst* von Below of the last chance to leave by road, in order to avoid the inevitable reproaches to the *Luftwaffe*. It would be extremely hazardous for the Supreme Command to fly at a later time for the following reasons:

a. Lack of fuel in the northern zone: we need the fuel for the fighting units and cannot use it for the air transfer of large staffs.

b. Bombing of the last airfields can make it completely impossible to take off.

c. Enemy night fighters: it is impossible to protect slow transport aircraft from them.

d. It will be impossible to communicate with our own flak later. Everybody agrees. However it is impossible to get the *Führer* to make a decision at the time. The *Führer* later decided that he will remain here (Berlin) to the last. Göring obtained Hitler's permission for himself and the greater part of his staff to travel south and establish their headquarters at Berchtesgaden. Koller was to remain at the *Führer*'s headquarters, as Göring's deputy.

[Koller's comment: Naturally he leaves me here to take all the anger!]

21 April

During the day Berlin came under fire from Soviet artillery for the first time. Ordered by the *Führer*:

a. A great deal of excitement caused by enemy artillery fire falling on the city of Berlin. Supposed to be from a heavy battery. The enemy is supposed to have a railway bridge over the Oder. The *Luftwaffe* must immediately locate and destroy the battery.

After checking with Flak Operations at the Flak Division Battle HQ, I found that an enemy battery had gone into position near Marzahn during the morning (observed by our own flak), twelve kilometres from the centre of the city. The fire on the city was probably coming from this battery.

Notified the *Führer*'s HQ.

b. The *Führer* requests several times exact figures on the operation of aircraft against the enemy south of Berlin.

These figures cannot be supplied because, owing to continual transfers [of units moving back] there is simply no means of communicating with the units in such a manner that such requests can be answered immediately. That takes many hours and days at the present time. (That provoked the *Führer*!)

c. The *Führer* criticizes the fact that the jet aircraft did not take off from their airfields near Prague yesterday.

I point out that they were continually being attacked by western enemy fighters and could not take off because no fighter cover for these airfields could be supplied from other airfields. The *Führer* answers: 'In that case we don't need the jet fighters any more and the *Luftwaffe* is superfluous.'

[Koller's comments: In spite of the continually narrowing and changing combat area – the *Luftwaffe* is encircled in a small pocket, surrounded on all sides by much stronger enemies – the greatest difficulties in the maintenance of communications and supply – in spite of all this everything that is humanly possible is being done. But decisive victories are no longer possible and the *Luftwaffe* will be completely dead in a few days . . .]

The OKL [*Oberkommando der Luftwaffe* – the Luftwaffe High Command] was not represented at the *Führer* Briefing on 21 April. I had intended to go and was to have been informed of the time by the *Führerbunker*. When no notification had been received up to 18.00hrs, a telephone call to the bunker brought to light the fact that it had been forgotten to notify the OKL. At the same time an order was given that [*General*] Christian and I had to be at the bunker all day on 22 April, from 10.00hrs. This would have been impossible because of the necessary command work (furthermore I should never be able to stand being insulted all day long), so I decided to send *Gen.* Christian and to relieve him in the course of the afternoon if necessary. As it turned out, this was not necessary.

22 April

After having previously informed me by telephone from the bunker that events of historical importance were taking place and that he has something important to tell me, *Gen.* Christian reaches me at 20.45hrs and reports verbally:

'The *Führer* has had a breakdown, considers continuation of the war to be hopeless, does not want to leave Berlin, wants to remain in the bunker and accept the consequences. Keitel, Jodl, Bormann, *Grossadmiral* Dönitz and the *Reichsführer* [Himmler] (the latter by telephone) all tried to get the *Führer* to change his mind and leave Berlin because it is impossible to maintain control from there and the *Führer* must remain in charge of the Reich. All in vain. The *Führer* had all his documents and papers brought into the courtyard from the bunker and then burned them . . .'

When asked what the staff officers who took part in the briefing are doing and what is now going to happen, Christian answers:

'The *Führer* has said that he is remaining there, the others can all leave the bunker, they can go where they please. The OKW [*Oberkommando der Wehrmacht* – Armed Forces High Command], Keitel and Jodl, now want to take charge, they want to turn the troops on the Elbe about and throw everything to the east. The OKW is leaving Berlin and is going to assemble in Krampnitz tonight. So much has broken up inside of me today, that I still can't grasp it. I do not believe that the *Führer* will leave. The atmosphere in the bunker has affected me deeply. An impression I cannot begin to explain.'

When asked whether I am now free to act independently or whether the *Führer* has ordered us to make a transfer, and where to, north or south, Christian answers: 'I don't know that either. The *Führer* has not issued any orders. He said only that the others can go where they please.'

That is of no use to me at all . . . I must be given clear instructions.

23 April

[By now Soviet troops had broken into the north-east part of Berlin, and the city was under artillery fire from several directions. Because of the momentous import of what Christian had said and because he was obviously upset, shortly after midnight Koller called on *Generalfeldmarschall* Jodl to discuss the matter. Jodl confirmed that Christian's report was accurate. Koller said that in that case it was his duty to fly to Berchtesgaden and inform Göring of what had happened. Jodl agreed.]

Von Below telephones from the bunker at 02.30hrs and asks if I have spoken to Jodl. I answered in the affirmative and informed von Below that Christian, along with a few other officers, will remain at OKW as Liaison Staff and that I will fly south in order to report to the *Reichsmarschall*. Below answered, 'Everything is in order then'.

Take off [in Ju 52] from Gatow airfield at 03.30hrs. Flight in clear moonlight. I am the first to take off, the other aircraft follow. Except for some flak the flight is without incident . . . Landed at Neubiberg, near Munich, at 06.00hrs.

[At noon Koller arrived at Berchtesgaden, where he recounted to Göring his conversations with Christian and Jodl.]

The *Reichsmarschall* is in a difficult position and reflects on what arrangements to make and where his duty lies. The *Reichsmarschall* has the law dealing with the *Führer*'s succession brought to him from a tin box, reads it to himself and then to us. The law clearly provides that should the *Führer* be prevented from or unable to carry out his duties for any reason whatsoever, then the *Reichsmarschall* is to become his deputy or his successor, as the case may be, with all powers in the affairs of State, the Armed Forces and the Party.

Anxious to secure his position before all contact was lost with Berlin, and after a lengthy discussion with Koller and *Reichsminister* Lammers, Göring sent the following telegram to Hitler:

Mein Führer!

In view of your decision to remain in the fortress of Berlin, are you agreed that I immediately assume overall leadership of the Reich as your Deputy, in accordance with your decree of June 29, 1941, with complete freedom of action at home and abroad?

Unless an answer is given by 10 p.m., I will assume you have been deprived of your freedom of action. I shall then regard the conditions laid down by your decree as being met, and shall act in the best interests of the people and Fatherland.

You know my feelings for you in these the hardest hours of my life. I cannot express them adequately.

May God protect you and allow you to come here soon despite everything.

Your loyal Hermann Göring

As well as the telegram to Hitler, Göring sent others to Keitel and Ribbentrop to join him at Berchtesgaden the next day unless they received further orders from him or from the *Führer*.

Meanwhile, in Berlin, the mood had changed completely since the previous afternoon. Hitler had largely recovered his spirits and at the next war conference he devoted himself once more to planning moves to stiffen the defences around the capital. Afterwards he discussed with Keitel the idea of beginning peace talks with the enemy, but insisted that these would start only after the Soviet attack on Berlin had been defeated and his negotiators had an improved bargaining position.

That was the mood in the *Führerbunker* when Göring's telegram arrived from Berchtesgarden. Among those with the *Führer* when it came were Martin Bormann, Albert Speer and *General* Keitel, people with little love for the *Reichsmarschall* and who were only too happy to bring about his downfall. With one voice they denounced the telegram as a treacherous ultimatum and a thinly veiled attempt to seize the reigns of power.

Somebody also let slip that the *Reichsmarschall* had plans to open peace talks with the Western Allies (he had indeed made such plans). Enraged at these moves behind his back by an old friend in whom he had placed his trust, Hitler sent a strongly worded cable to Göring forbidding any of the steps mentioned in the telegram. Simultaneously, the *Führer* sent orders to the commander of the SS guard at Berchtesgaden to place the *Reichsmarschall* under immediate house arrest, together with *General* Koller and senior *Luftwaffe* officers on their staffs. Thus, at the time when the *Luftwaffe* was under the greatest imaginable pressure, the force was deprived of its entire top leadership.

Once he had received confirmation that Göring was under arrest, Hitler sent him a further cable:

> Your actions are punishable by the death sentence, but because of your valuable services in the past I shall refrain from instituting proceedings if you will voluntary relinquish your offices and titles. Otherwise, other steps will have to be taken.

This was an offer the *Reichsmarschall* could not afford to refuse, and he immediately complied with his *Führer*'s 'request'. A few hours later, Hitler ordered that Koller be released from house arrest and allowed to resume his duties.

On the next day, 24 April, Hitler appointed *Generaloberst* Robert von Greim, previously commanding *Luftflotte* 6, to the post of Commander-in-Chief of the *Luftwaffe* in succession to Göring. The new commander was immediately summoned to Berlin.

Meanwhile, however, the disintegration of the Third Reich was proceeding apace. On 25 April the two arms of the Soviet pincers met west of Berlin to complete the encirclement of the city. On the same day, Soviet and American troops linked up on the River Elbe at Torgau, thus severing in two the diminishing area of Germany that remained unoccupied. Men and materials could now be moved from one part of Germany to the other only by air and at night, and then only by aircraft flying at low altitude to avoid marauding enemy night fighters.

Despite the hazards involved, von Greim obeyed his *Führer*'s summons to Berlin. The final part of his journey took place on 26 April, with a flight from Gatow airfield west of Berlin to a improvised landing strip cleared near the *Führerbunker*. On the way von Greim's Fieseler Storch flew past Soviet anti-aircraft positions and came under fire. An accurate burst struck the aircraft, wounding von Greim in the foot. The limping general was brought to Hitler's bunker and, after his wounds had been tended, he was put to bed in a room next to the main conference room. Soon afterwards Hitler went to the bedside to discuss the war situation with his new Air Force commander. That night, German radio broadcast the news that the *Führer* had promoted von Greim to *Generalfeldmarschall* and appointed him Commander-in-Chief of the *Luftwaffe* in place of Göring.

The land battle around Berlin was now entering its most

critical phase. After his release from arrest *General* Koller was summoned back to Berlin, and during the early morning darkness on 27 April he flew to Rechlin. He wrote:

Take off from Schleissheim [near Munich]: 03.30hrs.
   Landing at Rechlin: 05.45hrs.
   Some flak on the Elbe and south-west of Berlin. No night fighters in spite of bright moonlight . . . The last Ju's taking part in the Berlin night operations [Ju 52s attempting to fly troops and supplies into the Berlin pocket] landed again with their troops still on board. The air movement controller believed that last night was the last on which it would be possible to reach Berlin; the latest planes were no longer able to land. Over the city very large columns of smoke and haze coming from the innumerable fires. Orientation is almost impossible. Extremely heavy defensive fire along the approach to the axis [the city's main east-west axis, where previously aircraft had been landing]. All airfields closed, even Gatow; furthermore, it is no longer possible to reach the inner part of Berlin from Gatow. The crews of transport Ju's to whom I spoke supplemented and confirmed this picture.

Unable to reach the city, Koller visited the OKW command post where he discussed the deteriorating military situation with *Generalfeldmarschall* Jodl. Afterwards the *Luftwaffe* Chief of Staff noted:

As everywhere else, I got the impression here that everybody is expecting the coming collapse but tries to avoid discussing it at all costs. They pretend that continuation of the war will lead to disagreement between the Russians and the Western Powers and that Germany will then be given better conditions.

Meanwhile, the desperate attacks against the Soviet crossings over the River Oder continued. On the afternoon of the 27th *Leutnant* Eckard Dittmann of *II./KG 200* led a seven-*Mistel* attack against the bridge over the Oder at Küstrin that had been captured intact by Soviet troops. Three pathfinder Junkers Ju 188s led the force and a *Gruppe* of Fw 190 fighters provided top cover. As they approached the target the aircraft came under heavy fire from the numerous anti-aircraft guns positioned to protect the crossings. Dittmann gave a vivid account of the operation:

Suddenly, a river bend shimmers through the haze – the Oder! I had memorized the map of this area and recognized at once that I was a few miles too far south. Right – another 270 turn; that should lead me to the railway line and the bridges at the end of it! The haze closed in and all ground detail disappeared once more. *Mistel* was now way below 1,000m [3,280ft] and must have been clearly visible to the Ivans [Soviet troops] who were blazing away at me like mad.
   The rest happened very quickly. The ground features appeared like shadows from out of the haze and then there was a darker line – the railway. I had flown past it. Then in the next moment I caught sight of a bridge, then several. The target! I banked steeply to starboard, switched on the steering controls, uncaged the gyro, made a quick correction – there was no time for a really 'clean job' – then I had to release the Ju 88.
   There was a bang and I felt a blow from beneath me. My Fw 190 suddenly went into a roll to port and I thought they had got me. But

THE COLLAPSE OF
THE BATTLE FRONTS

- – German front lines, Jan 1945
- German-held, Apr 1945
- Neutral countries

0   100   200 miles

the aircraft simply needed retrimming and I soon had her under control again. With the haze and all that tracer, for a while I could not tell which way was up and which was down. I turned towards the lighter, redder part of the sky – that must have been the low-lying sun. The flak followed me all the way.

Dittmann had no idea what his explosive-laden Ju 88 hit. He sped clear of the target at low altitude at maximum speed, heading west for his recovery airfield at Werneuchen to the north-east of Berlin. Of the seven *Misteln* that had taken off, only his own and one other Fw 190 control aircraft reached the airfield. The other five *Mistel* pilots were missing.

Later on the 27th there was a further attempt to fly men and supplies into the beleaguered capital. Six Fieseler Storch aircraft carrying key personnel, with an escort of 30 fighters, assembled at Rechlin to fly into Berlin at dusk. The operation was a failure. On the way to the objective the formation ran into a rainstorm which scattered the aircraft. Only one Storch reached the centre of the city, but on account of dense smoke from the numerous fires its pilot was unable to find the improvised landing ground. Two aircraft were lost during the abortive operation.

During the early hours of the 28th, four Junkers 52s left Rechlin intending to land in the centre of Berlin with supplies and troops. One aircraft reached the city but spent an hour searching vainly for the Axis runway before being forced to return to Rechlin with its cargo; a second aircraft suffered serious flak damage and was forced to return with its load. Only one Ju 52 reached the Axis, but it crashed on landing and the remaining transport was ordered to return to Rechlin.

On the 29th, as Soviet forces tightened their grip around Berlin, von Greim was ordered to leave his sick bed and fly to Rechlin. From there he was to direct the 'all-out aerial bombardment' to support a powerful attack by German ground forces outside the city to lift the siege.

As was so often the case, the *Führer* was strong on objectives but weak on the means by which they would be achieved. Von Greim left in one of the last aircraft to fly out of the capital and arrived at Rechlin to find that his combat units in the area were in a poor state. Having had to change bases repeatedly to keep ahead of the enemy advance, the flying units were short of fuel, munitions and aircraft. Other *Luftwaffe* units had been ordered to give up their aircraft, and their men were going into action as infantry. The Army units earmarked for Hitler's breakthrough operation were in a similar state of disarray, and when the 'all out' counter-attack was launched it smashed itself uselessly against Soviet forces ringing the city.

Meanwhile, in Berlin itself, conditions deteriorated by the hour. With the defenders' fuel and ammunition almost exhausted, the *Luftwaffe* was ordered to air-drop supplies at night. Such measures could only prolong the agony, and it was clear that the rapidly contracting perimeter around the Chancery Building could not hold out for much longer.

On 30 April Hitler nominated *Grossadmiral* Karl Dönitz his successor as *Führer* as the Third Reich, then committed suicide. On the following day German forces in Berlin laid down their arms.

From the time he assumed power, *Grossadmiral* Dönitz worked to end the war as rapidly as possible. But he needed to slow the Soviet advance as much as he could, to buy time for German civilians to get themselves to areas occupied by the Western Allies. He immediately opened peace negotiations with the Allies, and in the west German forces surrendered in large numbers. One German pilot, at Leck in Schleswig-Holstein when the cease-fire order took effect, noted in his diary:

> *6 May 1945.* We lined up the aircraft ground equipment in parade order. The English were astonished at the imposing scene at the airfield: a view of more than a hundred aircraft, standing with a pride born of sadness. The newer types, the Me 262s and the He 162s, which had hardly begun operations, stood between the well-blooded Bf 109 and Fw 190s, victors in thousands of air battles; all of these were to be handed over to the enemy.
> *7 May 1945.* We have removed the propellers, rudders and guns from the aircraft. For us pilots the sight at the airfield is indescribably sad and painful. Our pride, our air force, our world, forced to be placed on exhibition, naked. At least thirty or forty Me 262s, the fastest fighters in the world, stand nose by nose next to each other, ready to be handed over.

Those *Luftwaffe* units who were able to surrender to Western Allies were content to do so. In the east it was a different matter. Several units continued a desperate resistance up to the time of the general cease-fire on 8 May. *Unteroffizier* Bernhard Ellwanger, an Fw 190 ground-attack pilot with *III./SG 77*, recalled:

> On 8 May all aircraft, with the exception of four, were drained of fuel. Why my 'crate' was one of those four, I don't know to this day. Led by *Hauptmann* Günther Ludigkeit, *Kapitän* of *7. Staffel*, we took off in the direction of Prague. Our mission was to destroy Prague radio station which was in the hands of Czech partisans. When we were at 4,000m Prague came in sight. Then I saw something I couldn't take my eyes off: hundreds of American fighters filled the sky like some gigantic fly-past at an air show. The whole mass flashed silver in the sun. The sight almost made me miss our attack. Our *Schwarm* dived away to port with me following. With the target centred in my *Revi* [gunsight], I released my bomb at 1,500m. A direct hit. Then we got out of there, eastward back to base. So ended my last sortie on the very day of the capitulation; and with it my last chance of landing in the American zone.

Other units based on the Eastern Front strove to reach the west with as many of their people as possible. Werner Gail, an Fw 190 fighter-bomber pilot with *III./SG 3* cut off in the Courland peninsula pocket, told the author:

> My *Gruppe* stayed in the Courland pocket until the very end. Only on the day of the armistice, 8 May 1945, did we receive permission to fly our aircraft out. That afternoon I took off from Nikas with four

ground crewmen squeezed into my Focke Wulf. For my passengers the flight of almost 600 miles to Schleswig-Holstein was long and uncomfortable; but neither so long nor so uncomfortable as was the Russian captivity for those left behind.

So the *Luftwaffe* met its end. But need it have been defeated? Might history have run a different path had national and service leaders adopted other courses of action during the final year? These aspects will be considered in the next and final chapter.

EXCERPTS FROM THE WAR DIARY OF *KAMPFGESCHWADER 76*, APRIL 1945

Operating from Kaltenkirchen near Hamburg, the unit's Arado Ar 234 jet bombers went into action against targets on the Western and Eastern Fronts.

13.4.
III Gruppe. Owing to the presence of [enemy] low flyers, four Arados were unable to take off for a mission.

14.4.
6. Staffel, mid-day. Attack on [British] vehicle concentration in the bridge-head over the River Aller at Essel, 30km ENE Nienburg.

15.4.
6. Staffel, morning. Attack on [British] vehicles at Meine, 11km S of Gifhorn, and armoured columns on the autobahn Hannover-Brunswick. Four enemy fighters made a vain attempt to chase *Lt* Croissant over Gifhorn. Owing to the presence of fighters lurking [in the area] he flew at low altitude to Ratzeburg south of Lübeck.
During the landing at Kaltenkirchen a fighter, presumably a Tempest, shot down *Ofw.* Luther of *6. Staffel*. He was forced to make a crash-landing and suffered severe injuries.

18.4.
Early afternoon. Weather reconnaissance of the area of the bridges over the Aller near Rethem, 17km north-east Nienburg [over which British troops were advancing]. Attack on the bridges from 500m. Defended by fighters and flak of all calibres.

19.4.
Midday, operation as on previous day. *Major* Polletien, Ia [Operations Officer] of the *Geschwader*, returning to Lübeck-Blankensee from an operation in the Berlin area, and despite a radio warning from the airfield he was shot down by an English fighter and crashed to his death.

20.4.
III. Gruppe at Kaltenkirchen, evening. Attack from 2,500/1,000m on tanks and vehicles on the road between Zossen and Baruth, south of Berlin. Negligible defence. The flight to the target began with an easterly flight over the Baltic before heading from there to the area of Berlin.

26.4.
Stab, morning. Target: Russian tanks at the Hallenschen Tor in Berlin. *Ofw.* Breme reported: the area from Tempelhof–Neu Köln–Hermannplatz is already occupied by the Russians; here one could see no firing. North of the Hermannplatz blazed flames reaching up to 300m. By the Hallenschen Tor

was a sea of fire. I did not wish to drop my bombs there so I released them 'safe' into a lake ESE of Schwerin.

29.4.
Stab, morning. Target Berlin.

Evening. Attack on armoured column east of Berlin. *Ofw.* Breme praised the way in which *Fw.* Wördemann in the control tower at Blankensee airfield kept watch on the air situation [for patrolling enemy fighters] and guiding him safely by means of radio calls and light signals.

THE FINAL DAYS

Taken from the flying logbook of Leutnant *Helmut Wenk, who flew Fw 190F fighter-bombers with* III./SG 1, *this section details one man's part in the desperate actions around Berlin during the final week leading to the cease-fire.*

Date	Time	Route	Enemy activity	Result of flight
27.4	14.00 15.40	Neubrandenburg – west Prenzlau – Gollmitz – Neu-brandenburg	Light flak, fighters	1 × 250kg container with SD 4 hollow-charge bombs released in the dive from 1,500m [4,800ft], on the road through the wood near Gollmitz. Precise results not observed, but the bombs fell in the target area. Attacked a self-propelled gun from low altitude, results not observed. Air combat with four La 5s; the one fired at disappeared into a layer of cloud.
27.4	18.50 19.45	Neubrandenburg – west Prenzlau – near Boizen	Light and medium flak	1 × 250kg container and 4 × 50kg bombs released in the dive from 2,275m [7,400ft], on the briefed target at the corner of the wood near Zervelin. Owing to poor light, results not observed. Ten La 5s tried to intercept and fired at the second *Rotte*.
28.4	16.35	Neubrandenburg – east of Neu-brandenburg – Neubrandenburg	Light flak	Reconnaissance flight at between 1,000m and ground level. Enemy armour and troops to the east and south-east of Neubrandenburg, seen to be advancing. Bad weather and rain showers. Cloud base in places 200m [700ft]. After this report an operation was flown against this target, then the unit withdrew to Barth.

28.4	18.05 19.00	Neubrandenburg – east of town of Burgstargard – Barth	Light flak	1 × 500kg armour-piercing bomb from 400m [1,300ft] on the road through the wood on the outskirts of Burgstargard. Target hit.
29.4	15.40 16.25	Barth – Treptow – Barth	Light flak, fighters	1 × 500kg armour-piercing bomb on the road where columns passing, east of Treptow. Low-altitude attack, hit observed. Air combat with Yak 3, no results observed.
29.4	18.00 18.50	Barth – Treptow – Barth	Light flak	1 × 250kg container and 4 × 50kg bombs released on the column at the previous target. Owing to thick smoke, results not observed. *Oblt.* Lehn (my wing man) crashed on take-off and killed.
30.4	10.30 11.40	Barth – Neubrandenburg – Barth	Nil	*Schwarm* leader became disorientated in cloud, ran short of fuel. 1 × 500kg bomb jettisoned.
30.4	17.00 17.45	Barth – east of Greifswald – Barth	Nil	The roads in the target area were found to be in our hands and the roads in the enemy-held area were all packed with refugees. 1 × 500kg bomb jettisoned.
30.4	19.30 20.15	Barth – east of Greifswald – Wismar	Light flak	1 × 500kg and 4 × 50kg bombs on a column of enemy vehicles heading for the outskirts of the town. Bombs laid accurately. Tanker vehicle hit, thick smoke seen clearly.
2.5	14.00 15.00	Wismar – Barth – Flensburg	Fighters (Thunderbolts)	Russians and English almost at airfield. Transfer to Flensburg. Hit twice by own flak.

Cease-fire on 3.5.45 at 08.00hrs, on the orders of *Grossadmiral* Dönitz.

FOLLOWING A PARADE WITH A SOLEMN ADDRESS BY THE COMMANDER AND THE SINGING OF THE NATIONAL ANTHEM, SCHLACHTGESCHWADER 1 (WITH A TOTAL STRENGTH OF ONE GRUPPE OF ABOUT 30 AIRCRAFT), UNDEFEATED BY THE ENEMY, DISBANDED ITSELF INTO SMALL GROUPS TO MAKE THEIR WAY HOME, PLEDGED TO CONTINUE TO DO THEIR DUTY AND BUILD A NEW, BETTER, GERMANY.

CHAPTER 14

WITH HINDSIGHT

IN MAY 1944 there had been optimism within the *Luftwaffe* High Command that, once the advanced types of aircraft and weaponry were in large-scale service, the tide of the air war might swing in Germany's favour. Failing that, it seemed it might at least be possible to establish so effective an air defence that the American heavy bombers would be forced to cease their highly destructive daylight attacks on German industry.

As we have observed in the preceding chapters, when the war ended the new weapons had produced no significant effect upon its course. So questions need to be asked. Why did the new weapons fail to have the expected impact? Were there significant weaknesses that mitigated against their effectiveness? Had the *Luftwaffe* High Command failed to employ the new equipment properly? Or was it simply that far too much had been expected from it?

In examining the new aircraft and weapons being prepared for service during the final year of the war, each system will be considered from four main standpoints. First, there is the question of the quality of the system *vis-à-vis* that of the enemy systems countering it: in other words, was it likely to have been effective within the tactical constraints it would meet in action? Second, if the system were effective, the time factor has to be considered: was the system developed to the point where it was ready to for mass production? Third, there is the question of quantity: could the new system be built in large enough numbers to have a decisive effect? And fourth, did the *Luftwaffe* have the resources to support the system in action in the numbers required?

THE DEFENSIVE SYSTEMS

The Messerschmitt Me 262 There can be no doubt that if it had gone into action in sufficient numbers in the fighter role, the Me 262 could have brought to a halt the daylight attacks on German industry by B-17s and B-24s. In May 1944 it had seemed that the large-scale operational use of the Me 262 was imminent. Components for airframes were being turned out in large numbers at numerous small factories dispersed throughout the country, and final assembly of Me 262s was moving ahead rapidly.

The restricting factor was the Jumo 004 engine that powered the new fighter. The 004 was the first turbojet engine in the world to enter pilot production and initially its average running life was only about 10hr. That was too low for general service use, and until it was improved the design could not be frozen for mass production to begin. When engineers face technical problems never previously encountered, it is impossible to predict how long it will take to find a solution – hence the over-optimistic noises being made in May 1944 on when the 004 would be ready for mass production.

Much has been written about the delay to the Me 262 programme supposedly imposed by Hitler's edict that initially the aircraft be used as a fighter-bomber rather than an air defence fighter. Few commentators have considered the possibility that Hitler's edict might have been correct in military terms, and this author believes it was. If the Allied landings in Normandy had run into serious difficulties – as actually happened to American troops coming ashore at Omaha Beach on D-Day – repeated bombing and strafing attacks from a few score Me 262s could have tipped the balance and changed the operation from one that just succeeded to one that failed with heavy loss of life. If the jet aircraft were available only in small numbers they were better employed as fighter-bombers against the beach-head than in high-altitude jousts with Allied fighters aloof from the troops coming ashore. Yet the point is purely academic, for in June 1944 the Me 262 was quite unready for operations in any role.

It has become part of the accepted wisdom about the *Luftwaffe* that Hitler's decision was instrumental in preventing the large-scale deployment of the Me 262 in the fighter force. In fact his edict was not the main reason, or even a major reason, for the failure to deploy the fighter in the hoped-for numbers. Not until August 1944 was the average running life of the 004 jet engine raised to 25hr; that was still a very low figure, but it meant that the design could be frozen and mass production could begin. In September Hitler rescinded his order that all new Me 262s be delivered as fighter-bombers. By then more than a hundred fighter airframes were sitting around without engines, and as soon as 004s became available these aircraft were completed and delivered to the *Luftwaffe*. In fact Hitler's order delayed the introduction of the Me 262 into service in the fighter role by only about three weeks. For the real reason for the failure to deploy the fighter in large numbers, we must look elsewhere.

As a completely new combat aircraft, the Me 262 suffered its share of teething troubles when it entered service. Despite energetic efforts to eradicate these, serviceability was poor and its sortie rate was correspondingly low during the latter part of 1944. As we observed in Chapter 8, the first Me 262 fighter unit to see regular action, *Kommando Nowotny*, entered the fray at the end of September 1944. It soon became clear that the unit was inadequately prepared for combat and after six weeks of fighting, during which it achieved relatively little, *Kommando Nowotny* was withdrawn for its pilots to receive additional training and for the aircraft to be modified. By January 1945 more than six hundred Me 262s had been built, production was running at about 125 per month and the great majority were fighters. By then many of the teething troubles had been solved, though the average running life of the Jumo 004 would never exceed 25hr and the need for regular engine changes depressed serviceability.

Despite the sizeable number of Me 262s available, the programme was outpaced by the numerous problems that went with Germany's rapidly deteriorating war situation. The *Luftwaffe*'s Order of Battle for 10 January 1945 reveals that only about 60 of these aircraft were serving with front-line combat units and all operated in the fighter-bomber, tactical reconnaissance and night fighter roles. Despite the fact that Hitler's edict had been rescinded three months earlier, no Me 262 unit was operating in the day fighter role. What had gone wrong?

Following the experience with *Kommando Nowotny*, the Me 262 fighter units being formed received a more thorough training before they were committed to action. This took time. Not until the third week in February was the next Me 262 fighter unit, *III./JG 7*, declared ready for operations.

By this stage of the war many factors combined to slow the formation or conversion of *Luftwaffe* units to new aircraft types. Napoleon once commented that an army marches on its stomach; in a similar vein it may be said that an air force flies on its ground organization. The crippling shortage of fuel affected all aspects of *Luftwaffe* operations, both in the air and on the ground (there was little fuel for motor vehicles, either). The German rail and canal systems were under sustained attack and this compounded the problems: even when fuel and spare parts existed, it was difficult to transport them to the points where they were required. On top of all else there was the ever-present threat of air attack on the Me 262 bases: any airfield discovered to be operating jet aircraft immediately became a priority target for Allied bombers.

By the beginning of April 1945 the *Luftwaffe* had accepted more than 1,200 Me 262s. The month saw the high point in the fighter's deployment, yet at the peak fewer than 200 of these aircraft, or about one in six of those built, served with combat units. Serviceability remained poor, hovering around the 60 per cent mark. The largest number of Me 262 day fighter sorties flown on a single day, only 57, was on 7 April 1945.

By the time the Me 262 was effective as a fighter and it existed in sufficiently large numbers, the *Luftwaffe* was beset by so many problems that it could not exploit these advantages. By then the US Eighth Air Force, alone, was dispatching raiding forces of more than 1,200 heavy bombers and 800 fighters almost daily against targets in Germany. Against such massed attacks the jet fighters were no more than a minor irritant.

Had six times as many Me 262s gone into action, however, even that would not have had more than a transitory effect on the course of the air war. During the final months of the war many US heavy bomber units re-equipped with the B-29 Superfortress.

It had been decided to restrict the use of this aircraft to the Pacific theatre, but if necessary units could have moved to Europe. Cruising at altitudes around 30,000ft and well protected by large numbers of machine guns, the B-29 formations would not have been easy targets for the first-generation jet fighters.

The Messerschmitt Me 163 With hindsight it is clear that the operational concept of the Me 163 target-defence interceptor was not viable. The fighter had a superb speed and climb performance but the high rate of fuel consumption, and the consequent short endurance, confined it to operating within 25 miles of base. Until several Me 163 units had been deployed – and they never would be – it would be relatively easy to route bomber formations outside the reach of the rocket fighters unless the target were close to one of their base airfields. The Me 163's limited endurance ruled out co-ordinated attacks by more than a couple of fighters, and on most occasions they attacked singly. Once it had exhausted its fuel the Me 163 became a glider, and as such it was extremely vulnerable if caught by an enemy fighter.

The Bachem Ba 349 The Bachem Ba 349 vertical take-off interceptor, on the point of going into action when the war ended, had an even shorter radius of action than the Me 163 and operationally it suffered even greater constraints.

The Focke Wulf Fw 190 *Sturmbock* This aircraft and its special tactics might have been very effective had they been brought into action earlier. As it was, from the late spring of 1944 the American bombers had strong fighter escorts accompanying them to any part of Germany or German-occupied territory. If caught by escorts, the heavy and unwieldy *Sturmböcke* suffered heavy losses.

Other Focke Wulf Fw 190 developments The re-engined D version of the Fw 190 was as good as the P-51C Mustang or the Spitfire XIV but for the most part it was flown by less competent pilots and so the type brought about no change in the air situation. In terms of performance, the Tank Ta 152, the ultimate development of the Fw 190 design, was the equivalent of the P-51H Mustang and Supermarine Spiteful fighters in production in the West at the end of the war. Few examples of the German fighter saw action, however, and the type achieved little.

Messerschmitt Bf 109 developments By producing sub-types for restricted employment, the operational life of the Bf 109 design was successfully extended, but the fuel shortage and the generally poor standard of pilots flying many of the aircraft restricted its effect.

The Messerschmitt Me 410A-2/U4 The Me 410 fitted with the 5cm high-velocity cannon was effective in picking off heavy bombers at long range. However, the twin-engined fighter was more unwieldy even than the Fw 190 *Sturmbock* and it was unable to avoid the American escorts. The single *Gruppe* equipped with the aircraft, *II./ZG 26*, suffered heavy losses and after a few weeks' operations was disbanded.

The fighters that came too late The Heinkel He 162 and the

Dornier Do 335 were too late in entering production to go into action.

Schmetterling, *Wasserfall* and **X-4** In the light of what is now known about guided missiles and their limitations in combat, it is clear that the tactical concept of the early German weapons was naïve. Had these first-generation weapons been used in action there is little doubt that they would have been ineffective.

In their initial versions none of the missiles could home automatically on their targets; nor did they have proximity fuses to detonate the warhead in the vicinity of the target. In each case they had to be guided throughout their flight by a human operator using a joystick controller, and to achieve a 'kill' they had to score a direct hit. All three missiles employed optical command-to-line-of-sight guidance (as it is now known), and the target had to be visible to the missile operator throughout the entire engagement. If darkness, cloud or haze prevented this, there was virtually no chance of a successful engagement.

Moreover, the Kehl-Strassburg radio command guidance system fitted to the *Schmetterling* and *Wasserfall* surface-to-air weapons was vulnerable to electronic jamming. The radio receivers used were similar to those fitted to the Henschel Hs 293 glider bomb and that, as we observed in Chapter 4, was already being jammed. An airborne version of the jammer would have been effective in deflecting these missiles.

The wire guidance system fitted to the X-4 air-to-air missile was unjammable by electronic means, but this weapon had other problems. It was guided by the pilot of the launching fighter throughout its flight lasting about 15 seconds. During that time the fighter pilot had to maintain straight and level flight behind the target; if he carried out any evasive manoeuvre he had to abandon the missile attack. Given the likelihood of interference from escorting fighters, it is unlikely that the X-4 would have been effective in action.

THE OFFENSIVE SYSTEMS

The Fieseler Fi 103 (V-1) flying bomb and the A-4 (V-2) rocket Neither of the long-range bombardment weapons put into service by the Germans, the Fi 103 flying bomb and the A-4 rocket, was sufficiently accurate to strike effectively at targets smaller than a major city. As a result only London, Brussels and Antwerp suffered serious damage from these weapons.

Against London, the Fi 103 bombardment caused considerable damage to property and large numbers of civilian casualties. The attack also had important secondary effects. By forcing people in the target area to take cover repeatedly, it imposed a loss of production. Paradoxically, the fact that the weapon could itself be attacked greatly increased its military effectiveness. During the early part of 1944 a sizeable proportion of the Allied medium bomber force was tied down in attacking the flying bomb launching sites. Later, when the Fi 103 bombardment began against London, large numbers of anti-aircraft guns, large quantities of the most modern fire control equipment, almost the entire production of proximity-fuzed anti-aircraft shells and several squadrons of the Royal Air Force's newest and fastest fighters had all to be concentrated in south-east England to meet the threat. This diversion of resources was the most serious military effect of the flying-bomb attack, and far more damaging than the few lucky hits on military targets that resulted.

In contrast to the flying-bomb, the A-4 rocket was almost invulnerable to enemy counter-action. The only impediment to that attack came from the disruption to the Dutch and German rail networks caused by Allied bombers supporting the land operations. The A-4 struck 'like a bolt from the blue', giving no warning of its approach, and its effect was restricted to the immediate area around the point of impact. The rocket attack diverted virtually no Allied military resources and as a result its military effect was considerably less than that of the Fi 103.

The Arado Ar 234 The largest of the jet aircraft to see operational service during the war, the Arado Ar 234 was hugely successful in the reconnaissance role. Its excellent performance enabled it to penetrate the most powerful defences, and it had the range to take in all of Holland and Belgium and most of France, Italy and south-east England. At no time were more than thirty Ar 234s operating with reconnaissance units, but this is a role in which a relatively small number of aircraft can achieve a great deal. The fact that by the time the German High Command had the ability to observe enemy movements it could no longer exploit this information does not detract from the capability of the aircraft or its pilots.

Technically the Ar 234 was also successful in the bomber role – it was able to get through to its targets – but militarily the attacks achieved little because they were mounted with insufficient force. Shorn of its mystique, effective bombing is a question of depositing a sufficient weight of explosive on the target to destroy it – it can be regarded as a transport operation. The greatest weight of bombs put down by *Kampfgeschwader 76* in a single day, about 18 tons, was when the unit flew 37 jet-bomber sorties against British troop positions in the Clève area on 21 February 1945. Dug-in troops and dispersed vehicles present a poor target for bombers, and it is significant that the attack receives no special mention in British Army accounts of the day's fighting.

In contrast, British and American tactical bombers delivered more than twenty times that tonnage against each of the ten or more targets they attacked each day. Compared with that effort the jet bombers were only a minor nuisance.

The Heinkel He 177 Several commentators have criticized the *Luftwaffe* for its failure to assemble a strategic bomber force comparable in size with those of the Western Allies. The heavy bomber type intended for this role was the four-engined Heinkel He 177 and, as we have seen, its over-ambitious design resulted in serious teething troubles that prevented it from entering large-scale service before the summer of 1944. By then moves were in train to equip nine *Gruppen* with the type, with a total establishment of 270 aircraft. About one-tenth the size of the heavy bomber fleets operated by each of the Western Allies, this planned effort was modest indeed. Yet it was the largest the *Luftwaffe* could realistically expect to support in action.

As in so many areas of endeavour by the *Luftwaffe*, a major limiting factor for its strategic bomber force was the supply of fuel. If the heavy bomber force mounted ten sorties per aircraft per month, and the operational training organization turned out new crews at a rate sufficient to replace moderate attrition, about 35,000 tons of aviation fuel would have been required per month. That was nearly *one-fifth* of the total German aviation fuel production in May 1944, the month when production reached its peak. Any increase in heavy bomber sorties would mean reducing other types of flying. The build-up of the He 177 force reached an advanced stage in the summer of 1944, but then the 'fuel famine' took effect. A single medium-range attack by a *Geschwader* of He 177s required about 480 tons of high-octane fuel; in August 1944 that represented an average day's output *from the entire German industry*. There could be no arguing with the arithmetic: the *Luftwaffe* could not maintain its heavy bomber force in action. Most He 177 units were disbanded and at the end of the year only one *Gruppe* remained.

Even had the necessary fuel been available, other factors would have prevented the German heavy bombers from reaching a level of effectiveness – plane for plane – comparable with those of the Western Allies. In attacks on distant targets the He 177s would have had no fighter escort, for the *Luftwaffe* possessed no long-range fighter that could engage Allied fighters on near-equal terms. On deep penetration daylight attacks the German heavy bombers would have faced heavy attrition, and would almost certainly have had to switch to night attacks. But for effective night attacks the bombers required sophisticated radio or radar devices to locate their targets. Hard pressed to meet the demands of the Army and the night fighter force, the German electronics industry had no spare capacity to produce such equipment.

From the beginning of the war the *Luftwaffe* had served mainly as a tactical arm to support the Army. Given the lack of any sustainable alternative, the decision to use it in that way was fundamentally correct.

The *Mistel* The largest weapon carried by conventional German bombers was the 5,500lb bomb. The *Mistel* provided a means of delivering an 8,400lb warhead against high-value tactical targets (to achieve a similar end the Royal Air Force modified a small number of Lancasters to drop 12,000lb and 22,000lb super-heavy bombs). *Misteln* could have been effective against targets that were lightly or moderately defended, and had Operation 'Eisenhammer' been launched against the Soviet power stations they might have produced spectacular results.

181

In the event, however, the *Mistel* was used only against targets of high tactical importance close to the battle area. In the nature of things, such targets were heavily defended by anti-aircraft guns and fighters. For an accurate attack the *Mistel* pilot needed to be brave and determined enough to close to within 1,200yd of the target before releasing the explosive component, and as a result pilot losses were heavy during these operations. Moreover, on several occasions the explosive Ju 88s were brought down by anti-aircraft fire following their release. Despite an intensive search, this author has found no case where a *Mistel* attack secured any major military effect. Looked at in retrospect, the *Mistel* has to get high marks for novelty of concept but low marks for military achievement.

The Henschel Hs 129 with 7.5cm cannon Although the airborne heavy cannon was effective against enemy tanks, the Hs 129 carrying it was so unwieldy that it could not survive long over enemy territory without fighter escort. Since that condition would be met only rarely during the closing stages of the war, the weapon achieved little.

When a new weapon is about to be introduced into action, there comes a glittering moment when it reaches the pinnacle of its perceived effectiveness. Its tactical shortcomings are either unknown or tend to be played down, it is viewed in the most optimistic light and the cushioning effect of enemy counter-measures is not yet apparent. In time of war all nations are guilty of this phenomenon, and it was axiomatic that the Germans would come to expect too much – singly and collectively – from the new weapons they were about to introduce. And so it proved.

After the war every aircraft or weapon built for the *Luftwaffe* was studied in great detail by the victorious Allies. The subsequent fate of each system provides an invaluable pointer to its military value, for we can see which were subsequently taken up by the victorious nations and which were not.

Plane for plane, the Me 262 was the most effective fighter type in the world in 1945. Yet after the war no nation attempted to introduce it into service in its original form. Several of its features were incorporated in post-war fighter designs, however. Several nations toyed with the concept of lightweight jet fighters along the lines of the Heinkel He 162 and rocket fighters along the lines of the Messerschmitt Me 163 but, here again, it was German ideas that were used rather than German designs. Most of the outlandish systems sank without trace after the war. Nobody bothered to take up the Bachem Ba 349 'manned missile', the *Sturmbock* fighter concept, the novel layout of the Dornier Do 335 or the *Mistel* attack system.

During the 1950s, when surface-to-air missile systems went into service in the USA, the USSR and Great Britain, these weapons owed little to *Schmetterling* or *Wasserfall*. The new weapons all employed centimetric wavelength radar for control to make them effective at night or in poor weather, and proximity fuses to increase the effectiveness of their warheads. The wire command guidance system used with the X-4 air-to-air missile has been employed in several post-war battlefield tactical surface-to-surface missiles; but since 1945 all air-to-air weapons have employed infra-red homing or some form of radar guidance.

The Fieseler Fi 103 flying bomb and the A-4 ballistic missile sired genres of weapon systems whose descendants are in use to this day. In their original forms, however, these weapons were too inaccurate and they carried insufficient explosive power to achieve decisive results (in many cases attacks with these weapons cost more to mount than the damage they inflicted cost to repair). Only when they were fitted with inertial or terrain-matching navigation systems, conferring greatly improved accuracy, and nuclear or thermo-nuclear warheads, would the potential of these weapons be realized.

Given that the new weapons were incapable of overturning the all-pervading air superiority enjoyed by the Allies, it goes without saying that the most brilliant and imaginative leadership from the *Luftwaffe* High Command would not have changed matters. Once again the point is purely academic, however, for such leadership was not forthcoming. Following his quarrel with Hitler in May 1944 about the Me 262, Göring kept away from the *Führer*'s headquarters as much as possible. By then the *Luftwaffe*'s Commander-in-Chief was a spent force, a tragi-comic figure trying to maintain a hand on events that had long since slipped from his control. His successor at the end of the war, *Generaloberst* von Greim, spent his time in office in great pain and hobbling on crutches after being wounded on the way to Hitler's headquarters.

In the absence of the C-in-C, a capable Chief of Staff could have ensured that the *Luftwaffe* was properly represented at Hitler's headquarters. Yet that did not happen either. The incumbent of the post in May 1944, Günter Korten, was fatally injured during the bomb attempt on the *Führer*'s life on 20 July 1944. His successor, Werner Kreipe, quickly fell out with Hitler and from mid-September was banished from the headquarters. Kreipe remained in office for two further months, during which the *Luftwaffe* was often represented by whichever senior officer happened to be present at the *Führer*'s headquarters. In November 1944 Karl Koller was appointed Chief of Staff and he held the post for the remainder of the war. As we have seen from his diary account in a previous chapter, Koller had little opportunity to influence events.

All of that said, it must be reiterated that by May 1944 the fortunes of the *Luftwaffe* had deteriorated to the point where even the finest leadership would not have extracted it from the morass in which it found itself.

The *Luftwaffe* had started the war as the best-equipped and the most powerful air force in the world, but following the initial relatively easy victories in Poland and Norway and in the west Hitler had become far too ambitious. By the end of 1941 his nation was at war not only with Britain but also with the USA and the Soviet Union. Once the German advance had been halted, the *Luftwaffe* was faced with a long war of attrition during which its enemies could mobilize their superior human and industrial resources and bring these to bear. In the long run that superiority was bound to decide the issue, and it did.

In hindsight, could the *Luftwaffe* have done any better than it did during the final year of the war? The force fought bravely, almost to the last drop of fuel if not to its last aircraft or pilot. At the time of the armistice it possessed some 3,000 front-line combat aircraft but most of them sat in camouflaged dispersal points with empty fuel tanks.

Supposing the *Luftwaffe* had been able to overcome all the major problems that beset it during the final year of the war? What if it had been able to attack the mass of Russian industry behind the Ural Mountains with its long-range heavy bomber force? What if, despite all the obstacles, the Me 262 had gone into service with fighter units on a large scale in the summer of 1944? What if the *Luftwaffe* pilot training organization had not broken down? What if its fuel supplies had remained intact and been sufficient to meet all needs? What then? Then the war might have continued on for a little longer, but the eventual outcome would have been no different. Had these moves extended the conflict to August 1945, it is likely that an atomic bomb attack would have forced Germany to surrender just as it forced capitulation on her yet more obdurate ally in the east.

APPENDICES

APPENDIX A: COMPARATIVE RANKS

Luftwaffe	Royal Air Force	USAAF
Generalfeldmarschal	Marshal of the RAF	–
Generaloberst	Air Chief Marshal	General (4-star)
General der Flieger	Air Marshal	General (3-star)
Generalleutnant	Air Vice-Marshal	General (2-star)
Generalmajor	Air Commodore	General (1-star)
Oberst	Group Captain	Colonel
Oberstleutnant	Wing Commander	Lieutenant Colonel
Major	Squadron Leader	Major
Hauptmann	Flight Lieutenant	Captain
Oberleutnant	Flying Officer	1st Lieutenant
Leutnant	Pilot Officer	2nd Lieutenant
Stabsfeldwebel	Warrant Officer	Warrant Officer
Oberfeldwebel	Flight Sergeant	Master Sergeant
Feldwebel	Sergeant	Technical Sergeant
Unterfeldwebel	–	–
Unteroffizier	Corporal	Staff Sergeant
Hauptgefreiter	–	–
Obergefreiter	Leading Aircraftman	Corporal
Gefreiter	Aircraftman First Class	Private First Class
Flieger	Aircraftman Second Class	Private Second Class

APPENDIX B: PREFIXES OF *LUFTWAFFE* FLYING UNITS

Aufklärungs	Reconnaissance
Bordflieger	Unit flew floatplanes, operated from warships
Erprobungs	Test
Fernauflärungs	Long-range reconnaissance
Jagd-	Fighter
Jagdbomber	Fighter-bomber
Kampf	Bomber
Küstenflieger	Unit operating in co-operation with the Navy
Lehr-	Tactical development unit
Luftlandes-	Unit operating with airborne forces
Minensuchs-	Mine search (aircraft fitted with magnetized ring equipment to explode magnetic mines)
Nachtjagd-	Night fighter
Nachtschlacht-	Night ground-attack
Nahaufklärungs-	Short-range reconnaissance
Panzer	Anti-tank (operated aircraft fitted with heavy cannon for use against tanks)
Schlepp-	Glider-towing
Schnellkampf-	Fast bomber
Seeaufklärungs-	Sea reconnaissance
Seenot-	Air–sea rescue
Seetransport-	Floatplane transport

Sturm	Operated heavily armoured Fw 190 fighters to engage enemy heavy bomber formations
Sturzkampf-	Dive-bomber
Transport-	Transport
Träger-	For operation from aircraft carrier
Wettererkundungs-	Weather reconnaissance
Zerstörer-	Twin-engined fighter

APPENDIX C: ORGANIZATION OF *LUFTWAFFE* FLYING UNITS

The *Kommando*

The *Kommando* was an *ad hoc* fighting unit, often named after its commander, that served in a specialized role. Usually the strength of a *Kommando* was less than that of a *Staffel*.

The *Staffel*

During the early part of the war the *Staffel* had a nominal strength of nine aircraft, and it was the smallest combat flying unit in general use in the *Luftwaffe*. By the late-war period the strength of a *Staffel* could be much greater or much smaller than that mentioned above, depending on the role of the unit. From the autumn of 1944 many day fighter *Staffeln* had their establishment raised to sixteen aircraft.

The unit was commanded by a *Staffelkapitän*, usually a *Leutnant*, an *Oberleutnant* or a *Hauptmann*.

The *Gruppe*

The *Gruppe* was the basic flying unit of the *Luftwaffe* for operational and administrative purposes. Initially it was established at three *Staffeln* each with nine aircraft, plus a Staff (*Stab*) unit with three, making 30 aircraft in all. After a period in action a *Gruppe* could be considerably smaller than that, as can be seen from the actual *Luftwaffe* Orders of Battle included in this book. If required for operational reasons, individual *Gruppen* were sometimes expanded greatly; for example, in May 1944 *IV./SG 9*, the sole unit operating the Henschel Hs 129 ground-attack aircraft, had on strength 67 machines.

During the reorganization of the night fighter force early in 1945, most of its *Gruppen* were regraded as *Staffeln* though in several cases they retained near-*Gruppe* strengths in aircraft. The *Gruppe* commander carried the title of *Kommandeur* and was usually a *Hauptmann* or a *Major*.

The *Geschwader*

The *Geschwader* was the largest flying unit in the *Luftwaffe* to have a fixed nominal strength, initially three *Gruppen* with a total of 90 aircraft plus a *Stab* unit of four, making a total of 94 aircraft. Originally it had been intended that the component *Gruppen* of each *Geschwader* would operate together from adjacent airfields but under the stress of war both this idea, and that of the fixed nominal strength for the unit, had to be abandoned. During the late-war period many fighter *Geschwader* and all bomber *Geschwader* had a fourth *Gruppe* added; in the case of the former, *IV. Gruppe* was a normal fighting unit, while in the case of bomber units it served as an operational training and aircrew holding unit for the other three operational *Gruppen*.

The *Geschwader* commander held the title of *Kommodore* and was usually a *Major*, an *Oberstleutnant* or an *Oberst*.

BIBLIOGRAPHY

Note: Editions marked * are German-language publications.

Aders, Gebhard. *History of the German Night Fighter Force 1917–1945.* Janes (London, 1978).

Air Ministry. *The Rise and Fall of the German Air Force 1933 to 1945.* Issued by the Assistant Chief of Air Staff (Intelligence) of the RAF in 1948; later published by Arms and Armour Press (London, 1982).

Balke, Ulf. *Kampfgeschwader 100 Wiking.* Motorbuch Verlag (Stuttgart, 1981).*

Bekker, Cajus. *The Luftwaffe War Diaries.* Macdonald (London, 1966).

Böhme, Manfred. *Jagdgeschwader 7.* Motorbuch Verlag (Stuttgart, 1983).*

Brütting, Georg. *Das waren die deutschen Kampfflieger-Asse 1939–1945.* Motorbuch Verlag (Stuttgart, 1975).*

——. *Das waren die deutschen Stuka-Asse 1939–1945.* Motorbuch Verlag (Stuttgart, 1976).*

Dierich, Wolfgang. *Die Verbände der Luftwaffe.* Motorbuch Verlag (Stuttgart, 1976).*

——. *Kampfgeschwader Edelweiss* (KG 51). Ian Allan (Shepperton, 1975).

——. *Kampfgeschwader 55.* Motorbuch Verlag (Stuttgart, 1975).*

Ethell, Jeffrey and Price, Alfred. *The German Jets in Combat.* Jane's (London, 1979).

Girbig, Werner. *Six Months to Oblivion.* Ian Allan (Shepperton, 1975).

Green, William. *Warplanes of the Third Reich.* Macdonald (London, 1970).

Gundelach, Karl. *Kampfgeschwader 'General Wever' 4.* Motorbuch Verlag (Stuttgart, 1978).*

Irving, David. *The Mare's Nest.* William Kimber (London, 1964).

——. *The Rise and Fall of the Luftwaffe: The Life of Erhard Milch.* Weidenfeld & Nicolson (London, 1973).

Kiehl, Heinz. *Kampfgeschwader 'Legion Condor' 53.* Motorbuch Verlag (Stuttgart, 1983).*

Koch, Horst Adalbert. *Flak: die Geschichte der deutschen Flakartillerie und der Einsatz der Luftwaffenhelfer.* Podzun Verlag (Bad Nauheim, 1954).*

Obermaier, Ernst. *Die Ritterkreuzträger der Luftwaffe, Jagdflieger 1939–1945.* Verlag Dieter Hoffmann (Mainz, 1966).*

Price, Alfred. *Battle Over The Reich.* Ian Allan (Shepperton, 1973).

——. *Blitz on Britain.* Ian Allan (Shepperton, 1976).

——. *Focke Wulf 190 At War.* Ian Allan (Shepperton, 1977).

——. *Luftwaffe Handbook.* Ian Allan (Shepperton, 1986).

Priller, Josef. *Geschichte Eines Jagdgeschwaders.* Kurt Wowinckel Verlag (Neckargemünd, 1969).*

Ring, Hans and Girbig, Werner. *Jagdgeschwader 27.* Motorbuch Verlag (Stuttgart, 1971).*

Schliephake, Hanfried. *Flugzeug Bewaffnung.* Motorbuch Verlag (Stuttgart, 1977).*

Smith, J. R. and Creek, E. J. *German Aircraft of the Second World War.* Putnam (London, 1972).

Stahl, P. W. *KG 200*. Janes (London, 1981).

Trenkle, Fritz. *Die deutsche Funkmessverfahren bis 1945*. Motorbuch Verlag (Stuttgart, 1979).*

——. *Die deutschen Funk-Navigations and Funk-Führungsverfahren bis 1945*. Motorbuch Verlag (Stuttgart, 1979).

United States Strategic Bombing Survey, The. Various reports. Unpublished.

Young, Richard. *The Flying Bomb*. Ian Allan (Shepperton, 1978).

USAF Historical Studies on the German Air Force in World War II, published by Arno Press Inc. (New York, 1968–70):

Deichmann, *General der Flieger* Paul. *German Air Force Operations in Support of the Army*.

Morzik, *Generalmajor* Fritz. *German Air Force Airlift Operations*.

Nielsen, *Generalleutnant* Andreas. *The German Air Force General Staff*.

Plocher, *Generalleutnant* Hermann. *The German Air Force Versus Russia, 1941*.

——. *The German Air Force Versus Russia, 1942*.

——. *The German Air Force Versus Russia, 1943*.

Suchenwirth, Richard. *Command and Leadership in the German Air Force*.

——. *Historical Turning Points in the German Air Force War Effort*.

——. *The Development of the German Air Force, 1919–1939*.

INDEX